M000213281

BOOKS

THOMAS LEIPER KANE

MORMON RESISTANCE

A Documentary Account of
the Utah Expedition, 1857–1858

2005

EDITED BY

LeRoy R. Hafen and
Ann W. Hafen

UNIVERSITY OF NEBRASKA PRESS
LINCOLN AND LONDON

⊗

First Nebraska paperback printing: 2005

Library of Congress Cataloging-in-Publication Data
Utah Expedition, 1857–1858.
Mormon resistance: a documentary account of the Utah Expedition, 1857–
1858 / edited by LeRoy R. Hafen and Ann W. Hafen.
p.   cm.
Originally published: Utah Expedition, 1857–1858. Glendale, Calif.: A. H.
Clark Co., 1958, in series: The Far West and the Rockies historical series,
1820–1875.
Includes index.
ISBN-13: 978-0-8032-7357-3 (pbk.: alk. paper)
ISBN-10: 0-8032-7357-6 (pbk.: alk. paper)
1. Utah Expedition, 1857–1858—Sources.   2. Mormon pioneers—Utah—
History—19th century—Sources.   3. Mormons—Utah—History—19th
century—Sources.   4. Utah—History—19th century—Sources.   I. Hafen,
Le Roy Reuben, 1893–   II. Hafen, Ann W. (Ann Woodbury), 1893–1970.
III. Title.
F826.U855   2005
979.2′02—dc22   2005012891

This Bison Books edition follows the original in beginning chapter 1 on
Arabic page 13; no material has been omitted.

The foldout map in the original edition has been converted to a two-page
spread. An unnumbered page has been inserted in order to retain the pagina-
tion of the original edition.

To

PRESIDENT ERNEST L. WILKINSON

outstanding builder of a great university

Contents

Illustrations

Introduction and Summary of Events

The Utah Expedition of 1857-58 was one of the strange episodes of American history. Misunderstanding, suspicion, and malice all contributed to create a situation that led to the sending of a military expedition against the Mormons and almost culminated in a tragic bloody war.

The story of that expedition, the reactions to it, the Mormon measures of resistance, and the heroic efforts that ultimately brought reconciliation, are the subject matter of this volume. The presentation will be documentary, with the actors in the drama each speaking his part and exhibiting his emotional reactions.

We take up the story at the launching of the expedition, and leave for others the presentation of the origin and previous history of the Mormons, and of the perennial conflicts between them and their neighbors. Even the more immediate causes of friction are omitted, except that the two documents most influential in producing the military movement – the letters of Judge Drummond and Mr. Magraw – are reprinted in the Appendix.

In the spring of 1857, with Congress adjourned, the new president, James Buchanan, and Secretary of War, John B. Floyd, decided to name new officials for Utah Territory and to send a military escort to support their authority. The President chose not to make a public announcement of his plans, presuming that he could thus carry them into effect before the Mormons were aware of his intentions. The secrecy shrouding the administration's program led to unfortunate suppositions and interpretations by the Mormons and caused them to fear more danger and hostility than were intended.

Had the President publicly announced a change of governors – though the Mormons would certainly have preferred to keep Brigham Young as their civil as well as their religious leader – an uprising by the Mormons would almost surely have been avoided, even though some troops were to be stationed in Utah.

General orders were issued on May 28, 1857, for the assemblage of twenty-five hundred troops at Fort Leavenworth, Kansas, to be dispatched to Utah. Two thousand head of beef cattle were to be procured and driven along the line of march. Equipment and supplies for the troops were to be freighted across the plains. General William S. Harney, veteran western campaigner, was designated to head the expedition.

The United States troops chosen were companies of the Tenth Infantry and the Fifth Infantry, Phelps' Battery and Reno's Battery, and later, companies of the Second Dragoons.

The first contingents began their westward march on July 18, each under its respective officers, without a unified command. Distraught conditions in "bloody Kansas" had caused General Harney's retention in that territory, and necessitated selection of a new commanding officer for the Utah Expedition. In late August, Albert Sidney Johnston was appointed to take over the command of the expedition, now well on its way to Utah. He did not catch up with the troops until early November.

Uncertainty marked the expedition. The late start brought criticism, and led to the forecast that the troops could not reach Utah that season and might have to winter at Fort Laramie. With General Harney detained in Kansas, Colonel E. B. Alexander, of the Tenth Infantry, was the senior officer among the troops. It was not until October 5, when the expedition forces had reached Green River Valley and were being attacked by the Mormons, that Alexander assumed command of the entire force.

Captain Stewart Van Vliet, of the Quartermaster's Department, was given instructions from army headquarters in the east, on July 28, "to proceed with the utmost dispatch to Salt Lake City, to make necessary arrangements for receiving and provisioning the troops in Utah." He carried a letter for Brigham Young, informing that official that Utah had been formed into a Military Department and that the troops assigned to that department were enroute to Utah. No mention was made that Young was being replaced as governor of the Territory.

Before Van Vliet could reach Utah, news was raced to the Mormons by couriers of their own people, saying an army was being sent to their Territory. The definite word was catapulted upon the Saints while they were enjoying a great celebration in a nearby canyon in honor of the tenth anniversary of their arrival in the Salt Lake Valley on July 24, 1847.

The mystery surrounding the movements of the troops led the Mormons to believe that the army was coming to annihilate them – the Latter Day Saints, or Mormons, as they were usually called. As a people, they recalled the numerous persecutions they had suf-

fered in New York, Ohio, Missouri, and Illinois; and
the occasions when organized militias were used against
them rather than to protect them from the local mobs.
Especially did they remember when Joseph Smith,
founder and leader of their sect, had been murdered
while in a county jail which was presumably under the
protection of state troops in Illinois. In the absence of
official notification from the United States government,
the Utah Mormons feared the worst. Rumors flew and
grew with the telling among the scattered settlements.
United States troops were marching against them, and
for what reason? The old religious prejudices could
not permit them to live their religion even in this inland
desert which they had subdued and made "to blossom
as the rose."

When Van Vliet, the government emissary, came
riding in alone to Salt Lake City on September 7, 1857,
he found the Mormons friendly to him personally; but
they were convinced of evil designs against them as a
people, on the part of the government. If civil commissioners were coming to investigate conditions here,
they would be welcomed; but not a shooting army.
Captain Van Vliet could not disabuse their minds of
the belief that the government wanted to destroy them
as a people. He was told with emphasis that the Mormons had made their last retreat; that they now would
fight to defend their homes and their families. Van
Vliet attended the large Sunday service in the new
tabernacle erected by the Mormons. He heard impassioned speeches and witnessed the unanimous resolution
to stand guard against any invader, be it government
or private organization.

On Captain Van Vliet's return east, he reported to

the advancing army, and then personally to the President of the United States, his reception by the people of Utah. He advised that the army should not attempt to push into the Salt Lake Valley during the present season; and he hoped that some reconciliation might be worked out to prevent a bloody conflict.

On the day following Van Vliet's departure from Salt Lake City, Brigham Young issued his Proclamation (September 15, 1857). It forbade the entry of armed forces into Utah, and declared martial law in the Territory. The territorial militia, still known as the Nauvoo Legion, was ordered to ready itself to repel invasion. In the various communities in Utah, Legion companies equipped themselves for defense, and were hastily dispatched eastward to prepare defenses to block the army's advance into the Territory.

Meanwhile, the United States army moved without difficulty westward over the well-beaten Oregon Trail toward South Pass – that low continental divide in present Wyoming. Already, Mormon scouts, dispatched in August, were attempting to reconnoitre the advancing troops, to scout their movements, and to learn their intentions. These horsemen heard common soldiers brag about what they would do to the Mormon leaders and to Mormon women when they reached Utah. All information learned was rushed by couriers to Salt Lake City.

On September 28, Colonel Alexander and his Tenth Infantry reached Ham's Fork near the Green River in Utah, about fifteen miles above the junction with the Black Fork. Phelps' Battery arrived there the next day. Here they caught up with a one-hundred-wagon freight train of provisions and supplies, and made camp to await the arrival of the other detachments. On October 4, the Fifth Infantry and Reno's Battery arrived.

The day after his arrival at this camp, Colonel Alexander received Brigham Young's Military Proclamation of September 15, whereby he forbade the entry of armed forces into Utah Territory. Along with it he received a letter from Brigham Young, written September 29, stating that the troops might winter in the vicinity of Black's Fork or Green River unmolested, providing they deposit their arms with the Utah Territorial Quartermaster and leave in the spring.

Colonel Alexander gave a calm and dignified answer saying, the "troops are here by orders of the President of the United States, and their future movements and operations will depend entirely upon orders issued by competent military authority."

When Mormon military leaders saw that the United States army ignored Governor Young's Proclamation, they decided to evidence their serious determination to keep the troops from entering Salt Lake Valley. On October 5, Lot Smith and his band of Mormons captured and burned two trains (52 freight wagons) of army provisions east of Green River. They also drove off oxen and beef cattle belonging to the provision train.

Colonel Alexander, senior officer in the absence of the late coming commander, had no choice but to take over direction of affairs. Although, as he said, "in utter ignorance of the objects of the government in sending troops here, or the instructions given for their conduct after reaching here," he assumed command of the expedition on October 5. He immediately convened a council of war and found opinions of the officers divided. Some were for pushing on to Salt Lake City; others voted for going into winter quarters.

It was decided to press forward – but by what route? The Mormons blocked the direct emigrant road, and they had burned their own outposts of Fort Bridger and Fort Supply. So Alexander decided to move up Ham's Fork toward Soda Springs, and thus proceed on a roundabout route to Salt Lake City. As the army and its supply trains stretched out on October 11, the caravan extended for nine miles. Half-heartedly, Alexander moved along, making but thirty-five miles in seven days. When snow and cold struck, he decided that safe winter quarters must be reached. Fort Bridger, or Henry's Fork farther south, being the most eligible locations, Alexander ordered, on October 18, a return march down Ham's Fork with Fort Bridger as the destination. To Alexander's relief, word came saying that Colonel Albert Sidney Johnston would soon arrive to take over the command. On November 3, he reached the camp on Black's Fork.

A squadron of dragoons was ordered to protect the supply trains. Because of the condition of the worn-down animals and the increasing cold, Johnston decided to push on to Fort Bridger and take up winter quarters in that vicinity. Then came terrific storms and cold that reached 16° below zero. Without shelter and almost no grass, the animals died by hundreds. The push of thirty-five miles across the barren desert required fifteen terrible days to reach Fort Bridger. When milder weather returned, the army settled itself nearby into winter quarters, which they called Camp Scott. Enough cattle and supplies had been saved to assure subsistence for the winter.

The loss of stock not only prevented any forward movement during the winter, but also necessitated procuring a new supply before an advance could be made in the spring. Colonel Johnston now despatched Captain R. B. Marcy to New Mexico to purchase new mounts and draught animals to be brought to Green River as early as possible for spring travel.

On November 19, Governor Alfred Cumming, of Georgia, and the other newly-appointed civil officers for Utah Territory, came rolling into Camp Scott, under the escort of Colonel Philip St. George Cooke's six companies of the Second Dragoons. As evidence of the painful storms encountered, Cooke reached the haven of Johnston's headquarters with 144 horses, after losing 134 head en route. Not being able to advance into Utah, the officials were made as comfortable as possible, and settled in their tents for a long and uneventful winter. As the weather moderated, and the remainder of the winter was not severe, the troops suffered little, except for shortages of salt and other supplies.

With the army stalled east of the Wasatch Mountains, that rimmed the Great Basin where the Saints had settled, there was plenty of time for Congress and the nation to contemplate. Condemnation of the Mormons, on the one hand, and on the other, criticisms of the management of the Utah expedition were voiced vigorously by Congress and the press. President Buchanan was denounced for having launched a large military undertaking without having first made an investigation; and also, for having dispatched the troops so late in the season that winter snow stopped their progress by blocking the mountain passes.

At this juncture the philanthropist, Thomas L. Kane of Philadelphia, visited the President and offered his services as a conciliator between the Mormons and the military expedition. Impelled by his friendship for the Mormons and his concern for the welfare of the nation, Kane obtained semi-official authorization for his trip to Utah. Knowing it was almost impossible to make an overland journey in the dead of winter, he took a ship to Panama – sea-sick all the way – crossed the isthmus on the new railroad, and voyaged northward by steamship. After disembarking at San Pedro Bay, near Los Angeles, he went to San Bernardino, and from thence with an escort of Mormons, he rode horseback through the deserts and mountains northeast to Salt Lake City. Using an assumed name, he wearily entered Salt Lake City in late February.

After a series of understanding conferences with Brigham Young, Kane traveled eastward through the mountains and the cold to the army headquarters at Fort Bridger. Against the advice of General Johnston, Governor Cumming agreed to accompany Kane back to Salt Lake City without a military escort. Entering under such circumstances, the Mormons accepted the new governor peacefully, as Kane had assured the Georgian they would. Upon arrival in the Mormon capital, Cumming was properly recognized by the Mormons as the new executive of the Territory. With diplomatic skill, he won the confidence of the citizens.

By March, the Mormon leaders had decided that military resistance to United States troops would be futile; instead of fighting, they would retreat southward, and if pushed, would adopt a "scorched earth" policy. They were engaged in this organized abandonment of their lands when Governor Cumming arrived with Kane. The "move south," which the new governor saw in full swing, he attempted to halt but without success. The Mormons insisted that they could not trust the army, and that they were prepared to burn their houses and lay waste the land if the troops and camp followers attempted to occupy their homes.

Again Colonel Kane, with Governor Cumming, traveled to the army headquarters. They advised Johnston – now a general – that Cumming had been accepted as Governor of Utah Territory and that peace existed. In April, Thomas Kane virtually disabled by his arduous months of travel, continued overland on his eastward journey to report the results of his mission to the President of the United States.

General Johnston insisted that his orders were explicit; that he would march into Salt Lake City. However, he consented to issue an order, reassuring the Mormons that they had nothing to fear concerning molestation of life or property at the hands of the soldiers.

In these days of difficult communication, without telegraph, regular express or mail service, it was hard to co-ordinate actions across a two-thousand-mile expanse. The President, in Washington, unaware of the success of Kane's mission, finally decided to send an official Commission of Reconciliation to Utah to deal with the Mormons. With Messrs. Powell and McCulloch, the two men chosen, he sent a signed pardon that was to be tendered the citizens if they would accept it and reaffirm obedience to the laws. Carrying their instructions, of April 12, the Commissioners left Washington, D.C., and hurried westward. At Fort Leavenworth they set out with a party of thirteen men, traveling in five four-mule ambulances that carried provisions for the men and feed for the animals.

Upon arrival at Camp Scott on May 29, they held conferences with General Johnston and Governor Cumming. Though doubting the capitulation of the Mormons, the Commissioners accompanied Cumming to Salt Lake City, arriving on June 7. After conferences with Brigham Young and his associates they reported, on June 12, that they had "settled the unfortunate difficulties existing between the government of the United States and the people of Utah." They thereupon sent word of this to General Johnston and suggested that he proceed to Salt Lake Valley at his convenience.

On June 26 the army marched through Salt Lake City and encamped on the Jordan River, west of the city. It was a quiet city, deserted by all its inhabitants except those men detailed to remain behind and fire the houses should the army not abide by its pledge to respect the abandoned property. General Johnston selected a permanent camp site in Cedar Valley, some thirty-five miles from Salt Lake City, and began the erection of quarters there, which were to be named Camp Floyd, in honor of the Secretary of War.

The Mormons, who had united in the exodus from northern Utah and the territory southward, were finally convinced of their safety from military or mob violence, and gratefully trekked back to their former residences, returning the herds of livestock to their farms, and the wagon loads of household goods to their homes.

Thus ended an extraordinary episode. Both sides of the controversy were glad for a settlement; both were perhaps a bit chastened; but each felt that its own stand had been justified and its position vindicated.

In assembling the materials for this volume we have selected the principal official documents pertaining to the expedition, a number of diary and journal extracts from actors in the affair, quotations from speeches in Congress and in Utah, and miscellaneous related items.

As announced in the prospectus of this *Series,* we had intended originally to include the letters of Lieut. Thomas Williams. But these are devoted almost entirely to a report of the movement of 1858 military reenforcements that did not reach Utah. So the letters were supplanted by other more pertinent materials.

We are pleased to acknowledge the ready cooperation of the following in making historical sources available to us: the National Archives, Duke University, New York Public Library, Tulane University, Brigham Young University, Stanford University, the Historian's Office of the Church of Jesus Christ of Latter Day Saints, and Lewis Pulsipher of Mesquite, Nevada.

Students in a Seminar at Brigham Young University during the summer of 1957 studied various aspects of the Utah Expedition and gave help in assembling material. These were: Kay Crabtree, Dean Green, Eldon Haag, Ikeda Toshiko, Robert Lambson, Homer Sheffield, Ted Warner, and Keith Worthington.

The Utah Expedition
Documents

I
General Orders
for the Military Expedition

INTRODUCTION

To newly-installed President James Buchanan came such complaints about the Mormons as those made by Judge Drummond and Mr. Magraw. The President was induced, while Congress was recessed, to send new officials and a supporting army to Utah.

Secrecy enveloped the project. No public announcement by the President as to his purposes or program was made prior to his launching of the undertaking. The first official pronouncement was the general order issued from United States Army Headquarters by General of the Army Winfield Scott. It came in the form of a circular to the heads of the Staff Departments of the army.

1. INSTRUCTIONS FROM GENERAL WINFIELD SCOTT [1]

CIRCULAR [2]

To the Adjutant General, Quartermaster General, Commissary General, Surgeon General, Paymaster General, and Chief of Ordnance.

HEADQUARTERS OF THE ARMY,   May 28, 1857
Orders having been dispatched in haste for the assemblage of a body of troops at Fort Leavenworth, to

---

[1] This and subsequent titles are supplied by the editors, and are given consecutive numbers for convenience of reference.

march thence to Utah as soon as assembled. The general-in-chief, in concert with the War Department, issues the following instructions, to be executed by the chiefs of the respective staff departments, in connexion with his general orders of this date:

1.   The force – 2d dragoons, 5th infantry, 10th infantry and Phelps' battery of the 4th artillery – to be provided with transportation and supplies, will be estimated at not less than 2,500 men.

2.   The Adjutant General will, in concert with the chiefs of the respective departments, issue the necessary orders for assigning to this force a full complement of disbursing and medical officers, an officer of ordnance and an Assistant Adjutant General, if the latter be required.

He will relieve Captains Phelps' 4th artillery and Hawes' 2d dragoons from special duty, and order them to join their companies. He will also give the necessary orders for the movement of any available officers, whose services may be desired by the Quartermaster General or Commissary General in making purchases. Lieutenant Col. Taylor and Brevet Major Waggaman will be ordered to exchange stations.

All available recruits are to be assigned to the above named regiments up to the time of departure.

---

2 Copied from "The Utah Expedition," *House Exec. Doc. 71*, 35 Cong., 1 sess., pp. 4-5 (Ser. no. 956). This collection of official papers will hereafter be cited as *Doc. 71*. It embraces the reports submitted by President Buchanan on Feb. 26, 1858, in response to the Resolution of the House of Representatives of Jan. 27, 1858, requesting "the President, if not incompatible with the public interest, to communicate to the House of Representatives the information which gave rise to the military expeditions ordered to Utah Territory, the instructions to the army officers in connexion with the same, and all correspondence which has taken place with said army officers, with Brigham Young and his followers, or with others, throwing light upon the question as to how far said Brigham Young and his followers are in a state of rebellion or resistance to the government of the United States."

3. About 2,000 head of beef cattle must be procured and driven to Utah.

Six months' supply of bacon (for two days in the week) must be sent – desiccated vegetables in sufficient quantity to guard the health of the troops for the coming winter.

4. Arrangements will be made for the concentration and temporary halt of the 5th infantry at Jefferson Barracks.

The squadron of dragoons at Fort Randall taking their horse equipments with them will leave their horses at that post, and remounts must be provided for them at Fort Leavenworth. Also, horses must be sent out to the squadron at Fort Kearny, and the whole regiment, as also Phelps' battery, brought to the highest point of efficiency.

Besides the necessary trains and supplies, the quartermaster's department will procure for the expedition 250 tents of Sibley's pattern,[3] to provide for the case that the troops shall not be able to hut themselves the ensuing winter. Storage tents are needed for the like reason. Stoves enough to provide, at least, for the sick, must accompany the tents.

5. The Surgeon General will cause the necessary medical supplies to be provided, and requisition made for the means of transporting them with the expedition.

6. The chief of ordnance will take measures immediately to put in position for the use of this force, three travelling forges and a full supply of ammunition, and will make requisition for the necessary transportation of the same.

WINFIELD SCOTT.

---

[3] Round tents, much like the Plains Indian lodges, except that the covering was canvas, instead of buffalo skins.

2. INSTRUCTIONS TO GENERAL W. S. HARNEY [4]

HEADQUARTERS OF THE ARMY,
New York, June 29, 1857

BREVET BRIGADIER GENERAL W. S. HARNEY [5]
Commanding &c., Fort Leavenworth, K.T.

SIR: The letter which I addressed to you in the name of the general-in-chief, on the 28th ultimo; his circular to the chiefs of staff departments, same date; his general orders No. 8, current series, and another now in press, have indicated your assignment to the command of an expedition to Utah Territory, and the preparatory measures to be taken.

The general-in-chief desires me to add in his name the following instructions, prepared in concert with the War Department, and sanctioned by its authority.

The community and, in part, the civil government of Utah Territory are in a state of substantial rebellion against the laws and authority of the United States. A new civil governor is about to be designated, and to be charged with the establishment and maintenance of law and order. Your able and energetic aid, with that of the troops to be placed under your command, is relied to insure the success of his mission.

---

[4] Copied from *Doc. 71, op. cit.*, pp. 7-9.

[5] The addressee in this and in many subsequent documents is named at the end of the document, instead of at the beginning, but for uniformity and for the more ready identification of the person to whom the communication is sent, the addressee will be indicated at the beginning of each document. Where the address is evident, or is unimportant, it will be omitted.

General William Selby Harney, commander of Fort Leavenworth, and a well known and experienced leader of Western campaigns, was at first chosen to lead the expedition to Utah. Later he was given an assignment in Kansas and was superceded by Colonel Albert Sidney Johnston. Harney, a native of Louisiana, became a Captain in 1825, a Colonel in 1846. He fought Indians in Florida and in the West. He was made a Brigadier General for gallant conduct in the Mexican War. He died May 9, 1889.– F. B. Heitman, *Historical Register and Dictionary of the United States Army,* etc. (Washington, Government Printing Office, 1903), I, p. 502.

The principles by which you should be guided have been already indicated in a somewhat similar case, and are here substantially repeated.

If the governor of the Territory, finding the ordinary course of judicial proceedings of the power vested in the United States' marshals and other proper officers inadequate for the preservation of the public peace and the due execution of the laws, should make requisition upon you for a military force to aid him as a *posse comitatus* in the performance of that official duty, you are hereby directed to employ for that purpose the whole or such part of your command as may be required; or should the governor, the judges, or marshals of the Territory find it necessary directly to summon a part of your troops, to aid either in the performance of his duties, you will take care that the summons be promptly obeyed. And in no case will you, your officers or men, attack any body of citizens whatever, except on such requisition or summons, or in sheer self-defence.[6]

In executing this delicate function of the military power of the United States the civil responsibility will be upon the governor, the judges and marshals of the Territory. While you are not to be, and cannot be subjected to the orders, strictly speaking, of the governor, you will be responsible for a jealous, harmonious and thorough cooperation with him, or frequent and full consultation, and will conform your action to his requests and views in all cases where your military judgment and prudence do not forbid, nor compel you to modify, in execution, the movements he may suggest.[7] No doubt is entertained that your conduct will fully

---

[6] This specific order was to restrain the troops on occasions when they might otherwise have initiated military action.

[7] This directive helps to explain the strained relations that later existed between the heads of the military and the civil authority.

meet the moral and professional responsibilities of your trust, and justify the high confidence already reposed in you by the government.

The lateness of the season, the dispersed condition of the troops, and the smallness of the numbers available, have seemed to present elements of difficulty, if not hazard, in this expedition. But it is believed that these may be compensated by unusual care in its outfit, and great prudence in its conduct. All disposable recruits have been reserved for it.

So well is the nature of this service appreciated, and so deeply are the honor and interests of the United States involved in its success, that I am authorized to say the government will hesitate at no expense requisite to complete the efficiency of your little army, and to insure health and comfort to it, as far as attainable. Hence, in addition to the liberal orders for its supply heretofore given – and it is known that ample measures, with every confidence of success, have been dictated by the chiefs of staff departments here – a large discretion will be made over to you in the general orders for the movement. The employment of spies, guides, inter-preters or laborers may be made to any reasonable extent you may think desireable.

The prudence expected of you requires that you should anticipate resistance, general, organized and formidable, at the threshold, and shape your move-ments as if they were certain, keeping the troops well massed and in hand when meeting expected resistance.[8] Your army will be equipped, for a time, as least, as a self sustaining machine. Detachments will, therefore, not be lightly hazarded, and you are warned not to be betrayed into premature security or over confidence.

---

[8] This indicates the uncertainty that existed as to the reaction of the Mormons and their reception of the army.

A small but sufficient force must, however, move separately from the main column, guarding the beef cattle and such other supplies as you may think would too much encumber the march of the main body. The cattle may require to be marched more slowly than the troops, so as to arrive in Salt Lake Valley in good condition, or they may not survive the inclemency and scanty sustenance of the winter. This detachment, though afterward to become the rear guard, may, it is hoped, be put in route before the main body, to gain as much time as possible before the latter passes it.

The general-in-chief suggests that feeble animals, of draught and cavalry, should be left ten or twelve days behind the main column, at Fort Laramie, to recruit and follow.

It should be a primary object on arriving in the valley, if the condition of things permit, to procure not only fuel, but materials for hutting the troops. Should it be too late for the latter purpose, or should such employment of the troops be unsafe or impracticable, the tents (of Sibley's pattern) furnished will, it is hoped, afford a sufficient shelter.

It is not doubted that a surplus of provisions and forage, beyond the wants of the resident population, will be found in the valley of Utah; and that the inhabitants, if assured by energy and justice, will be ready to sell them to the troops. Hence no instructions are given you for the extreme event of the troops being in absolute need of such supplies and their being withheld by the inhabitants. The necessities of such an occasion would furnish the law for your guidance.

Besides the stated reports required by regulations, special reports will be expected from you, at the headquarters of the army, as opportunity may offer.

The general-in-chief desires to express his best wishes, official and personal, for your complete success and added reputation.

I have the honor to be, sir, very respectfully, your obedient servant.   GEORGE W. LAY
Lieutenant Colonel Aid-de-camp.[9]

P.S. The general-in-chief (in my letter of the 26th instant) has already conveyed to you a suggestion – not an order, nor even a recommendation – that it might be well to send forward in advance a part of your horse to Fort Laramie, there to halt and be recruited in strength, by rest and by grain, before the main body comes up. Respectfully,   G.W.L.,

3. DEPARTURE OF TROOPS [10]

HEADQUARTERS, ARMY OF UTAH
Fort Leavenworth, K.T., July 21, 1858
COL. SAM'L COOPER,   Adjt. General, U.S.A.
Washington, D.C.   (by telegraph)

Your telegraphic dispatch of July 17 received. Tenth Infantry marched on the 18th, about 650 strong. Phelps Battery on the 19th, 70 strong; and the Fifth Infantry will march on the 22d about 525 strong.

In consequence of the force being so much diminished by sickness and desertion, I feel bound to take the responsibility of allowing the battery to continue its march. I will fit up a battery now here to meet any emergency.   Very respectfully your obt. servant

WM S. HARNEY
Colonel 2d Dragoons, B.B.B. Gen. Comdg.

---

[9] Aid-de-camp to General Scott. Lay graduated from the United States Military Academy in 1842, and served in the Mexican War. He served the Confederacy through the Civil War and died May 7, 1867.– Heitman, *op. cit.*, I, p. 620.

[10] Department, Army of Utah, Letters Sent, 1857-61. Old War Records, no. 18, National Archives, Washington, D.C.

II
Mission of Captain Van Vliet

INTRODUCTION

Not until after the army was on the march did the commanding officer send a quartermaster department representative to Utah to investigate the availability of supplies and to arrange for procurement of provisions.

This was not a routine assignment, for there was considerable uncertainty as to the attitude of the Mormons and whether they would resist entry of troops into Salt Lake Valley.

For the dual role of a quartermaster's agent and diplomat, a man of character, wisdom, and discretion was needed. The officer finally chosen was Stewart Van Vliet.[1] He had graduated from the United States Mili-

---

[1] Orders had been issued by Gen. Harney, on July 27, to Capt. John H. Dickerson to proceed ahead of the troops from Fort Laramie, to procure forage between South Pass and Salt Lake City. The order continued:

"The General also directs that upon your arrival in Utah, you ascertain if possible, the general feeling of the inhabitants towards us, and if there is a likelyhood of any opposition being made to the troops entering the Territory. You will use all possible discretion in the matter and will, as soon as possible, send an express to meet the officer commanding the advance, informing him of the results of your observations, and also giving him such information concerning the route as you conceive would facilitate the march." – U.S. Army Commands; Army and Department of Utah, Letters Sent, July 1857 – November, 1858, no. 21 (War Department Records, National Archives).

The same day an order to Capt. H. F. Clarke directed him to proceed to Utah without delay to superintend the operations of the Subsistence Department (Order no. 22). Both of these orders were signed by Capt. Stewart Van Vliet, as Asst. Qr. Master and A. Asst. Adjt. Gen.

The next day both of these orders (nos. 24 and 25) were rescinded by Gen. Harney and were superseded by the one to Capt. Van Vliet (no. 26) directing him to go to Utah ahead of the troops.

tary Academy in 1840 and was a man of wide experience in the army.[2] Especially important for this mission was the fact that he had had previous contact with Mormons at Winter Quarters (near present Omaha) and had employed some of them. The Mormons admired him for his fair dealings and just treatment.[3] He would doubtless be as well received by the Mormons as any officer the United States Army could send to them.

The record of Captain Van Vliet's mission follows.

1. INSTRUCTIONS TO CAPTAIN VAN VLIET [4]

HEADQUARTERS ARMY FOR UTAH,
Fort Leavenworth,   July 28, 1857
CAPTAIN: By special orders No. 13, from these

---

[2] He became a Captain and Asst. Quartermaster in 1847 and a Major in 1861. He served as a Brig. Gen. of Vols. in the Civil War and was made a Maj. Gen. in 1865 for faithful and distinguished service. He retired in 1881 and died March 28, 1901.–Heitman, *op. cit.*, I, p. 984.

[3] After arrival in Utah, Van Vliet was invited to attend the general meeting of the Mormons on Sunday, Sept. 13. Pres. Young thus introduced him to the audience: "The officer in command of the United States Army on its way to Utah detailed one of his staff, Captain Van Vliet, who is now on the stand, to come here and learn whether he could procure the necessary supplies for the army. Many of you are already aware of this, and some of you have been previously acquainted with the captain. Captain Van Vliet visited us in winter quarters (now Florence), and if I remember correctly, he was then officiating as Assistant Quartermaster; he is again in our midst in the capacity of Assistant Quartermaster. From the day of his visit to winter quarters many of this people have become personally acquainted with him, both through casual intercourse with and working for him. He has invariably treated them kindly, as he would a Baptist, a Methodist, or any other person, for that is his character. He has always been found to be free and frank, and to be a man who wishes to do right; and no doubt he would deal out justice to all, if he had the power. Many of you have labored for him and found him to be a kind, good man; and I understand he has much influence in the army through his kind treatment to the soldiers. He treats them as human beings, while there are those who treat them worse than brute beasts."–*Deseret News*, Sept. 23, 1857.

[4] *House Ex. Doc. 2*, 35 Cong., 1 Sess., II, pp. 27-28 (Ser. no. 943).

headquarters, of this date, you are directed to proceed with the utmost despatch to Salt Lake City, Territory of Utah, for the purpose of making the necessary arrangements and purchases for providing the troops of the army for Utah with sufficient forage, fuel, &c., on their arrival at or near that place.

The general commanding has deemed it proper and courteous to inform President Young, of the Society of Mormons, of the object of your visit, and has also requested of him the required facilities to enable you to execute your instructions certainly and effectively. You will, therefore, call upon President Young in person, in the first instance, and deliver to him the enclosed communication; at the same time you will explain freely and fully the object of your mission and the steps you propose to take for its accomplishment.

You will ascertain as soon as possible to what points on the road forage can be furnished the troops, and in what quantities; also, the amounts to be obtained near the Salt Lake City, together with such other information as you can gather which will be useful to the general commanding, all of which you will forward by special express to these headquarters, sending a copy of that portion relating to the supplies of forage on the road, and whatever else may be essential, to the senior officer with the troops *en route,* for his information and guidance.

You will obtain a suitable location for the troops in the vicinity of Salt Lake City, sufficiently near to be effective in supporting the civil authority in the maintenance of the territorial laws, but allowing ample room to prevent an improper association of the troops with the citizens – an object in this selection of primary importance.

A position called Scull Valley,[5] some sixty miles from the city, has been mentioned as favorable for this purpose; the distance, however, is too great. Any place some twenty or thirty miles from the city, possessing the necessary requisites of wood, water, and grazing, would be most advantageous. In this selection great care, judgment, and discretion will be observed.

You have authority to contract for such lumber and other articles which, in your opinion, will be necessary for hutting the troops, stabling the animals, &c., during the winter.

The quartermaster general will be requested to place at your disposal the funds required to meet your expenses.

You will impress upon the officer in charge of your escort the imperious necessity for a very careful circumspection of conduct in his command. The men should not only be carefully selected for this service, but they should be repeatedly admonished never to comment upon or ridicule anything they may either see or hear, and to treat the inhabitants of Utah with kindness and consideration.

After completing the duties thus assigned to you, you are instructed to report in person to the quartermaster general, in the event of the general commanding being absent from this post.

In conclusion, the general tenders you his best wishes for success in a mission requiring the high bearing, intelligence, and devotion which have confirmed your selection in this instance.

I am, captain, very respectfully, your obedient servant
A. PLEASONTON,
Captain 2d Dragoons, A. Asst. Adjt. General

5 Southwest of Great Salt Lake.

2. GENERAL HARNEY'S LETTER TO
BRIGHAM YOUNG [6]

HEAD QUARTERS, ARMY FOR UTAH
Fort Leavenworth, July 28th 1857

PRESIDENT BRIGHAM YOUNG, OF THE
SOCIETY OF MORMONS
Salt Lake City Utah Territory

SIR: The Government of the United States have decided to form the Territory of Utah into a Military Department, similar in all respects to the Military Department of New Mexico, the Pacific, and other geographical Military districts into which our country has been subdivided; at the same time, the undersigned has been named to the honor of commanding the troops assigned to the Department of Utah.

The great distance to be passed over, with the shortness of the season in the Rocky Mountains, have urged the expediency of placing the troops on the march – and they are now en route to some suitable position in Utah, the better to protect the interests with which they have been charged. The large number of men and animals connected with such a movement, necessitates the provision of supplies of grain and other articles of forage and subsistence at different points on the road, and also at the terminus; and the undersigned, confident you are fully alive to the advantages accruing to any community by the promotion of a proper intercourse and understanding between themselves and their Government, is induced to address you, the representative of the Society residing in Utah, to request from you such

[6] Department of Utah; Letters Sent, 1857-1861, Vol. II (Records of the War Department, U.S. Army Commands), no. 27. This large volume of official orders and letters is in the War Records, National Archives, Washington, D.C. A microfilm copy is in the library of Brigham Young University. Hereafter cited as Dept. of Ut., Letters Sent.

assistance, according to your place and position, as will facilitate and secure the purchase of the various amounts of the above mentioned necessaries required for the use of the troops upon their arrival in Utah. Liberal prices will be paid for all the supplies needed.

That the subject may be clearly and fully understood, both by yourself and the people of Utah, I have commissioned one of my staff officers, Captain S. Van Vliet, Assistant Quartermaster, to present to you this communication, and to render at the same time the necessary explanations of the measures to be adopted for the attainment of the object herein designed.

Captain Van Vliet's many high and most estimable traits of character with your previous knowledge of his acquaintance, have been the inducements for his selection to the service; which the undersigned feels assured will convey the conviction to yourself and the people of Utah, that his intentions as well as the intentions of the Government, are dictated by a spirit of honor, fairness and impartiality.

With every consideration of respect.

WM S. HARNEY
Colonel, 2nd Dragoons, & Brt. Brig Genl,
Commanding

[It is interesting to note that neither Van Vliet's orders nor the letter to Brigham Young hints at the replacement of Young as Governor, nor that the Mormons were considered to be in a state of rebellion. The dispatch of troops to the Territory was to be officially for the purpose only of establishing a military district. However, both communications indicate an undercurrent of hesitation and caution. Van Vliet was to avoid any unpleasant incidents with the Mormons and to admonish his escort to abstain from ridiculing the Utah inhabitants. Compare the tone of these documents with that of the instructions to General Harney, June 29, reprinted in Part I.

Captain Van Vliet left Fort Leavenworth on July 30, and reached the advance troops at Fort Kearny on the Platte, August 9.[7] Here Captain Jesse A. Gove, of the 10th Infantry, recorded: "Captain Van Vliet, quartermaster's department, arrived by express, under orders to go to Utah in 25 days; has an escort from the 10th Infantry of one officer (Lt. Deshler), 1 sergt. (Preston), 1 corporal and 28 privates, to go in wagons." [8]

After remaining one day at the fort, Van Vliet pushed ahead, traveling as fast as six-mule wagons would permit. On the road he met several parties from Utah and some mountain traders. All told him he would not be allowed to enter Salt Lake Valley.[9] At Ham's Fork, in the Green River Valley, he decided to leave his escort behind and to continue with two Mormons who were returning from the now-abandoned mail station on Deer Creek.

The Captain's arrival in Utah and his visit there are thus reported in the *Deseret News*.]

3. *DESERET NEWS* ACCOUNT OF VAN VLIET'S VISIT [10]

Captain Stewart Van Vliet, Assistant Quartermaster, U.S.A., arrived in this city on the afternoon of the 8th instant. . .

During the evening of the 8th Governor Young, accompanied by Hon. H. C. Kimball, Lieut. Gen. D. H. Wells, Hon. J. M. Bernhisel, Adjutant Gen. J. Ferguson, Architect T. O. Angel and the Editor of the *Deseret News*[11] called upon Captain Van Vliet at the

---

[7] See his report of Sept. 16, 1857, given below.

[8] O. G. Hammond (ed.), *The Utah Expedition, 1857-1858; Letters of Capt. Jesse A. Gove,* etc. (Concord, New Hampshire Historical Society, 1928), p. 31. Hereafter cited as *Gove's Letters.*

[9] Van Vliet's report of Sept. 16, *op. cit.*

[10] *Deseret News* (Salt Lake City), Sept. 16, 1857.

[11] The editor of the *News* was Albert Carrington. This newspaper was a Mormon organ, owned and published by the Church.

The others who accompanied Pres. Young were men of importance. Heber C. Kimball was First Counsellor to Pres. Young. Daniel H. Wells was Second Counsellor and he headed the Nauvoo Legion, which was the Utah militia and the Mormon military organization. John M. Bernhisel was Utah's delegate to Congress. James Ferguson was Adjutant General of the Nauvoo Legion. Truman O. Angell was Church Architect.

residence of Hon. W. H. Hooper, Secretary for Utah, and passed some time in a mutually frank and friendly interchange of queries and ideas.

At 9 a.m. of the 9th, Governor Young, Hon. H. C. Kimball, Lieut. Gen. D. H. Wells, Hon. J. M. Bernhisel, those of the Quorum of the Twelve [12] now in this city, Hon. William Hooper and a large number of our prominent citizens met Captain Van Vliet in the Social Hall, where he was very favorably introduced to the audience by the Governor and gave a general outline of the object in view with General Harney in sending him here on express, and at the conclusion of his remarks presented a letter to Gov. Young from Gen. Harney, addressed, "President Brigham Young, of the Society of the Mormons."

At the conclusion of the interview, Governor Young invited Captain Van Vliet and several others to accompany him to his private office and, (after a time spent in a style of conversation very pleasing to upright and loyal American citizens,) [13] to a stroll through the adjacent orchard, vineyard, and garden. . .

On the 10th, as the Captain had expressed a desire to see the domestic workings of the "peculiar institution," [14] Governor Young showed him the finishing and furnishing of his Bee Hive and Lion Mansions,[15] from garret to cellar, and introduced him to his numerous family of wives and children. . .

In the afternoon, with Hon. W. H. Hooper and

---

[12] The Quorum of Twelve Apostles ranks next to the First Presidency in the Church of Jesus Christ of Latter-Day Saints (Mormon Church).

[13] The essence of the conversations, as recorded in H. C. Kimball's diary, follows this newspaper report.

[14] Polygamy.

[15] These unique historic buildings still stand on the city block east of Temple Square, Salt Lake City.

Territorial Surveyor Gen. J. W. Fox, Captain Van Vliet left on a visit to the military reservation in Rush Valley,[16] returned on the 11th and participated in a supper at the Globe, and in the course of the evening he voluntarily arose and requested the privilege of making a few remarks, which was at once most cheerfully granted, in which he warmly expressed his gratitude for his former and present acquaintance and associations with this people, and said that his prayer should ever be that the Angel of Peace should extend his wings over Utah.

On the 12th he partook of a sumptuous dinner at the residence of Pres. Heber C. Kimball, at which President Brigham Young and Daniel Wells, Hon. J. M. Bernhisel, Hon. W. H. Hooper, Bp. L. D. Young,[17] Elders John Taylor,[18] Feramorz Little[19] and Albert Carrington, and numerous ladies were guests. . .

On Sunday, the 13th, Captain Van Vliet, attending forenoon service in the Bowery, politely accepted an invitation from the President to take a seat on the stand. . .

In the evening the Captain was again visited by Governor Young and numerous friends, as he wished to start for Washington very early in the morning, and after another very friendly interview the company separated with a cordial shake of the hand and wishing the Captain a speedy journey and safe arrival, with the blessings of Jehovah to attend him.

---

[16] This reservation was selected by Col. Steptoe. It was located west of Salt Lake City.

[17] Lorenzo D. Young, a brother of Brigham, was Bishop of the 18th Ward, Salt Lake City.

[18] John Taylor, editor and church leader, was to succeed to the Presidency of the Mormon Church upon the death of Brigham Young in 1877.

[19] Feramorz Little was a prominent churchman and writer.

At about 6 a.m. of the 14th, Captain Van Vliet, placed himself in the care of Brothers N. V. Jones,[20] O. P. Rockwell[21] and S. Taylor, with animals, carriage and baggage wagon furnished by Governor Young, to proceed to his escort on Ham's Fork, from whence he will use all diligence to make a short trip to Washington City .

. . . Captain Van Vliet often expressed a regret that the Government had not first sent one or more responsible men as a committee to investigate. He constantly appeared exceedingly anxious that a collision, threatened solely upon false rumors and reports, might be avoided, (as every law abiding and peace and union loving citizen should,) and fondly anticipated that the war clouds now so causelessly lowering might be peacefully scattered and give place to the clear, serene and just administration of true rights and privileges to every class of citizens throughout our wide spread Republic, which, it is well known by all in power, is all that we have ever asked.

Bernhisel accompanied Van Vliet in his carriage to Ham's Fork.[22]

4. CONVERSATIONS OF PRES. YOUNG AND CAPT. VAN VLIET [23]

PRESIDENT YOUNG: We do not want to fight the United States, but if they drive us to it, we shall do the best we can; and I will tell you, as the Lord lives, we

---

[20] Nathaniel V. Jones was one of the officers of the Nauvoo Legion.

[21] Orrin Porter Rockwell, bodyguard of Joseph Smith, was a famous Mormon scout and pioneer.

[22] The two continued on to Washington together.

[23] This report of the conversations is from Wilford Woodruff's Journal, as reproduced in Edward W. Tullidge, *Life of Brigham Young; or Utah and her Founders* (New York, 1876), 262-65. Woodruff later became President of the Mormon Church.

shall come off conquerors, for we trust in Him. . . The United States are sending their armies here to simply hold us still until a mob can come and butcher us, as has been done before. . . We are the supporters of the constitution of the United States, and we love that constitution and respect the laws of the United States; but it is by the corrupt administration of those laws that we are made to suffer. If the law had been vindicated in Missouri, it would have sent Governor Boggs [24] to the gallows, along with those who murdered Joseph and Hyrum,[25] and those other fiends who accomplished our expulsion from the States. . . Most of the Government officers who have been sent here have taken no interest in us, but on the contrary, have tried many times to destroy us.

CAPTAIN VAN VLIET: This is the case with most men sent to the Territories. They receive their offices as a political reward, or as a stepping-stone to the Senatorship; but they have no interest in common with the people. . . This people has been lied about the worst of any people I ever saw. . .

PRESIDENT YOUNG: . . . but the United States seem determined to drive us into a fight. They will kill us if they can. A mob killed Joseph and Hyrum in jail, notwithstanding the faith of the State was pledged to protect them. . . I have broken no law, and under the present state of affairs I will not suffer myself to be taken by any United States officer, to be killed as they killed Joseph.

CAPTAIN VAN VLIET: I do not think it is the in-

---

[24] Governor Lilburn W. Boggs issued the notorious "extermination order" against the Mormons in Missouri.

[25] Joseph Smith, founder of the Latter-Day Saints (Mormon) Church, and his brother Hyrum were murdered in the jail at Carthage, Illinois, by a mob in June, 1844.

tention of the Government to arrest you, but to install a new Governor in the Territory.

PRESIDENT YOUNG: I believe you tell the truth – that you believe this – but you do not know their intentions as well as I do. . . If the Government persists in sending an army to destroy us, in the name of the Lord we shall conquer them. If they dare to force the issue, I shall not hold the Indians by the wrist any longer, for white men to shoot at them; they shall go ahead and do as they please. If the issue comes, you may tell the Government to stop all emigration across this continent, for the Indians will kill all who attempt it. And if an army succeeds in penetrating this valley, tell the Government to see that it has forage and provisions in store, for they will find here only a charred and barren waste.

CAPTAIN VAN VLIET: . . . If our Government pushed this matter to the extent of making war upon you, I will withdraw from the army, for I will not have a hand in shedding the blood of American citizens.

PRESIDENT YOUNG: We shall trust in God. . . Congress has promptly sent investigating committees to Kansas and other places, as occasion has required; but upon the merest rumor it has sent 2,000 armed soldiers to destroy the people of Utah, without investigating the subject at all.

CAPTAIN VAN VLIET: The Government may yet send an investigating committee to Utah, and consider it good policy, before they get through.[26]

PRESIDENT YOUNG: I believe God has sent you here, and that good will grow out of it. I was glad when I heard you were coming.

---

[26] At Washington, Capt. Van Vliet appears to have joined others in urging the despatch of an investigating committee to Utah – which was ultimately done, as recorded later in this volume.

CAPTAIN VAN VLIET: I am anxious to get back to Washington as soon as I can. I have heard officially that General Harney has been recalled to Kansas to officiate as Governor. I shall stop the train on Ham's Fork, on my own responsibility.[27]

PRESIDENT YOUNG: If we can keep the peace for this Winter I do think there will be something turn up that may save the shedding of blood.

5. CAPTAIN VAN VLIET'S LETTER TO GOVERNOR YOUNG [28]

GREAT SALT LAKE CITY,   September 10, 1857

GOVERNOR: The communication from General Harney, which I had the honor to deliver to you yesterday, has made you acquainted with the object of my visit to this Territory, viz: to procure certain supplies for the troops now "en route" for Utah.

As it is late in the season, it is possible that the troops may not be able to reach here the present year; but should they succeed in doing so, the following articles will be required, viz: from 50,000 to 75,000 bushels of oats, corn, or barley; 1,000 tons of hay, and some 150,000 to 200,000 feet of assorted lumber.

[27] He doubtless advised it, but the troops and trains did not stop there. They pushed on to the vicinity of Fort Bridger, where they were halted, primarily as the result of severe winter weather. Van Vliet reached the oncoming troops on Sept. 21. Capt. Gove reports: "He brings intelligence that the Mormons will oppose us in entering the city of Salt Lake. They have burnt the grass for many miles along the road and are determined to resist at all hazards. This much of it is talk, but that some seven hundred Mormons are in the mountains there can be no doubt. Capt. Van Vliet is silent, as his instructions were secret, but he says that we cannot go into Salt Lake this fall. If we do not it will verify all I have written before, and what everyone who knows anything about the country says, and that is 'it was too late to start the expedition.' Had the blockheads in Washington had an idea in their heads, or listened to those who were able to give advice, all this would have been avoided, and in the spring a splendid fit-out might have been made, and supplies of grass, wood and water obtained."– *Gove's Letters*, pp. 59-60.

[28] Printed in *House Ex. Doc. 2,* 35 Cong., 1 Sess., II, pp. 35-36.

I do not deem it proper to make contracts for the delivery of the above articles, owing to the uncertainty attendant upon the arrival of the troops; but I should be glad to ascertain if they can be obtained by purchase in open market, at fair market prices, by the assistant quartermasters who accompany the troops when they arrive here.

When the troops get through the mountains, they will also require some fuel on their march to Rush Valley, or whatever other point may be selected, and I should be glad to know if fifty cords of dry wood could be had in the city to be taken up by the wagons as they pass through it.

I am, governor, very respectfully, your obedient servant,

STEWART VAN VLIET,
Capt., Ass't Quartermaster

6. GOVERNOR YOUNG'S REPLY [29]

GOVERNOR'S OFFICE, TERRITORY OF UTAH,
Great Salt Lake City,   September 11, 1857.

CAPTAIN: Your communication of the 10th instant is before me, and, as you state, the letter from General Harney, addressed by him to "President Brigham Young, of the society of Mormons," and which you, in person, presented to me on the 9th, gave me a general outline of the official duties expected to be devolved upon you on your arrival in this Territory.

It is probable that the number of bushels of "oats, corn, or barley," and the quantity of hay and lumber, specified by you as likely to be required for certain troops "en route" for Utah, in case they should arrive here this season, could be procured. But it must be

---

[29] *Ibid.,* pp. 36-37.

obvious to yourself that, from the uncertainty of the arrival of the troops mentioned, even in your view, in consequence of the lateness of the season, and the already falling of snow in the mountains, and the consequent well-grounded hesitancy on your part to "make *contracts for the delivery of* the above mentioned stores," the question touching any definite amount, pending an uncertain future contingency which, owing to the instability of human affairs, may never arrive, and especially large amounts in so newly settled a country, which has so recently been pinched close upon starvation, is too difficult of solution to admit of being determined from the information at present before me. . .

As to the few cords of wood that you might require for troops passing from this city to Rush valley, should they get through the mountains and wish to pass upon that line, it is highly probable that the requirement for so small a quantity, should all the previous contingencies alluded to by you pave the way to that result, could be easily managed by the quartermasters accompanying the march, and be procured in the neighborhood where they might pass, as there are large quantities of the kind of wood specified by you already in the city.

I am, captain, very respectfully, your obedient servant,

BRIGHAM YOUNG
Governor and ex-officio Sup't of Indian Affairs.

[On Sunday, September 13th, Van Vliet attended the Mormon Church service and was invited to sit on the stand with the Church leaders. He listened to impassioned speeches by Brigham Young and John Taylor and noted the ready response of the audience.[30] Here again was effectively exhibited the distrust of the Mormons and the intense feeling against the coming of an army into their midst. Extracts from these speeches are given in Part VI.

Captain Van Vliet set out upon his return with the definite conviction that the Mormons distrusted the government and would resist the entry of its troops into Salt Lake Valley. Upon reaching Ham's Fork the Captain wrote the official report of his mission.]

7. VAN VLIET'S REPORT [31]

HAM'S FORK, September 16, 1857

CAPTAIN PLEASANTON,
Acting Assistant Adjutant General,
Army for Utah, Fort Leavenworth.

CAPTAIN: I have the honor to report, for the information of the commanding general, the result of my trip to the Territory of Utah.

In obedience to special instructions, dated headquarters army for Utah, Fort Leavenworth, July 28, 1857, I left Fort Leavenworth July 30th, and reached Fort Kearney in nine travelling days, Fort Laramie in ten, and Great Salt Lake City in thirty-three and a half. At Fort Kearney I was detained one day by the changes I had to make, and by sickness, and at Fort Laramie three days, as all the animals were forty miles from the post, and when brought in all had to be shod before they could take the road.

I travelled as rapidly as it is possible to do with six-mule wagons; several of my teams broke down, and at least half of my animals are unserviceable, and will remain so until they recruit. During my progress towards Utah I met many people from that Territory, and also several mountain men, at Green River, and all

---

[30] See Part VI, extracts from Young's speech on this occasion.
[31] *House Ex. Doc. 2,* 35 Cong., 1 Sess., II, pp. 24-27.

informed me that I would not be allowed to enter Utah, and if I did I would run great risk of losing my life; I treated all this, however, as idle talk, but it induced me to leave my wagons and escort at Ham's Fork, 143 miles this side of the city, and proceed alone.

I reached Great Salt Lake City without molestation, and immediately upon my arrival I informed Governor Brigham Young that I desired an interview, which he appointed for the next day. On the evening of the day of my arrival, Governor Young with many of the leading men of the city, called upon me at my quarters. The governor received me most cordially, and treated me during my stay, which continued some six days, with the greatest hospitality and kindness. In this interview the governor made known to me his views with regard to the approach of the United States troops, in plain and unmistakable language.

He stated that the Mormons had been persecuted, murdered, and robbed, in Missouri and Illinois, both by the mob and State authorities, and that now the United States were about to pursue the same course; and that, therefore, he and the people of Utah had determined to resist all persecution at the commencement, and that the *troops now on the march for Utah should not enter the Great Salt Lake Valley;* as he uttered these words, all there present concurred most heartily in what he said.

The next day, as agreed upon, I called upon the governor, and delivered in person the letters with which I had been entrusted.

In that interview, and in several subsequent ones, the same determination to resist to the death the entrance of the troops into the valley was expressed by Governor Young and those about him. The governor informed me that there was abundance of everything I required for the troops, such as lumber, forage, &c., but that none would be sold to us.

In the course of my conversations with the governor and the influential men in the Territory, I told them plainly and frankly what I conceived would be the result of their present course; I told them that they might prevent the small military force now approaching Utah from getting through the narrow defiles and rugged passes of the mountains this year, but that next season the United States government would send troops sufficient to overcome all opposition. The answer to this was invariably the same. "We are aware that such will be the case; but when those troops arrive they will find Utah a desert; every house will be burned to the ground, every tree cut down, and every field laid waste. We have three years' provisions on hand, which we will 'cache,' and then take to the mountains, and bid defiance to all the powers of the government." I attended their service on Sunday, and, in course of a sermon, delivered by Elder Taylor, he referred to the approach of the troops, and declared they should not enter the Territory. He then referred to the probability of an overpowering force being sent against them, and desired all present who would apply the torch to their own buildings, cut down their trees, and lay waste their fields, to hold up their hands; every hand in an audience numbering over 4,000 persons was raised at the same moment. During my stay in the city I visited several families, and all with whom I was thrown looked upon the present movement of the troops towards their Territory as the commencement of another religious persecution, and expressed a fixed determination to sustain Governor Young in any measures he might adopt.

From all these facts, I am forced to the conclusion that Governor Young and the people of Utah will prevent, if possible, the army for Utah from entering their Territory this season. This, in my opinion, will not be a difficult task, owing to the lateness of the season, the smallness of our force, and the defences that nature has thrown around the valley of the Great Salt Lake.

There is but one road running into the valley on the side which our troops are approaching, and for over fifty miles it passes through narrow canons and over rugged mountains, which a small force could hold against great odds. I am inclined, however, to believe that the Mormons will not resort to actual hostilities until the last moment. Their plan of operations will be, burn the grass, cut up the roads, and stampede the animals, so as to delay the troops until snow commences to fall, which will render the road impassable. Snow falls early in this region; in fact, last night it commenced falling at Fort Bridger, and this morning the surrounding mountains are clothed in white. Were it one month earlier in the season, I believe the troops could force their way in, and they may be able to do so even now; but the attempt will be fraught with considerable danger, arising from the filling up of the canons and passes with snow.

I do not wish it to be considered that I am advocating either the one course or the other; I simply wish to lay the facts before the general, leaving it to his better judgment to decide upon the proper movements.

Notwithstanding my inability to make the purchases I was ordered to, and all that Governor Young said in regard to opposing the entrance of the troops into the valley, I examined the country in the vicinity of the city with the view of selecting a proper military site.

I visited the military reserve, Rush Valley, but found it, in my opinion, entirely unsuited for a military station. It contains but little grass, and is very much exposed to the cold winds of winter, its only advantage being the close proximity of fine wood; it is too far from the city, being between forty and forty-five miles, and will require teams four days to go there and return. I examined another point on the road to Rush Valley, and only about thirty miles from the city, which I consider a much more eligible position; it is in Tuella Valley, three miles to the north of Tuella[32] City, and possesses wood, water, and grass, but it is occupied by Mormons, who have some sixty acres under cultivation, with houses and barns on their land. These persons would have to be dispossessed or bought out. In fact, there is no place within forty, fifty, or sixty miles of the city, suitable for a military position, that is not occupied by the inhabitants and under cultivation. Finding that I could neither make the purchases ordered to, nor shake the determination of the people to resist the authority of the United States, I left the city and returned to my camp on Ham's Fork. On my return I examined the vicinity of Fort Bridger, and found it a very suitable position for wintering the troops and grazing the animals, should it be necessary to stop at that point. The Mormons occupy the fort at present, and also have a settlement about ten miles further up Black's Fork, called Fort Supply. These two places contain buildings sufficient to cover nearly half the troops now en route for Utah, but I was informed that they would all be laid in ashes as the army advanced.

I have thus stated fully the result of my visit to Utah,

---

[32] Tooele, about thirty miles southwest of Salt Lake City.

and, trusting that my conduct will meet the approval of the commanding general,

I am, very respectfully, your obedient servant,

STEWART VAN VLIET
Captain, Assistant Quartermaster

P.S. I shall start on my return to-morrow with an escort of ten men.

[Captain Van Vliet continued to Washington, where he amplified the above report by personal interviews and written statements. Delegate Bernhisel reported that Van Vliet's appearance before committees in Washington helped to effect the decision to send a peace commission to Utah.]

III
Colonel Alexander's Reports
on Advance of Troops
and Relations with Brigham Young

INTRODUCTION

Edmund B. Alexander, Colonel of the 10th Infantry, was the senior officer of the advance troops destined for Utah.[1] He was the ranking official throughout the march, for Colonel Albert Sidney Johnston, his superior officer, did not catch up with his army until it had reached Green River Valley. Alexander's reports are the official record of the army's progress; and his was the problem of handling the first dealings with the Mormons. His reports and correspondence follow.

1. COLONEL ALEXANDER'S REPORT OF AUGUST 10, 1857 [2]

HEADQUARTERS TENTH INFANTRY
Camp near Fort Kearny,[3]   August 10, 1857

COLONEL S. COOPER
Adjutant General   U.S.A.

SIR: I have the honor to transmit herewith a field return of the battalion under my command. I have been obliged to rule it, as no printed blanks of the prescribed form have been received. The march from Fort Leaven-

---

[1] Edmund Brooke Alexander was born in Virginia and appointed to the United States Military Academy from Kentucky. He became a 2nd Lt. in 1823, a 1st Lt. in 1827, and a Captain in 1838. He fought in the Mexican

worth here occupied nineteen days, giving an average of fifteen and a half miles per day. The men are in good health and condition, and have surprised me by the endurance they exhibited from the commencement. Though raw recruits when we left Fort Leavenworth, I consider them now fit for any kind of service, and have no doubt they would do credit to themselves and the army. I would respectfully suggest the propriety of ordering the officers detached from the regiment to join their companies as soon as practicable.

If the regiment is to serve long in Utah, it is very desirable to have all the officers with it.

I am, sir, very respectfully, your obedient servant,

E. B. ALEXANDER
Colonel Tenth Infantry, Commanding

2. ALEXANDER'S REPORT OF SEPTEMBER 3 [4]

HEADQUARTERS TENTH REGIMENT OF INFANTRY,
Camp near Fort Laramie,[5] N.T.

COLONEL S. COOPER,   September 3, 1857
Adjutant General U.S. Army.

SIR: I have the honor to transmit herewith a field

War and was made a Brevet Lt. Col. in 1847 for gallant and meritorious conduct in battle. He was made Colonel of the 10th Infantry on March 3, 1855.

Subsequent to the Utah Expedition, he did recruiting service during the Civil War. He retired in 1869 and died Jan. 3, 1888.– F. B. Heitman, *Historical Register and Dictionary of the United Army,* etc. (Washington, Government Printing Office, 1903), I, p. 156.

During the Utah campaign of 1857 some of the officers criticized Col. Alexander severely for indecision, referring to him as the "Old Woman." *Gove's Letters, op. cit.,* pp. 66, 71, 77, 81, and elsewhere.

[2] This report is from *Doc. 71, op. cit.,* pp. 18-19.

[3] Fort Kearny, named for Gen. Stephen W. Kearny, was built in 1848. Located on the south side of the Platte River, a short distance from the present city of Kearney, Nebraska, it was an important station on the Oregon and California Trail.

[4] *Doc. 71,* pp. 19-20.

return of my command for the month of August. As this is the last place from which I can depend upon a communication, I respectfully submit the following remarks upon the march of the eight companies of the tenth infantry under my command from Fort Leavenworth to this place, a distance of 625 miles. The battalion marched from Fort Leavenworth, July 18, and being composed mainly of recruits, the length of the march for the first four or five days was inconsiderable, not exceeding ten or twelve miles. The men, however, became accustomed to marching very soon, and unless the heat was powerful, very few fell out. The march across the prairie country from Fort Leavenworth to the Platte river was made within the time allowed by General Harney's orders, and was, perhaps, the most exempt from loss and accident ever known.

With a train of ninety-seven wagons, and over six hundred animals, but five mules have been lost, one by straying and four by death, and not a wagon has been broken. The journey along the Platte was one of great ease, as the road is good, and grass abundant nearly everywhere, and men and animals improved in health and strength remarkably.

The sick report has never exceeded twenty, and has averaged twelve. This in a command of 500 is very small. No serious sickness has prevailed, though four cases of bilious fever, produced by great alternations

---

[5] Fort Laramie was founded as a fur trade post in 1834. The government purchased it in 1849 and converted it into an important military establishment. For its history, consult L. R. Hafen and F. M. Young, *Fort Laramie and the Pageant of the West, 1834-1890* (Glendale, Arthur H. Clark Co., 1938).

of temperature and miasma of the Platte bottom, have occurred, which the assistant surgeon has recommended to be left at this post. Colonel Hoffman[6] having kindly consented, I have determined to leave them until the two companies of the regiment under Colonel Smith[7] comes up, when they can be brought on. The order of march has been strictly preserved, and the column marched by platoon fronts, with regular intervals, at the rate of 96 or 100 steps per minute. The company arrangements have also been as regular as the ground would admit, having in view the proper guard over the mules and wagons. I have adopted the plan of detailing a company of guard, and posting it in the most convenient place the commander is enabled to post pickets and sentinels, so as to guard every approach. This plan saves many details, lessens labor, and excites a spirit of emulation which insures great vigilance. The officers of the command have attended faithfully to their several duties, and many have shown great powers of enduring fatigue, being on foot all the time. Brevet Lieutenant Colonel Canby[8] has ably assisted in conducting the march, and much of the good fortune is due to his constant attention to the duties immediately devolved upon him.

[6] Lt. Col. William Hoffman was in command at Fort Laramie. He was born in New York and graduated from the West Point Military Academy in 1829. He served in the War with Mexico and the Civil War. He retired from the Army in 1870 and died Aug. 12, 1884. Heitman, *op. cit.*, I, p. 535.

[7] Lt. Col. Charles Ferguson Smith was born in Pennsylvania, and graduated from West Point in 1825. He served in the Mexican War. He died April 25, 1862. *Ibid.,* I, p. 895.

[8] Col. Edward R. S. Canby, a native of Kentucky, graduated at West Point in 1839 and became a Major of the 10th Infantry in 1855. He fought in the Mexican War and Civil War. He was killed by the Modoc Indians of California while negotiating with them in 1873. *Ibid.,* I, p. 279.

On the 5th the march to Utah will be resumed, and although the accounts of the road as regards grass makes it much more difficult than anything we have yet experienced, I hope to give as favorable a report upon my arrival at the Salt Lake City.

I may be excused from expressing the pride I feel in the successful accomplishment by my regiment of so much of its first arduous duty, and I confidently express the belief that unless some very unforseen accident occurs, I will reach the Territory of Utah in a condition of perfect efficiency and discipline.

I am, sir, very respectfully, your obedient servant,

E. B. ALEXANDER
Colonel Commanding

3. BRIGHAM YOUNG TO COLONEL ALEXANDER [9]

GOVERNOR'S OFFICE, UTAH TERRITORY
Great Salt Lake City, September 29, 1857

THE OFFICER COMMANDING THE FORCES
NOW INVADING UTAH TERRITORY:

SIR: By reference to the act of Congress passed September 9, 1850, organizing the Territory of Utah, published in a copy of the Laws of Utah, herewith forwarded, pp. 146-7, you will find the following:

"Sec. 2. *And be it further enacted,* That the executive power and authority in and over said Territory of Utah shall be vested in a governor, who shall hold his office for four years, *and until his successor shall be appointed and qualified,* unless sooner removed by the President of the United States. The governor shall reside within said Territory, shall be commander-in-chief of the militia thereof," &c. &c.

---

[9] Printed in *Doc. 71*, p. 33.

I am still the governor and superintendent of Indian affairs for this Territory, no successor having been appointed and qualified, as provided by law; nor have I been removed by the President of the United States.

By virtue of the authority thus vested in me, I have issued, and forwarded you a copy of, my proclamation forbidding the entrance of armed forces into this Territory.[10] This you have disregarded. I now further direct that you retire forthwith from the Territory, by the same route you entered. Should you deem this impracticable, and prefer to remain until spring in the vicinity of your present encampment, Black's Fork, or Green River, you can do so in peace and unmolested, on conditions that you deposit your arms and amunition with Lewis Robison, quartermaster general of the Territory, and leave in the spring,[11] as soon as the conditions of the roads will permit you to march; and should you fall short of provisions, they can be furnished you, upon making the proper applications therefor. General D. H. Wells[12] will forward this, and receive any communications you may have to make. Very respectfully, BRIGHAM YOUNG

Governor and Superintendent of Indian Affairs

Utah Territory

---

[10] This Proclamation, issued on Sept. 15, 1857, is reproduced following this letter.

[11] This is a strange communication to issue from the Governor of a Territory and be directed against officers and troops of the United States. Capt. Gove reacted vigorously to the proclamation: "The old fool! Did you ever see such impudence, such braggadocio? Such an old idiot! We will show him on which side of his bread the butter should be spread." *Gove's Letters, op. cit.*, p. 70.

[12] Daniel H. Wells was in command of the Mormon troops. For his biography see Bryant S. Hinckley, *Daniel Hanmer Wells and Events of his Time* (Salt Lake City, Deseret News Press, 1942).

4. PROCLAMATION OF GOVERNOR YOUNG [13]

CITIZENS OF UTAH: We are invaded by a hostile force, who are evidently assailing us to accomplish our overthrow and destruction.

For the last twenty-five years we have trusted officials of the government, from constables and justices to judges, governors, and Presidents, only to be scorned, held in derision, insulted, and betrayed. Our houses have been plundered and then burned, our fields laid waste, our principal men butchered while under the pledged faith of the government for their safety, and our families driven from their homes to find that shelter in the barren wilderness, and that protection among hostile savages, which were denied them in the boasted abodes of Christianity and civilization.

The Constitution of our common country guarantees unto us all that we do now, or have ever claimed. If the constitutional rights which pertain unto us, as American citizens, were extended to Utah, according to the spirit and meaning thereof, and fairly and impartially administered, it is all that we could ask; all that we have ever asked.

Our opponents have availed themselves of prejudice existing against us, because of our religious faith, to send out a formidable host to accomplish our destruction. We have had no privilege or opportunity of defending ourselves from the false, foul, and unjust aspersions against us before the nation. The government has not condescended to cause an investigating committee, or other person, to be sent to inquire into

---

[13] Printed in *Doc. 71*, pp. 34-35.

and ascertain the truth, as is customary in such cases.[14] We know those aspersions to be false; but that avails us nothing. We are condemned unheard, and forced to an issue with an armed mercenary mob, which has been sent against us at the instigation of anonymous letter writers, ashamed to father the base, slanderous falsehoods, which they have given to the public; of corrupt officials, who have brought false accusations against us to screen themselves in their own infamy; and of hireling priests and howling editors, who prostitute the truth for filthy lucre's sake.

The issue which has thus been forced upon us compels us to resort to the great first law of self-preservation, and stand in our own defence, a right guaranteed to us by the genius of the institutions of our country, and upon which the government is based. Our duty to ourselves, to our families, requires us not to tamely submit to be driven and slain, without an attempt to preserve ourselves; our duty to our country, our holy religion, our God, to freedom and liberty, requires that we not quietly stand still and see those fetters forging around us which are calculated to enslave, and bring us in subjection to an unlawful military despotism, such as can only emanate, in a country of constitutional law, from usurpation, tyranny, and oppression.

Therefore, I, Brigham Young, governor and superintendent of Indian affairs for the Territory of Utah, in the name of the people of the United States, in the Territory of Utah forbid:

First. All armed forces of every description from

---

[14] This was a strong point in the Mormon case, and one that was subsequently to be noted by non-Mormons. The President was finally to accede and send an investigating committee.

coming into this Territory, under any pretence whatever.

Second. That all the forces in said Territory hold
themselves in readiness to march at a moment's notice
to repel any and all such invasion.

Third. Martial law is hereby declared to exist in
this Territory from and after the publication of this
proclamation, and no person shall be allowed to pass or
repass into or through or from the Territory without a
permit from the proper officer.

Given under my hand and seal, at Great Salt Lake
City, Territory of Utah, this fifteenth day of September, A.D. eighteen hundred and fifty-seven, and of the
independence of the United States of America the
eighty-second.

BRIGHAM YOUNG

5. COLONEL ALEXANDER'S REPLY
TO BRIGHAM YOUNG [15]

HEADQUARTERS 10TH REGIMENT OF INFANTRY,
Camp Winfield,[16] on Ham's Fork,   October 2, 1857

SIR: I have the honor to acknowledge the receipt
of your communication of September 29, 1857, with
two copies of Proclamation and one of "Laws of Utah,"
and have given it an attentive consideration.

I am at present the senior and commanding officer
of the troops of the United States at this point, and I
will submit your letter to the general commanding as
soon as he arrives here.

In the meantime I have only to say that these troops
are here by orders of the President of the United States,

---

[15] *Doc. 71*, p. 35.

[16] This temporary camp, named in honor of Winfield Scott, General of the
Army, was located on Ham's Fork, about fifteen miles above its junction
with Black's Fork of Green River.

and their future movements and operations will depend entirely upon orders issued by competent military authority.

I am, sir, very respectfully, &c., E. B. ALEXANDER,
Col. 10th U.S. Infantry, Commanding.

6. ALEXANDER'S REPORT OF OCTOBER 8 [17]

HEADQUARTERS ARMY FOR UTAH
Camp Winfield, on Ham's Fork, October 8, 1857
TO THE OFFICERS OF THE UNITED STATES ARMY
COMMANDING FORCES EN ROUTE TO UTAH

GENTLEMEN: I feel it my duty to address you the following remarks upon the condition of the troops of the United States, which are now here, and to inform you of the disposition to be made of them. The 5th and 10th regiments of infantry, and the batteries under Captains Phelps and Reno, have been encamped here for the last eight or ten days. Seven ox trains have arrived here and are now guarded by the troops, thus furnishing a supply of provisions for about six months. The Mormons are committing acts of hostility and depredation, and have already burnt three trains containing supplies.[18]

The season is late and the time in which military operations can be effected is very limited; the total supply of forage will last only fourteen days, and it is evident that before the expiration of that time the troops must either be at their wintering place, or from loss of animals they will be unable to transport supplies to it. No information of the position or intentions of the commanding officer has reached me, and I am in

---

[17] *Doc. 71*, pp. 38-40.
[18] Accounts of this activity will be presented in Part VII.

utter ignorance of the objects of the government in sending troops here, or the instructions given for their conduct after reaching here.[19] I have had to decide upon the following points: 1st. The necessity of a speedy move to winter quarters. 2d. The selection of a point for wintering, and 3d. The best method of conducting the troops and supplies to the point selected. In regard to the first, the question was, "Should I, in virtue of my seniority, and the circumstances of the case, move the troops on, or await the arrival of the commander?" I received, about this time, reliable information that Colonel Johnston was placed in command, and that he had not left Fort Leavenworth on the 10th of September. I decided to move, as it would jeopardize everything to wait Colonel Johnson's arrival, which could not take place before the 20th of October. The selecting of a wintering place was next to be considered, and of those suggested, the following were deliberated upon: 1st The east side of Wind River mountains,[20] going back to the South Pass. 2d Henry's Fork of Green River and Brown's Hole.[21] 3d. The vicinity of Fort Hall on Beaver Head mountain.[22] The

---

[19] This has placed Col. Alexander in a difficult position. He has hesitated to assume responsibility and to take positive action. Some of his junior officers have fretted uneasily, and have criticized and condemned the Colonel for his failure to push on toward Salt Lake City. Capt. Gove, as noted above, has been especially strong in his condemnation.

[20] This would be northeast of his present location, and in the vicinity of present Riverton, Wyoming.

[21] Henry's Fork, of Green River, lay south of his present position. Brown's Hole was a mountain-encircled valley on Green River. It would have provided good feed for his stock, but would have been inaccessible to his wagons.

[22] Fort Hall, on Snake River, was established as a trading post in 1834 by Nathaniel Wyeth. He sold it to the Hudson's Bay Fur Company, which operated it for several years. It was a notable way station on the Oregon Trail.

distances from the present position would be, respectively, about 110, 90, and 140 miles.

Independent of its being a retrograde movement, the scarcity of grass, and uncertainty of finding a wintering place of suitable character in the Wind River mountains, were sufficient objections to the first. The second position was accessible and convenient, but the strong probability that the Mormons would burn the grass, and the well-established fact that it would be very late in the spring before the troops could leave their winter quarters and become effective, decided me against this project. The third I have adopted, and I will move as soon as practicable by the following route: Up Ham's Fork, on which we are now encamped, about eighteen miles, to the road called Sublette's Cut-off,[23] then by that road to Bear River and Soda Spring, thence by the emigrant road to the north and east, where I am assured good wintering vallies can be easily found. There are also, in that vicinity, and at Fort Hall, many herds of good cattle which can be depended upon for subsistence. It is believed, on some authority, that the Mormons will make a stand at a fortified place near Soda Spring, and if so, an engagement will take place. This, if successful for us, which I do not doubt, may lead the head of the Mormon church to treat, and by following up a success totally, we may be enabled to obtain quarters and provisions in Salt Lake Valley. But, in any event, we have good wintering open to us outside of the Territory of Utah, and abundant supplies of cattle, and in the spring we will be ready to march down by the broad valley of Bear River to the great Salt Lake City.

To reach this point commands should take Kenney's

---

[23] This was a short-cut from Green River to Bear River, avoiding the much longer route by way of Fort Bridger.

Cut-off from Green River to Soda Spring, a road which runs nearly parallel to Sublette's Cut-off, and which is said to be better for grass and water. After reaching the South Pass, where all trains have been directed to stop until they can be overtaken by troops for escort, the road lies nearly due west, and if any doubts are entertained, persons can be found on Green River who will point it out. The road from Green River to the Bear River valley will be passable for three weeks yet, and as soon as your arrival at Bear River is known, information will be furnished for your guidance.

Very respectfully, your obedient servant,

E. B. ALEXANDER,
Colonel 10th Infantry, Commanding

Received, headquarters army of Utah,
8 p.m., 16th October.

7. COLONEL ALEXANDER ASSUMES COMMAND [24]

HEADQUARTERS ARMY FOR UTAH,
Camp Winfield, Utah Territory, October 9, 1857

COL. S. COOPER,
Adjutant General, U.S.A.

SIR: I have the honor to report that I have assumed command of the troops of the United States, constituting part of the army for Utah, which are now encamped at this point. These troops are the 5th regiment of infantry, eight companies of the 10th infantry, and the batteries of artillery (6 and 12-pounder) commanded by Captain Phelps,[25] 4th artillery, and Reno,[26] ordnance depot, respectively. This

---

[24] *Doc. 71,* pp. 30-32.

[25] John W. Phelps, whose biographical sketch and diary will be found in Part IV.

[26] Jesse Lee Reno, born in Virginia, went to West Point from Pennsylvania, and graduated in 1846. He served in the Mexican War and was killed in the Civil War, in 1862. Heitman, *op. cit.,* I, p. 823.

camp is situated on Ham's Fork, a tributary of Black Fork, which is in turn a tributary of Green River, about 15 miles above the junction of the two forks. Fort Bridger is distant, in a southeast direction, about 30 miles. The 10th infantry reached here on the 28th of September; Phelp's battery on the following day; and the 5th infantry arrived on the 4th of October, and Reno's battery on the same day. On the 5th instant I assumed command, for reasons which I conceive to be of the greatest importance to the troops and their supplies, and of which I shall have the honor to make a full report when a safer and more certain opportunity of sending despatches presents itself. At present, I can give only a statement of what has occurred since my arrival and report the disposition I have determined to make of the troops.

On the day after reaching Ham's Fork, and at the first camp I made on it, I received the enclosed letters from Governor Young[27] and Lieutenant General Wells. The propositions they contain, however absurd they are, showed conclusively that a determined opposition to the power of the government was intended.

I had met Captain Van Vliet on the 21st of September, returning from Salt Lake City, and was informed by him, that although the Mormons, or rather Governor Young, were determined to oppose an entrance into the city, yet he was assured that no armed resistance would be attempted, if we went no further than Fort Bridger and Fort Supply.[28] I was still further convinced of this by the circumstance that a train of more than one hundred contractor's wagons had been

[27] These are printed above.
[28] See the account of Van Vliet's mission, in Part II.

packed for nearly three weeks on Ham's Fork without defence, and had been unmolested, although they contained provisions and supplies which would have been of great use to the Mormons. Upon securing these letters I prepared for defence, and to guard the supplies near us until the nearest troops came up. I replied to Governor Young's letter, a copy of which I enclose, and have not had any further correspondence with him. On the morning of the 5th of October, the Mormons burnt two trains of government stores on Green River, and one on the Big Sandy, and a few wagons belonging to Mr. Perry, sutler of the 10th infantry, which were a few miles behind the latter train. Colonel Waite,[29] of the 5th, though not anticipating any act of the kind, was preparing to send back a detachment to these trains from his camp on Black Fork when he received from some teamsters who came in, the intelligence of their being burnt. No doubt now existed that the most determined hostility might be expected on the part of the Mormons, and it became necessary from the extreme lateness of the season to adopt some immediate course for wintering the troops and preserving the supply trains with us. After much deliberation, and assisted by the counsel of the senior officers, I have determined to move the troops by the following route:

Up Ham's Fork about 18 miles to a road called Sublette's Cut-off, along that road to Bear River and Soda Spring. On arriving at Soda Spring two routes will be open, one down Bear River valley towards Salt Lake, and one to the northeast towards the Wind River

---

[29] Col. Carlos A. Waite, born in New York, attended the U.S. Military Academy. He became a Captain in 1838, a Major in 1847, and Lt. Col. of the 5th Infantry in 1851. He was honored for gallant conduct in the Mexican War. He retired in 1864 and died May 7, 1866. Heitman, *op. cit.,* I, p. 993.

mountains, where good valleys for wintering the troops and stock can be found. The adoption of one of these will be decided by the following circumstances: If the force under my command is sufficient to overcome the resistance which I expect to meet at Soda Spring, I shall endeavor to force my way into the valley of Bear River and occupy some of the Mormon villages, because I am under the impression that the Mormons, after a defeat, will be willing to treat and bring provisions for sale. The supplies on hand will last six months, and if I can get possession of a town in Bear River valley, I can easily fortify and hold it all the winter. There are also several supply trains in the rear to which I have communicated, and if they receive my letter in time they will be saved, and can join us. If the Mormons are too strong for us, which I do not anticipate, the other road will be adopted, and I will make the best of my way to the mountains and hut for the winter. I desire to impress upon you the fact that I, though *not* the commander appointed to this army, have adopted this course, because the safety of the troops absolutely depends upon an *immediate* effort, and having information which makes it certain that the commander will not reach here before the 20th instant, and if we wait until that time we cannot leave this valley. The information I allude to is to the effect that Colonel Johnston had relieved General Harney, and had not left Fort Leavenworth on the 10th of September; and thirty days is the least possible time in which he can arrive here. I cannot, for fear of this being intercepted, tell you the strength of my command or send returns of it. It is strong enough to defend itself and its supplies; whether it is able to assume and sustain an offensive position remains to be seen, but should the commands which I have heard are in the rear come up in time, I think we will have sufficient force to carry out an active invasion. If we are obliged to winter in the mountains you can perceive, by a reference to Stansbury's maps,[30] that we will have an open road to Salt Lake City in the spring, and one which I am told is open early. By this one attack can be made and attention called from the main road (that by Fort Bridger) which may then be traversed by troops. The Bear River route is, however, said to be the best one into the valley; the other passes through canons that can be defended by a handful against thousands, and it is moreover so easily obstructed, that in a week it could be made utterly impassable. The want of cavalry is severely felt, and we are powerless on account of this deficiency to effect any chastisement of the marauding bands that are constantly hovering about us. On the 7th instant I detached Captain Marcy,[31] 5th infantry, with 4 companies to Green River, to collect what he could find serviceable from the burnt trains and to disperse any bodies of Mormons he found.

In conclusion, permit me to express the hope that my acts will meet the approval of the government, and on

---

[30] Capt. Howard Stansbury conducted a survey to and of Great Salt Lake in 1849-50. See his *Exploration and Survey of the Valley of the Great Salt Lake of Utah,* etc. (Washington, Robert Armstrong, Public Printer, 1853), one vol. of text and one of maps.

[31] Randolph B. Marcy was born in Massachusetts and graduated at West Point in 1832. He was made a Captain in 1846, a Major in 1859, a Colonel in 1861, and a Brigadier General in 1861. He retired in 1881 and died Nov. 22, 1887. Heitman, I, p. 689. He was not only an experienced western officer, but he wrote rather extensively. See especially his *The Prairie Traveler,* etc. (New York, Harper & Brothers, 1859); *Thirty Years of Army Life on the Border* (New York, 1866); and *Border Reminiscences* (New York, 1871).

the first opportunity I will make a fuller and more detailed report. It is unquestionably the duty of the government to quell, by overwhelming force, this treasonable rebellion of the governor and people of Utah; and I must most urgently impress upon the War Department the fact that the small body of troops here will need reinforcement and supplies as soon as they can possibly be got here next spring. I would further respectfully suggest that troops should be sent from California and Oregon. It is said that the road from California to Salt Lake is passable all winter,[32] and it is certainly so much earlier in the spring than that from the States.

I am, sir, very respectfully, your obedient servant,

E. B. ALEXANDER
Colonel 10th Infantry, Commanding

8. COLONEL ALEXANDER TO GOVERNOR YOUNG [33]

HEADQUARTERS ARMY FOR UTAH,
Camp on Ham's Fork,   October 12, 1857.

SIR: Yesterday two young men, named Hickman, were arrested by the rear guard of the army, and are now held in confinement. They brought a letter from W. A. Hickman [34] to Mr. Perry, a sutler of one of the regiments, but came under none of the privileges of bearers of despatches, and are, perhaps, liable to be considered and treated as spies. But I am convinced, from conversation with them, that their conduct does not merit the serious punishment awarded to persons

---

[32] This would be true of the Southern route from Los Angeles to Salt Lake City, but not of the Northern route, east from Sacramento.

[33] *Doc. 71,* pp. 83-85.

[34] The notorious Bill Hickman. See his story in W. A. Hickman, *Brigham's Destroying Angel* (New York, 1872). The two Hickmans arrested were presumably his brothers.

of that character, and I have accordingly resolved to release the younger one, especially in consideration of his having a wife and three children dependent upon him, and to make him the bearer of this letter. The elder I shall keep until I know how this communication is received, and until I receive an answer to it, reserving, even then, the right to hold him a prisoner, if, in my judgment, circumstances require it. I need hardly assure you that his life will be protracted, and that he will receive every comfort and indulgence proper to be afforded him.

I desire now, sir, to set before you the following facts: the forces under my command are ordered by the President of the United States to establish a military post at or near Salt Lake City. They set out on their long and arduous march, anticipating a reception similar to that which they would receive in any other State or Territory in the Union. They were met at the boundary of the Territory of which you are the governor, and in which capacity alone I have any business with you, by a proclamation issued by yourself, forbidding them to come upon soil belonging to the United States, and calling upon the inhabitants to resist them with arms. You have ordered them to return, and have called upon them to give up their arms in default of obeying your mandate. You have resorted to open hostilities, and of a kind, permit me to say, very far beneath the usages of civilized warfare, and only resorted to by those who are conscious of inability to resist by more honorable means, by authorizing persons under your control, some of the very citizens, doubtless, whom you have called to arms, to burn the grass, apparently with the intention of starving a few beasts,

and hoping that men would starve after them. Citizens
of Utah, acting, I am bound to believe, under your
authority, have destroyed trains containing public
stores, with a similar humane purpose of starving the
army. I infer also from your communication received
day before yesterday, refering to "a dearth of news
from the east and from home," [35] that you have caused
public and private letters to be diverted from their
proper destination, and this, too, when carried by a
public messenger on a public highway. It is unnecessary
for me to adduce further instances to show that you
have placed yourself, in your capacity of governor, and
so many of the citizens of the Territory of Utah as have
obeyed your decree, in a position of rebellion and hostility to the general government of the United States.
It becomes you to look to the consequences, for you
must be aware that so unequal a contest can never be
successfully sustained by the people you govern.

It is my duty to inform you that I shall use the force
under my control, and all honorable means in my
power, to obey literally and strictly the orders under
which I am acting. If you, or any acting under your
orders, oppose me, I will use force, and I warn you
that the blood that is shed in this contest will be upon
your head. My means I consider ample to overcome
any obstacle; and I assure you that any idea you may
have formed of forcing these troops back, or of prevent-
ing them from carrying out the views of the government, will result in unnecessary violence and utter

[35] This communication from Brigham Young, dated at Salt Lake City, Oct.
7, reads: "Presuming that during a dearth of news from the east and your
home, news from the west might enliven the monotonous routine of camp life,
I have the honor to forward to you two copies each of the latest numbers of
the *Deseret News*." *Doc. 71*, p. 47.

failure. Should you reply to this in a spirit which our relative positions give me a right to demand, I will be prepared to propose an arrangement with you. I have also the honor to inform you that all persons found lurking around or in any of our camps, will be put under guard and held prisoners as long as circumstances may require.

I remain sir, very respectfully, your obedient servant

E. B. ALEXANDER
Colonel 10th Infantry, Commanding.

9. BRIGHAM YOUNG TO COLONEL ALEXANDER [36]

GREAT SALT LAKE CITY, U.T.,   October 14, 1857

COLONEL: In consideration of our relative positions – you acting in your capacity as commander of the United States forces, and in obedience, as you have stated, to orders from the President of the United States, and I as governor of this Territory, impelled by every sense of justice, honor, integrity and patriotism to resist what I consider to be a direct infringement of the rights of the citizens of Utah, and an act of usurpation and tyranny unprecedented in the history of the United States – permit me to address you frankly as a citizen of the United States, untrammelled by the usages of official dignity or military etiquette.

As citizens of the United States, we both, it is presumable, feel strongly attached to the Constitution and institutions of our common country; and, as gentlemen, should probably agree in sustaining the dear bought liberties bequeathed by our fathers – the position in which we are individually placed being the only apparent cause of our present antagonism; you, as colonel commanding, feeling that you have a rigid duty to

[36] *Doc. 71*, pp. 48-50.

perform in obedience to orders, and I, a still more important duty to the people of this Territory.

I need not here reiterate what I have already mentioned in my official proclamation, and what I and the people of this Territory universally believe firmly to be the object of the administration in the present expedition against Utah, viz: the destruction, if not the entire annihilation of the Mormon community, solely upon religious grounds.   . .

We have sought diligently for peace. We have sacrificed millions of dollars worth of property to obtain it, and wandered a thousand miles from the confines of civilization, severing ourselves from home, the society of friends, and everything that makes life worth enjoyment. If we have war, it is not of our seeking; we have never gone nor sought to interfere with the rights of others, but they have come and sent to interfere with us. We had hoped that, in this barren and desolate country, we could have remained unmolested; but it would seem that our implacable, blood-thirsty foes envy us even these barren deserts. Now, if our real enemies, the mobocrats, priests, editors and politicians, at whose instigation the present storm has been gathered, had come against us, instead of you and your command, I would never have addressed them thus. They never would have been allowed to reach the South Pass. In you we recognize only the agents and instruments of the administration, and with you personally, have no quarrel. I believe it would have been more consonant with your feelings to have made war upon the enemies of your country than upon American citizens. But, to us, the end to be accomplished is the same, and while I appreciate the unpleasantness of your position, you

GOVERNOR ALFRED CUMMING

must be aware that circumstances compel the people of Utah to look upon you, in your present belligerent attitude, as their enemies and the enemies of our common country, and notwithstanding my most sincere desire to promote amicable relations with you, I shall feel it my duty, as do the people of the Territory, universally, to resist to the utmost every attempt to encroach further upon their rights.

It therefore becomes a matter for your serious consideration, whether it would not be more in accordance with the spirit and institutions of our country to return with your present force, rather than force an issue so unpleasant to all, and which must result in much misery and, perhaps, bloodshed, and, if persisted in, the total destruction of your army. And, furthermore, does it not become a question whether it is more patriotic for officers of the United States army to ward off, by all honorable means, a collision with American citizens, or to further the precipitate move of an indiscreet and rash administration, in plunging a whole Territory into a horrible, fratricidal and sanguinary war.

Trusting that the foregoing considerations may be duly weighed by you, and that the difficulties now impending may be brought to an amicable adjustment, with sentiments of esteem, I have the honor to remain, most respectfully, &c.,

BRIGHAM YOUNG [37]

---

[37] Another long letter of a similar tone was written by Brigham Young on Oct. 16 (*Doc. 71*, pp. 50-54) in answer to Alexander's letter of the 12th. Col. Alexander answered Young's second letter on the 19th (*Doc. 71*, p. 54) with a brief response in which he said, "It is not necessary for me to argue the points advanced by you. . . My disposition of the troops depend upon grave considerations not necessary to enumerate, and considering your order to leave the Territory illegal and beyond your authority to issue, or power to enforce, I shall not obey it."

10. COLONEL ALEXANDER'S APPEAL
OF OCTOBER 14 [38]

HEADQUARTERS ARMY FOR UTAH
Camp on Ham's Fork, October 14, 1857
TO ANY OFFICER OF THE UNITED STATES ARMY
EN ROUTE TO UTAH, OR GOVERNOR CUMMING

SIR: The bearer of this, Eli Dufor, is a trustworthy person whom I send to obtain information of the position of any trains or bodies of troops coming this way. If my expresses have been received all troops and trains should be on Kenney's Road, and I will be on that with the troops under my command by the 17th, or perhaps the 16th, where that road crosses Ham's Fork or near it. I will wait one day and by that time the forces can be joined; should this be seen by Colonel Johnston or Governor Cumming, I desire to impress upon them the necessity of a rapid march to join us. Eli will tell all that has occurred and his statements may be relied on. I wish him sent back to me as soon as possible with the fullest information concerning the troops. This column is so encumbered with ox wagons that its march is very slow, and it will be easy to overtake it.

The Mormons are preparing, as I learn, to attack us, and it will require all the troops that can be got up to defend the supplies, and overcome resistance. I can hold a position, however, against any force, but the trains will prevent my going on in the face of an attack.

Very respectfully, your obedient servant,

E. B. ALEXANDER
Colonel Commanding

Note.– I am extremely anxious to hear from Colonel Johnston or the governor, and hope they will join or send me their views. No expresses have reached us.

E.B.A.

11. REPORT OF ALEXANDER'S RETURN MARCH [39]

HEADQUARTERS ARMY FOR UTAH
Camp on Ham's Fork, October 18, 1857 [40]
HEADQUARTERS ARMY

COLONEL: In view of the lateness of the season, and the severity with which the winter has already set in, as well as the deficiency of supplies of clothing, forage, and provisions, it becomes necessary to place the troops in winter quarters.

The best available place for this is on Henry's Fork, and the column will march today down this stream, (Ham's Fork,) towards Fort Bridger, and thence to Henry's Fork. [41] It will require about nine days to make the journey, and as soon as I can get matters in train for wintering, I will send you two companies, (about 130 men,) and such additional transportation as I can furnish to bring your trains on to us. Use every effort to bring on the trains, as not a wagon can be spared; and from the nature of that country, (Henry's Fork,) we may have to remain there until May next. Mr. Fickling will tell you how we are off, and can take you by the best route to Henry's Fork.

Send on first the wagons containing clothing and

---

[39] *Ibid.*, pp. 66-67.

[40] On this same day Col. Alexander had his Asst. Quartermaster, Capt. John H. Dickerson, write to Col. C. F. Smith that the soldiers were almost destitute of clothing: "Please bring up with you a few wagon loads of socks, flannel drawers and shirts, shoes and blankets. These are indispensible to the comfort of the soldiers." He also asked for medicines. *Doc. 71*, p. 66.

[41] Capt. Gove wrote on Oct. 14: "A report is out that we are going back. God forbid! The Colonel is not the man for his position; he is harassed nearly to death. He does not know what to do. He consults no one, not even Col. Canby. He will find that his true course is to advise with men of sense and practice. It has now become a matter of judgement and practical sense, and if he desires to be successful he must rely upon his company officers.

[Oct. 15] . . . Rumor has it that we go back. The Colonel has said so already. You never saw such a disgusted set of men as the officers are. They are furious. What his final determination will be I do not know. If we do go back we are in a fair way to be disgraced." *Gove's Letters, op. cit.,* p. 77.

medicines, which are much needed. We have provisions for three or four months, but we still require all that can be got up. If the governor, or General Harney, or Colonel Johnston are anywhere near you, please communicate with them, and tell them the disposition to be made of the troops. Nothing causes me such poignant regret as to be obliged to give up my design of penetrating to Salt Lake City. But the odds against me are too powerful, and the lives of all require me to move to Henry's Fork to winter.

Very respectfully, your obedient servant,

E. B. ALEXANDER
Colonel Commanding

P.S.– When I leave Ham's Fork to go to Fort Bridger, I will try and send a detachment to you to assist in guarding the trains. This will be about the 23d or 24th. Please keep this, as there is not time to take a copy.

E.B.A.

12. COLONEL ALEXANDER TO MAJOR PORTER [42]

HEADQUARTERS ADVANCE OF THE ARMY FOR UTAH
Camp on Ham's Fork, October 22, 1857

MAJOR F. J. PORTER,[43] Assistant Adjutant General

SIR: I have the honor to report that my command is now encamped on Ham's Fork, about 16 miles above the crossing of the Fort Bridger road, and near the point where the route to Fontenelle Creek [44] leaves this stream and takes across the prairie. When I received

---

[42] Doc. 71, pp. 67-68.

[43] Fitz John Porter is the Asst. Adjt. Gen., accompanying Col. A. S. Johnston. Porter, a native of New Hampshire, graduated from West Point in 1845. He served in the Mexican War and the Civil War. He retired in 1886 and died May 21, 1901. Heitman, I, p. 799.

[44] Fontenelle Creek enters Green River from the west side, about 25 miles above the mouth of Big Sandy.

your letter by Eli Dufour,[45] I was already a day's march below the crossing of Ham's Fork by the Sublette road, having been obliged to return to seek winter quarters.

The road from here to Fontenelle Creek will be more, I am afraid, than my teams can stand, and if it does not interfere with the plans of the colonel commanding, I would respectfully suggest that they be spared the travel across, (30 miles.) As long as I am on a stream I can get along, because, no matter how short the march, I can always get grass and water; but to attempt 30 miles with only one watering place, will, in my opinion, prove fatal to the artillery horses and a great many of the mules and oxen. I request, therefore, to be informed, as soon as possible, whether I am to await the colonel on this creek, going slowly down it, or to make the march to Fontenelle Creek at all risks.[46]

I am, sir, very respectfully, your obedient servant,
E. B. ALEXANDER
Colonel 10th Infantry, Commanding

13. COLONEL ALEXANDER'S SUMMARY REPORT [47]

HEADQUARTERS 10TH REGIMENT OF INFANTRY
Camp on Black's Fork, November 17, 1857
ASSISTANT ADJUTANT GENERAL,
Headquarters, Army of Utah.

SIR: I have the honor to submit the following report of my operations from the time I reached the boundary of the Territory of Utah until the arrival of

---

[45] This was the letter from Maj. Porter written Oct. 16th. In it Johnston orders Alexander to move to the mouth of Fontenelle Creek. This letter is not found in the printed documents, but is no. 112 in Department of Utah, Letters Sent. It is printed in Part v.

[46] Johnston apparently reconsidered, and did not insist upon Alexander making the 30-mile eastward march to the mouth of Fontenelle Creek.

[47] *Doc. 71*, pp. 80-81.

Colonel Johnston at Black's Fork. After a long march on the 26th of September, 1857, I encamped, with eight companies of the 10th infantry, at the Big Timbers on Big Sandy, this being my first camp in Utah. On the 27th, I marched across to Green River, and camped near the trading house of one Yates,[48] reaching that point about half-past-eleven a.m., with my troops and trains very much exhausted by the previous three days' marches, which had been, of necessity, very long. At 9 o'clock a.m. on the 27th, an express had been sent to Ham's Fork to Lieutenant Deshler,[49] who was left by Captain Van Vliet at the rendezvous of the supply trains with a small guard. An answer from Lieutenant Deshler was received at 4½ p.m. on the 27th, stating that he was in no immediate apprehension of being molested, and thought he could abide the arrival of the troops, without being immediately reinforced. I felt much relieved by this statement, but upon further reflection, I determined to forestall any attempt of the Mormons, by a change in the usual hour of march, thinking that they would count upon my taking two days to go from Green River to Ham's Fork, or at least that I could not reach there until late in the evening, if I went in one. I accordingly struck camp at 12 o'clock on the night of the 27th, and set out for Ham's Fork. At 7 a.m. on the 28th I came in sight of the trains, and by 11 the regiment was camped near them, guards and pickets established, and everything

[48] Richard Yates, later killed during the conflict.

[49] Lt. James Deshler, of the 10th Infantry, had accompanied Capt. Van Vliet on his westward journey to Ham's Fork. He had been appointed to the Military Academy from Alabama, and graduated in 1854. He served the Confederacy in the Civil War and was killed at the Battle of Chickamauga in 1863. Heitman, I, p. 369.

prepared for defence. I have since learned that a party of Mormons had determined to attack Lieut. Deshler, and destroy the trains on that day, and were prevented by the arrival of the troops about seven hours earlier than they anticipated.

A few days after I reached Ham's Fork, I received a letter from Brevet Colonel Waite, commanding the 5th infantry, stating that he was at Green River, and asking advice as to his remaining there or coming on. I advised him to come to Ham's Fork, as the grazing was very fine, and I knew there was but little at Green River.

Captain Phelps' battery had come up with me on the 29th of September, and on the 5th of October the 5th infantry and Reno's battery arrived. On the morning of the 5th I received information that three supply trains, which had been marching in rear some distance, since leaving Fort Leavenworth, without reference to protection from troops, had been burnt. On the 7th of October I despatched two companies under Captain Marcy, 5th infantry, to Green River, to collect and bring up what was serviceable of the contents of the burnt trains. This service was well and promptly executed. Having, on the 5th of October, assumed command of the troops near me, I determined to march up Ham's Fork, where I would be in a position to reach Fort Bridger as near as from the crossing, or to go into the valley of Bear River, and, by way of Soda Spring and the Malade River, to Salt Lake City. This route gave me the alternative of choosing at Soda Spring whether I would continue towards the city or go to Snake River to winter, according to what might be learned relative to the power of the Mormons, and state of my supplies, and the nature of the season. I was under the impression at this time that Brevet Colonel Smith, who was in command of the only force I had any knowledge of, could join me on Bear River by taking Sublette's Cut-off. I proceeded up Ham's Fork, marching from October 11 [50] to October 19, making about 35 miles,[51] and reaching a point two miles from the Sublette road. On the 19th I ordered a return,[52] having heard from Brevet Colonel Smith, who was so far in the rear, and so much encumbered with supply trains, that it was not likely he could join me; I was also actuated in coming to this decision by hearing that Colonel Johnston was assigned to the command and was coming up.[53] For convenience of moving and grazing, the force was divided into three columns, and, by slow marches, the whole reached Black's Fork on the 2d of November.[54]

Very respectfully, your obedient servant,

E. B. ALEXANDER,
Colonel 10th Infantry, Commanding

---

[50] Capt. Gove wrote, on Oct. 12: "Yesterday we made a march en route for Salt Lake City. . . Our whole train is 9 miles long. It takes about 6 companies to guard it. . . It snowed yesterday morning and also last night. It goes off readily; all this is excellent for us as it wets the grass so they cannot burn it." *Gove's Letters*, pp. 75-76.

[51] This slow progress was largely the result of indecision as to what to do. But on Oct. 17 the snow began to fall.

[52] By the 18th snow was seven inches deep and the weather turned very cold. *Gove's Letters*, pp. 79-80. A retreat to safe winter quarters seemed advisable.

[53] See Part v for Col. Johnston's progress.

[54] Col. Johnston came up the next day. See *Gove's Letters*, p. 89; and Johnston's reports in Part v.

IV
Diary of Captain Phelps

INTRODUCTION

John Wolcott Phelps was a well matured soldier and gentleman when he led his Battery to Utah. Son of a lawyer, he was born in Guilford, Vermont, November 13, 1813. After graduation from West Point in 1836 he served against the Creeks and Seminoles and then escorted the Cherokees on their westward migration in 1838. He served under General Scott in the Mexican War and was breveted a captain for gallant conduct.

After his service in the Utah Expedition Phelps resigned from the army in 1859, but two years later was leading Vermont volunteers in the Civil War as a brigadier general. In 1865 he was chosen President of the Vermont Teachers' Association. He traveled in Europe, was known as a scholar and linguist, and was author of several volumes. In 1880 he was candidate of the American Party for President of the United States. He died in Vermont on February 2, 1885.[1]

Captain Phelps kept extensive diaries. The New York Public Library has some twenty-five of these little black volumes, of which Books 15 to 17 have generously been made available for publication here. The part published reveals an observant man, one with wide interests and calm judgment. The Captain had a great

---

[1] J. G. Wilson and John Fiske (eds.), *Appleton's Cyclopaedia of American Biography* (New York, D. Appleton & Co., 1888), IV, p. 751.

fondness for clouds, and devoted much space to their description. Limitations of space have induced the editors to omit most of these descriptions, those concerned with the nature of the soil and topography, and also some observations irrelevant to present purposes.

In Chicago, on June 7, 1857, Phelps received orders to join his Battery at Fort Leavenworth. His appraisal of President Buchanan at this time was of a man who "has not the firmness, either from habit or character for the epoch in which he finds himself in power." Phelps did not underestimate the Utahns. "The fanatacism of the Mormons," he wrote, "in its effect, is equal to military organization and discipline." [2] We pick up Phelps' record after his arrival at Fort Leavenworth.

THE DIARY

FORT LEAVENWORTH, K.T.   June 14, 1857

Arrived yesterday at about midday. There are here six companies of 2nd Dragoons which average about 50 men each & 50 horses, besides my company which has a total of 49 men present and absent, and 27 horses. It has about 16 horses besides in its possession which belong to the Qr. Master, making a total number of 43 horses. . .

---

[2] He continues in his diary: "They have no sympathies with our Government or people, being generally foreigners without much stay among our people and taught to consider us as persecutors.

"Their opposition to government cannot be overcome without the destruction of its cause, which involves the complete destruction of their life as a public body, and to effect this a large physical force – at least man to man – and all the force of martial law is necessary. They number from 10 to 20,000 men who are capable of bearing arms; and many of whom have born arms in actual service, and have been disciplined.

"Our government reckons upon their division, but with greater reason they could reckon upon divisions among us."

JUNE 23RD 1857.[3] Col. Thomas[4] the Qr. Master who is to superintend the movement of the troops to Utah, arrived yesterday. Governor Walker[5] came into garrison on the evening of the 20th and the next day 6 companies of Dragoons marched in review and my Battery fired a salute.

JUNE 24. A party at Genl Harney's last night – Govr Walker, Capt Walker one of his aid-de-camps, officers and officers ladies and daughters present.

It is said that the Qr. Master, Col Thomas states that he is getting off this expedition he has instructions to annihilate space and time by money.

JUNE 25. A lot of horses arrived yesterday by Steam Boat from St. Louis – of which I have taken 46 – making altogether – good, bad and indifferent 89 –. . .

JUNE 27. Eight companies of the 10th Infy arrived yesterday from Minnesota by way of St. Louis. They are only about half full. They are commanded by their Colonel, Alexander, and are encamped near by. . .

JUNE 28. Rain and much lightening and thunder last evening. It was very much needed; for the air was full of dust. Yesterday morning a row of thunder heads, crossed with strata, as if an array of troops with shields were looking over the western hills, viewing the scene of their contemplated operations.

Some 172 recruits have arrived to-day – 39 for my company and the rest for the 10th Infy. Took 6 more horses yesterday, with 2 halters.

---

[3] The year, where given in the diary, is hereafter omitted. Some short paragraphs are combined.

[4] Col. Charles Thomas, a native of Pennsylvania, became a Captain in 1833 and Col. Asst. Quartermaster General in 1856. He retired in 1866 and died Feb. 1, 1878. F. B. Heitman, *Historical Register and Dictionary of the United States Army,* etc. (Washington, Government Printing Office, 1903), I, p. 953.

[5] Governor of Kansas Territory.

Capt Jones and 3 other officers came with the recruits from N.Y. They left on the 22nd inst. and lost 21 men by desertion on the way – mostly, if not entirely between St. Louis and this post.

JULY 3. Horses and mules have been purchased gradually by the Qr. Mr. Department. To-day another detachment of recruits numbering 119 arrived for the 10th Infantry.

It is said that Governor Walker wrote on the 14th of June that he had been promised the assistance of General Harney, and that he should consider it a breach of faith on the part of the Government if General H was taken away from him; but the General to-day informed me that he has orders to go to Utah, never-the-less.[6]

Took six more horses to-day. The detachment of recruits came from New Port under Lieut Whistler. Lost three on the way.

The sun peered over the nor-eastern hills and a low cloud of interneous fog like the benevolent right eye of my grandfather over the rim of his golden spectacles – beaming thro a hase of joy. . .

JULY 5. Govr. Cummings[7] appeared in Garrison to-day. He is to return immediately to Washington.

JULY 6. 120 Recruits arrived last evening for the 10th Infantry – from New York. Day before yesterday a lot of mules arrived, it is said, from New Orleans, while Mules generally go from this region to New Orleans.

JULY 7. Took 8 more horses yesterday – making 96 in all. They were said to be from Ohio – not so good as

---

[6] However, he remained in Kansas.

[7] He was not to receive his commission as Governor until July 11th; see Part X.

those from Missouri. We have had hay for several days. . . Large wagons loaded with stores of all kinds for the troops and drawn by eight yoke of oxen have been passing continually since my arrival here, toward the far West. Forts Riley, Kearny, Laramie, and Utah, Russel and Majors are the contractors. . .

JULY 9. Three companies of the 5th Infantry arrived last evening by steamer from St. Louis. Saw a whirl-wind moving contrary to the hands of a watch.

JULY 10. Three other companies of the 5th Infantry have arrived. The regiment has lost 200 men by desertion since leaving Florida, and is suffering from the scurvy. It is hot, dry and dusty – offering but a poor chance at grasing. . .

8 p.m. 220 recruits have just arrived for the Dragoons – brought up the River on one boat. The 8 companies of the 10th Infy came on two boats – 5 on one boat and 3 with the field and staff on the other. The five companies amounted to 200 which, the officers who commanded them considered enough for one boat.

JULY 12. About one hundred recruits arrived this morning for the 5th infantry. A copious shower last evening, laying the durt and starting the herbage.

JULY 14. Col. Mansfield, Inspector General, arrived last evening. 8 companies of the 5th Infy are present. Two are yet to come. It rained yesterday. It is a clear bright, cool morning. . .

JULY 15. The remaining two companies of the 5th arrived yesterday. Horses still continue to arrive from St. Louis. It is very hot. Cirrius flecks the sky in all quarters and moves to the Eastward. . . There has been talk yesterday and to-day of sending the Dragoons to Lawrence.

JULY 16. Another very hot day. It was hot and clear during the night. Seven companies of Dragoons left this morning for Lawrence – to reduce a rebellious people to submission to the law. The movement is accompanied with a proclamation of the governor dated yesterday.

JULY 18. Received orders for the march yesterday. They are dated the 15th. The 10th Infantry were reviewed and inspected previous to their marching, which is ordered for to-day.[8] My Battery is to go to-morrow, and the 5th Infy the next day. We are none of us prepared for such a move and my Battery less so than the other commands.

It is very hot. Yesterday at inspection many of the 10th, it is said, fell out of the ranks, overcome by heat. The nights, tho' clear, are oppressively warm.

Capt Reno[9] arrived yesterday from St. Louis. All his stores have not yet come and some of mine are still behind. . .

JULY 19. Weather still hot. Reviewed yesterday, previous to the march to Utah. The 10th Infantry got off yesterday towards night-fall, and encamped three miles from here.

---

[8] Capt. Jesse Gove of the 10th Infantry, reports: "It is complimentary to the 10th that they lead the van. Gen. Harney allowed each company of the regiment to wear shirts and hats, provided they were all alike, the knapsack to be carried in wagons. Accordingly, to commence on the right, Capt. Gardner, gray shirts, black hats; Co. B, Co. I, your humble servant, gray and gray hats, the only ones in the command and they are splendid; Co. C, Capt. Tidball, white shirts; Co. F, Lt. Forney, white; Co. G, Lt. Williams, light blue shirts, black hats; Co. H, Capt. Tracy, white shirts; Co. K, Capt. Dunovant, dark blue and black hats; Co. E, Lt. Dudley, gray and black hats. In all about 600 men when they passed Gen. Harney's quarters in the Fort, band playing and Col. Smith in command. It was a splendid sight. We marched about 8 miles to Salt Creek and encamped." *Gove's Letters, op. cit.,* p. 15.

[9] Jesse L. Reno was to lead the other Battery. See reference to him in Part III, fn. 26.

JULY 20.   Are encamped about 15 miles from Ft. Leavenworth on the way to Utah. Hurried off without due preparation – 3 officers, 1 acty judge, 65 enlisted men – 25 citizens employed as blacksmiths, teamsters, etc. 104 horses – 6 pieces of artillery – two battery wagons, one forge, 16 wagons and one ambulance, etc. Country hilly and undulating as it frequently is in level prairie regions on approaching rivers.

Grasing good. Too short handed by about one half. Ten beef cattle are taken along with two herdsmen. After a very hot spell, the weather this evening is pretty cool. Got off at near sunset on the 19th.

JULY 21ST.   Arrived at about ½ past 8 o'clock a.m. A few minutes after the 10th Infy had left. distance 6 or seven miles. Country thus far presents occassional cornfield whose dark green shows a rich soil. The squatters cabin is frequently seen, holding possession of the soil without occupants. Country very undulating, little timber, not much water, grazing good. Limestone crops out now and then.

Passed a school house yesterday full of boys and girls.

22ND.   Marched about 18 miles and encamped at a half dry creek called the Grasshopper.[10]

The settlements have become less and less until at last it seemed as if there was nothing but a sparse scattering of tenantless claimant's cabins. A load of lumber with a plow on its top would make one of these – the plow soon turning furrows only to give proof of tillage. Two of these huts were of sod. As far as the eye could reach, they could be seen among the undulations which look like immense waves in a stormy green sea. These huts, consisting of whitish boards, and shining

---

[10] The streams and other physical features along the road were by this time so well known that they need no identification here. For earlier descriptions, see vols. III - VI in this *Series*.

in the sun were like the last froth of the waves of immigration as they heave in from the old fort upon the unoccupied prairie.

There is but very little timber or water; soil very good.

Mr. Howard lost his horse last night. Met a train of 19 wagons loaded down with buffalo robes and other peltry from Fort Laramie. . .

23RD, THURSDAY. Got off ¼ before 6 a.m. and encamped at about 1 p.m. a mile off the road, on *Walnut Creek*. Distance about 18 miles, grazing good.

The cabins, with occassional residences continued until about 9 O'clock when we came near the Kickapoo Reserve. A large 3 story house was seen, which is presently occupied by a Presbyterian Mission to the Kickapoos. . .

A train of ox wagons from the westward encamped near us last night. With them were a number of seeceding Mormons who found the severity of the Saints untolerable and who left Utah last April. They said secret assassinations had occurred during the last winter.

In the ox train that we met yesterday morning there was one Mormon. A young Englishman who said that he wished his mother and sisters might be relieved from the thraldom of Mormonism. . .

We have passed two ox trains today on the way to Utah with Government Stores – large wagons carrying some 5000 pounds and drawn by five or six yoke of oxen. . .

24TH, FRIDAY. Marched 12 miles and encamped upon a half dry creek called "The Muddy." Two large ox trains are encamped near by on their way to Utah.

We entered settlements again about 8 O'clock. At one place we saw pins driven down to mark out the limits

CAPTAIN JOHN W. PHELPS

of a town. At this point there is a saw mill driven by horse power, and a blacksmith shop. . .

Killed a beef to-day. Lt. C. (?) of the 10 Infy, arrived in camp from Fort Leavenworth – says that the recruits designed for my Battery arrived at the Fort day before yesterday and that there is a prospect of my Battery being ordered back.

25, SATURDAY. We arrived at this point upon the Nemeha a half dry creek, a little after 11 O'clock a.m., having got under way a quarter before 6 – distance 15 miles. The 10th infantry are encamped near us – they have lost upwards of 100 men by desertion – their strength being about 550.

I lost two men last night by desertion, which reduces my strength to 63 enlisted men. . .

26TH SUNDAY. Agreeably to the order of the march, we have lain by to-day, washing and grazing. A tedious day – have read an old news-paper nearly thro, and visited the pebbly tops of the undulations near us several times. The ever rolling sea of green presented its expanse and over it moved a train of wagons far in the distance, as it were ships on the way to Utah. . . The 10th infantry left this morning. It rained last night. . .

Some dozen settlers have been round our camp to-day.

One of the horses that was kickt in the off fore leg three days ago still limps along on three legs. This is one of the small inconveniences attending the sudden bringing together of raw elements for taking the field; horses that are raised together are not likely to hurt each other by kicks.

27 MONDAY. Arrived at this point – The Vermillion, at ½ past 1 O'clock – distance 20 miles. A cool days march. . .

Two large ox trains and companions left soon after we came up. An enclosure is made of the wagons by night which might serve both as a pen and a military defence. The front part of one wagon is made to overlap the rear part of another in such a way that the whole forms the figure of a horse shoe.

Horses begin to gall badly. . .

TUESDAY 28TH. Commenced the march at 5½ and ended it at 12 distance 20 miles. We are on what is called "The Big Blue" a running stream. It is fordable, tho there is a broken down ferry boat near by. No cabins or houses until we arrived at this point, and here we came upon quite a settlement with a grocery store. . .

Several returned Californians are encamped near by. They say that they left Salt Lake on the 22nd of June – say that there are seceeding Mormons on the road hitherward.

WEDNESDAY 29TH . . . No settlements to-day nor any notable points except "Cotton Wood Creek." This was nearly dry; and near by were steep stony bluffs.

THURSDAY 30TH. Got under way at 5 a.m. and encamped at 10½ at "Rocky Creek"– distance 15 miles. But little water and poor grazing – country burnt up.

There is a party of surveyors near us, laying off townships and sections. We are in Nebraska. No water passed to-day – no huts. There is a trading post at this point for the sale of tobacco and whiskey. A man of the 10th infantry has been picked up at it.

Met a man on horseback this morning with a half filled sack of flour, without saddle and with a rope halter instead of bridle. Said he was from California.

Met a couple of covered wagons with traders from Fort Laramie – left there on the 30th inst.– say that the grazing beyond this is good. We are still entangled with ox trains – they have orders it is said to keep ahead of us. . .

FRIDAY 31ST. Marched 18 miles and encamped on the "Big Sandy" a running stream skirted with a few trees. There is a shop near by; and there were a hundred Cheyenne Indians here this morning, it is said. Country still parched and grasing bad.

Met several wagons containing Mormons of both sexes. Asked them if they were going out as missionaries. I told them that we were going as missionaries to Salt Lake. They said that the Mormons are sending out missionaries among the Indians.

Once in a while a solitary wolf and a few doves are all the moving things seen. . .

SATURDAY 1ST AUGUST. A hot day. Marched 18 miles and encamped on the "Little Blue," a fine running stream. There are large fish in it which one of the drovers assisted by a teamster has been hunting with rifle and revolver. They fired at one fish several times and chased him in the stream. . .

SUNDAY 2ND AUGUST. Marched about 17 miles along the left bank of the "Little Blue" and encamped at about 11 a.m. amidst good grazing. The 10th Infy are a mile or two below us. We lay over tomorrow. . .

Met a considerable number of mules with several wagons containing Mormons. The mules were those which had been used in carrying the Salt Lake mail; as the contract has been anulled the mules are now being driven down to the Missouri River for the purpose of carrying back goods. With the wagons was the sutler of Fort Laramie. An express man for Fort Laramie came into our camp last night.

AUG. 3.   Remain in camp – washing, grazing, greasing and resting. . . Col. Alexander of the 10th Infy with his Adjutant and Qr. Master called to see us while his regiment was passing by this morning. His command, numbering some 550, was followed out by several carriages belonging to officers and then by a long train of 85 wagons – nearly one wagon to 6 men. In my command there is one wagon to about 4 men. . .

TUESDAY AUG. 4TH.   Got off at ¼ past 5 and marched 17 miles and encamped, again on the "Little Blue." The road part of the way very muddy, since a copious shower had recently fallen. . .

Met the mail from Fort Kearney with an Infantry escort in wagons. They brought an open letter directed to commanding officers along the route and the Adjt. General of the army for Utah. It stated that some 800 head of cattle and a number of mules had passed Fort Kearny on the 1st of Aug. that when 28 miles west of that post the herdsmen (19 in number) were attacked by 150 Cheyanne Indians and the cattle and mules were driven off. These cattle were for the use of the expedition to Utah. One herdsmen and 2 Indians were killed.

The letter was from the commanding officer of Fort Kearny, Lt. Marshall 6 infy and went on to state that he had no troops of the proper kind to send after them. We ought to have dragoons along. Last night was a beautiful cool moonlight night – dew heavy. . .

WEDNESDAY AUG 5.   Detained passing a bad gully together with one of the ox trains that accompanies us and by stopping to send off three or four miles for some cattle which it appeared probable might be some of those recently driven off by the Indians. But they proved not to be.   .   .

Distance to-day 12 miles. We are encamped where the 10th Infantry encamped last night on the "The little blue." Capt. Dickerson, Asst Qr. Master with the sutler of Fort Kearny passed us today and brought a mail – also a deserter, McGiven.   .   .

THURSDAY AUG 6.   Marched 16 miles and encamped in a large basin where the grazing is good, and where unexpectedly, the water is also good, but there is no wood; we brought some along with us. Lost 21 of our 25 new cattle during the night, or rather early this morning.   .   .

Met a party of 14 returned Californians, with about one hundred and fifty animals – mules and mares, which they are bringing to the East on speculation. They gave 25 dollars apiece for the mares and will probably get a hundred for them. They were owned by two of the party; the 12 others were employees. They were a rough looking set, but some of them intelligent fine looking men. They came through Salt Lake City and saw about two thousand soldiers from the age of 12 up to sixty going thro drills.   .   .

The expressman on returning from Fort Kearny stopt at our camp last night and I sent official letters by him.

FRIDAY AUG 7.   Made a long march of 25 miles and encamped a mile or more above Fort Kearny. Hence, the distance from Fort Leavenworth to Fort Kearny, as I make it is 275 miles – tho it is generally considered as nearly 300.

The Fort consists of several edifices – some of wood and others of sod. The national flag is flying in their midst, and below it are several pieces of artillery.   .   .

On entering upon the border of the Platte we began to notice Indian lodges made of bushes. They had been recently occupied by the Pawnees and pieces of buffalo skin recently taken off were seen. These Indians are suffering from the small pox and Col. Alexander sent back a letter to me this morning cautioning me against admitting them into my camp – he had excluded them from his. As from the haste with which we got off from Fort Leavenworth we had not time to have our recruits innocculated. This caution was thankfully received. I could ill afford to lose men. The Pawnees have all retired beyond the sand hillocks.

The 10th Infantry are just below us. They arrived this morning. We have thus far seen but little animal life in this land of grass. We noticed the lark this morning and one small lizzard. . .

SATURDAY AUG 8. Lost a horse – a fine old Battery horse, by inflamatory cholic. He grazed heartily last evening and was well till Tattoo. A drench of whiskey was given him and he seemed a little saner. This morning he was led out to graze and soon laid down and died. His stomach had burst with the gas in it. This is the second case that I have had in about a month. It arises probably from something that the horse eats. Burn cotton rags under the nose is said to be good.

Capt Van Vliet arrived this morning, is going to Utah with some mission not generally known. . .

SUNDAY AUGUST 9. Grazing etc. Several of the wheel horses especially of the forge and battery wagons are badly ulcered on the top of the neck from the collars. . .

The Platte is probably the most peculiar river in the world. Tho nearly a mile wide at this point it could easily be waded across. Sand flats and islets are seen in its current everywhere. Its bottom is all sand. . .

MONDAY AUG. 10 The day passed in packing etc preparatory to the march.

The 5th Infy arrived this morning. It numbers 470 men or about 47 per company – has lost some 300 while in the vicinity of Fort Leavenworth. It suffers from the taint of secret societies – the scurvy of the soul as well as from the scurvy of the body. . .

WEDNESDAY AUG 12. Left camp near Ft. Kearny yesterday at about 3 O'clock p.m.; marched some 5 miles and encamped. Met half a dozen Californians with horses. They came thro Salt Lake City on the 9th of July. . .

THURSDAY AUG 13. Marched 15 miles and encamped. Left a distempered horse by the wayside and on sending back for him from camp found him dead. Saw a solitary Buffalo looking down upon us from the sand ridge and speculating, apparently upon the cause of our intrusion. . .

FRIDAY AUG 14. Marched 21 miles. Saw (61 miles from Fort K.) as many as a dozen buffalo. Two of the sergeants ran one down and shot him. Many of their skeletons, bones and chips have been seen during the after part of the march. The hollow places where they have wallowed are numerous. They remind one of the hog-wallow prairies of Texas. . .

Our grazing is very good to-day. We are close upon the bank of the river, where there is no wood, and we are in consequence using buffalo chips, or *Argols*. A number of ox wagons that had been to Fort Laramie with government presents for the Sioux have just passed along on their return. They left Fort Laramie on the 1st of August. . .

SATURDAY AUG 15. Marched 18 miles and encamped in a cold drizzle from the N.E. Have seen numerous buffalo to-day on both sides of the river – at least two hundred of them. The scenery remains unchanged. . .

We had some of our buffalo meat for breakfast this morning. It was the most of anything the meat kind that I ever tasted.

Crows have been seen to-day and indeed occasionally during the whole route. Also prickley pear and thistle.

Noticed a species of grass on the borders of pools of water that looked somewhat like wheat or barley.

[BOOK 16] SUNDAY AUG 16. Marched 18 miles, and encamped about half a mile from the road on a little rivlet of water that empties into the river.

Met a cavalcade of Californians with several Mormons. . . They passed thro Salt Lake City they said on the 22nd of July. Brigham Young was fortifying and intending to fight.

The road has run nearer the base of what I have called the sand ridge to-day than usual. . . Our route at one time lay among numerous holes made by the prairie dogs, and we saw one of these animals hieing to his retreat.

In the early part of our days march we passed a camp of several persons with three wagons and one tent. There was a woman among them. They were traders going to Fort Laramie, had left St. Joseph Mo. on the 22nd of July, had followed our column probably with whisky for sale. They had a surveyors compass with them – mounted on its tripod and said that they where laying out a city. . .

MONDAY, AUG 17. Marched 24 miles – a long march

which we were compelled to make chiefly on account of the troublesomeness of horse flies. During about 8 miles they were very numerous and exceedingly pertinacious, rendering some of the horses almost frantic.   .   . We encamped on the South Branch of the Platte, about a mile above the 10th Infantry, which arrived but a few minutes before us. Between us is a center herd of cattle for the Army for Utah which the contractor keeps along with the troops for safety.

The North and South branch of the Platte meet a few miles below this. This branch is like the main stream, only its valley and channel are not so wide. The first, at this point, is from one to two miles in width and is a deep channel.   .   .

We have seen no buffalo to-day. Perhaps they are driven off by the flies. And why these flies should be limited to localities, as they appear to be, is a question. They are green, like the grass, and the region occupied by them is a little more sandy than usual.   .   .

The *Argols* came extensively in use. The odor from them, while burning, is not unpleasant.

The day dawned beautifully. Venus, or some other bright star, led forth. Dian with her silver bow all bent as if to hunt buffalo upon the prairie, and then followed the "meek-eyed moon," while a train of dark cold yet blushing clouds moved towards her greetingly from the So West, promising us mortals a warmer day. A fog lay close along the river's course, but as the sun arose it filled the air and hid the world from view.   .   .

We have clumps of cotton wood trees near us; and the grazing is pretty good. While my horse was kicking at the flies to-day and occasionally hitting my left heel with his left hind foot, the idea occurred to me of a feat to be announced by some circus, viz: That of a saddled horse putting his left hind foot in his own stirrup, and mounting himself!! My horse would do it, I believe, if any one could. He would certainly rather ride than walk.

The 10th Infantry boast of having killed 10 buffalo. We have destroyed only three.

TUESDAY, AUG. 18. Grazing, washing, greasing, etc. and assigning the drivers to posts as Cannoneers in case of necessity. When in Battery the lead horses of the limber of the piece are to be brought up head to head with the lead horses of the Caisson, and the lead driver of the Caisson dismounts and holds both lead teams. The two wheel drivers remain mounted and hold their teams. The Chief of piece acts both as gunner and No. 4, and in this way we get 5 pretty reliable men to serve each piece.

5 men to each piece	.	. .	30
3 drivers to each 2 Carriage	.		18
3 " to each Limber	.	.	9
2 Musicians	.	. . .	2
Total	.	. . .	59

The Company being 64 strong, there are, under this arrangement, still 5 available men (recruits) if they are not sick. . .

Killed another beef to-day. How strange it is that life should exist only at the sacrifice of life. And it is sad to see that innocence is generally the sacrifice to wickedness. . .

Music from the band of the 10th Infantry is heard plainly in our Camp. It was very cold last night, as it was the night before, and we were again enveloped in fog this morning. Tho' the day has been clear and bright it has not been very warm. One of the men is suffering from fever and ague.

WEDNESDAY, AUG. 19. Remain in Camp. The 10th Infantry left this morning. A party of Californians passed by our camp pretty early on their way to the States. They left a couple of California papers with us – which are filled with accounts of murders and other such violences. They say that Brigham declared in one of his sermons That unless we bear ourselves pretty peaceably he will "spank us and send us back."

It has been a beautiful day, nearly clear, with a fresh breeze from the south. . . Grazing good, and we have mown enough for the night yesterday and to-day.

THURSDAY, AUG. 20. Commenced the march at ½ past 5 and ended it at ½ past 12 with a stoppage of 20 minutes to water – distance 20 miles. The route lies up the right bank of the South Fork of the Platte. This Fork resembles the main stream, tho its water is more confined, being proportionally in a narrower compass. It is still shallow. The valley thro which it runs is only about a mile in width. . .

Have seen no buffalo to-day, but started up a couple of deer. We have seen this animal occasionally, tho' not very often, since the beginning of our march. Another man is badly poisoned in the face. There is some weed or plant that has affected the troops in this way, more or less, ever since their first encampment upon the Missouri.

It is a pitty that our medical men of the Army are not more acquainted with Botany. They might with some information upon that subject not only enable the command to avoid poisonous plants but to point out such as when boiled as greens, might prevent the scurvy. They might too, be of a great use with mounted corps if they would acquire some knowledge of veterinary practice. . .

Yesterday and day before we used some of our desiccated vegetables. They are indeed very palatable, and undoubtedly very useful as a preventitive of the scurvy.

FRIDAY, AUG. 21. Made 19 miles, and encamped on the edge of the stream, 3 miles below the crossing. Grazing pretty good, but no fuel, except *argols*. These are numerous, tho' no buffalo have been seen to-day. We saw one prairie dog, barking in the mouth of his hole, two deer, and the Dr. saw two badgers. These are all the animals except a few birds that we have seen to-day. Among the birds is a species called the buffalo bird – small, darkish colored, and very familiar with our horses, lighting upon their backs while grazing.

Besides the plants heretofore mentioned, we have noticed from time to time the flag, a species of milk-weed, a dwarf sumach, and one or more varieties of cactus, besides the prickly pear. The botany of this region would be interesting to those who could understand it. . .

SATURDAY, AUG. 22ND. Commenced the march at 5 a.m. and ended it at ½ past 3 p.m. distance 22 miles. At about 4 miles from last night's camp we crossed the South Fork of the Platte. The water, at no time, came above the axles. Ascending the left bank of the valley by several long slopes we again found ourselves on the rolling prairie. It is dry and parched, showing but little evidence of rain. Finally at 10 minutes before twelve o'clock we reached the slope, the descent into Ash Hollow and to the North Fork of the Platte. The

10th Infantry were before us, clogging the way, and we were compelled to stop for one hour.

The view was down upon a basin of numerous gullies and ravines, with precipitous acclivities and dividing ridges, from which a grayish limestone was protuding. Here and there was a cedar tree; and way down through the broadest ravine the river could be seen with its margin of green. We had a very steep declivity to descend, and after the Infantry had passed down with their 85 wagons, we occupied an hour in descending with the battery and its train[11]– in all 33 carriages. Captains Dickerson and Clarke overtook us with their train while we were making the descent, and brought the news of a fight with the Cheyennes by Col. Sumner's command. The Indians had formed in line of battle and charged upon our troops. Some 12 of them were killed and a number wounded. Our side lost 2 killed and a few wounded. The Col. followed in pursuit; burnt one of their villages, and is continuing in the pursuit down to the Arkansas River.[12] Hence, we shall not have four of his companies, as we expected, to accompany us to Utah.

The fight occurred on the 29th of July, some where on the Republican Fork of the Kansas River, South of Fort Kearny.

Just before arriving at the crossing of the S. Fork of the Platte, we met Capt. Hendrick's Command of two Companies of the 6th Infantry, which were the escort of a surveying party under Lt. Bryant of the Topo-

---

[11] The descent to Ash Hollow was steep and difficult to negotiate. The numerous tracks may still be seen.

[12] A fuller account of this engagement is to be given in the next volume of this Series.

graphical Engineers. They have been to Bridger's Pass by a new route, which is not only shorter than the one that we are now following, but it affords good grazing.[13] Having accomplished their work they are returning by Fort Leavenworth. It is very much to be regretted that the authority directing this expedition has not been sufficiently active to have furnished us guides for this new route. It is very much to be feared that we shall lose some of our animals in consequence. I sent letters by this opportunity.

There were encamped near the crossing some of Col. Sumner's Command of the 1st Cavalry.[14] Leaving a kind of depot there of wagons, spare men, etc. the number of men over and above the number of his horses, and taking his supplies on pack mules, he left in search of the Cheyennes. . .

The vicinity of the Crossing for a short time exhibited a pretty animated appearance. As we were approaching it, the Exploring expedition was coming away from it; the 10th Infantry were winding up the opposite bank of the valley, and the encampment of the 1st Cavalry was nearby – making four different detachments of U.S. troops all brought together at the same point in the midst of the prairie. . .

We are encamped on the margin of the North Platte just below the 10th Infantry, right at the mouth of the ravine, and, with our tents, our hundred wagons, our seven hundred draught animals, some five hundred

---

[13] Lieut. Francis T. Bryan conducted various other western surveys for wagon roads. See accounts in W. Turrentine Jackson, *Wagon Roads West*, etc. (Berkeley and Los Angeles, University of California Press, 1952). Bryan graduated from West Point in 1846, served in the Topographical Engineers. He resigned June 10, 1861. Heitman, *op. cit.*, p. 257.

[14] Principally the wagon train. See Volume 9 of this *Series*.

beeves, and not least, six or seven hundred men, some getting wood, some grazing, others gazing upon the scene from the Cliffs, we occupy a long space along the river and form a stirring scene.

The Right bank of the River and the jaw of the Ravine rising in nearly perpendicular lime-stone steeps right above us, send back the light of our camp fires mingled from time to time with the softened and sweetly resounding echoes from the strains of our bugles. How strange that the serious old rocks should join in so harmoniously with such music! It has set all our men of musical qualities a-whistling their sweetest airs, showing how imperceptibly influences steal in upon and move our sensibilities. . . But besides sweet echoes, we have sweet odors too, for the burning cedars, cut and brought down from the cliffs, exhale a most pleasant perfume and agreeable incense.

Ash Hollow is near the scene of an Indian fight that occurred in consequence of the destruction of Lt. Grattan and his command by the Indians at Fort Laramie several years since. . .[15]

A little enclosure made of sods, close upon the bank of the river about a hundred paces from me, occupied

---

[15] Lt. John Lawrence Grattan graduated from West Point in 1853, went to the Sioux camp below Fort Laramie in August, 1854, to demand surrender of the Indians who had taken an emigrant's cow. When refused the culprits, young Grattan attacked the camp, and he and his 29 men were wiped out. The army launched a punitive expedition under Col. Harney the next year. The principal engagement, called variously the "Battle of Ash Hollow," the "Battle of Blue Water," or the "Harney Massacre," occurred on the Blue Water branch of the North Platte, some six miles from Ash Hollow. Harney reported 86 Indians killed, 5 wounded, and about 70 women and children captured. His own loss was 4 killed and 7 wounded.

For an account of these affairs, with sources cited, see the chapter, "The Grattan and Harney Massacres, 1854-1855," in L. R. Hafen and F. M. Young, *Fort Laramie and the Pageant of the West, 1834-1890* (Glendale, Arthur H. Clark Co., 1938).

for a while after the affair of Ash Hollow or Blue Water as it is called, by two companies of Infantry, but long since wholly deserted, bears the name of Fort Grattan [16]– in its loneliness and abandonment a fit symbol of the fate of him from whom it was named. . .

SUNDAY AUG. 23RD. Remain in Camp. A cold drizzling day with a fresh breeze from the S.E. . . The Infantry got off at about half past 5 this morning. . .

The North Platte is about the same width as the South Platte, and the two when joined, retain about their united width, without an increase of depth. My orderly sergeant rode across the river this morning to examine the grazing there, and horse twice sank in quicksand. . . A cold, comfortless day.

MONDAY, AUGUST 24. Marched 18 miles – a considerable portion of the way thro' heavy sand – a fatiguing day's work. One of the teams balked badly; and I was fairly softened by the excessive whipping that we gave one of its three pairs. As it was, tho one of the horses was all trembling, and his hide all welted, we had to affect a compromise by adding a fourth span to the other three – they then worked pretty well. The carriage was one of the Battery wagons.

Some of the horses have been galled very badly. I got 7 double trees – all I could get – at Ft. Kearny in order to give them some relief, if possible, and besides this we have some of the poles triced up by ropes passing over the limber chest, and made fast to the stock; but tho this relieves them somewhat their galls are still bad. One of the horses has had a hole in the top of his neck under the collar as large and deep as a common sized

---

[16] An outline of the fort was noted on the ground by the editors some years ago.

tumbler. It is needless to say that his driver was a raw recruit.

Many of the men are exceedingly stupid. They are such, the most of them, as would not be enlisted in the military service of the countries in Europe from which they came. Coming from the old and sophisticated society of the old world, and being naturally defective in intellect, they cannot possibly understand plain simple language and simple acts. Besides this, expecting unlimited freedom when they arrive in America, they are always suspicious that they are being robbed of their dues in this respect, and yield to authority grudgingly. It is impossible to understand them, or be understood by them. They will stand in helpless inactivity in face of a set of harness or a tent, as a piece of mechanism altogether too complicated to be understood or managed without due deliberation and a proper lapse of time. They would sell their best article of clothing for liquor, though they have reflection enough to know that they will suffer from bitter cold in consequence.

Such are the men that I have had in an American Light Battery that require considerable education during the last seven years. Only one of my eight non-commissioned officers is American. The 10th Infantry does not seem to be much better off in this respect than I am. In fact, as the Mormons are chiefly foreigners, we exhibit to the sun the ridiculous spectacle of an army of foreigners led by American officers going to attack a set of foreigners on American soil.

The few American soldiers who are found among these foreigners are generally the lowest of all Americans, and are frequently more worthless than the foreigners themselves. Once in a while, however, an

American of sense finds his way into the ranks – I have more now than I have had before for a long time – and it is a real relief and even a luxury when in the execution of duty to come in contact with them. You find that at least you have a community of ideas with them, that they understand you, and accomplish more in an hour than could be accomplished by the stolid stupidity of the foreigner in the course of a day. Such Americans, however, when they find themselves in the service and discover that it is not so agreeable or tolerable as they had fancied it, think it no harm to desert – so low have American moral notions become.   . .

If it were prohibited to enlist foreigners, Americans certainly would fill the ranks – Americans will not degrade and stultify themselves by putting themselves on a level with stupid stolid foreigners – as they would do by entering the ranks on an equality with them. These foreigners are driving Americans from Agricultural employments too, and for the same reason, and are thus demoralizing us in a variety of ways.

To see a nation so helpless as we are to rid ourselves of such an evident source of injury presents a lamentable view of human infirmity.

Soon after leaving camp this morning we saw several graves on an elevated site on the left of the road. They were of the soldiers who were killed in the battle of the Blue Water.   . .

No wild animals seen to-day except a rattlesnake which made its appearance on our arrival in camp.

We passed an ox train just before encamping. Several of them got ahead of us during our three days stay at Fort Kearny and we shall probably not overtake them very soon. They can travel about 18 miles a day.   . .

While I write, several wagons are passing on toward Salt Lake City loaded with goods for Livingstone and Kincaid, merchants there. They are driven by Mormons and the mules and wagons are those which used to be employed in carrying the mails.[17] A clerk accompanying the train stopped to see us, and says that his Mormon Company sometimes laugh at the Expedition sent against them, and sometimes talk threateningly. At any rate they say it will bring a great deal of money among them, something which is very much wanted in Salt Lake City.

TUESDAY, AUGUST 25. Marched 22 miles – farther than we should have done had we found a convenient camping place.

Passed our Mormon friends who passed us yesterday – a savage looking set, all squatted round a common center devouring their breakfast. . .

My horse is quite sick – coughs a great deal and looks often at his side. Twice to-day he came down upon his knees, as if too weak to stand. . .

WEDNESDAY, AUG. 26. As the Infantry is encamped a mile or two ahead of us, we remain in camp.

I awoke this morning with an intense headache, but by dint of dozing till 12, added to the virtue of a seidlitz powder, I find myself at 5 p.m. almost entirely relieved. It is a great happiness to be free from pain.

My horse has apparently got the distemper. He probably took cold in that cold Easterly storm, which

---

[17] The B. Y. Express Co. had the contract to carry the mail from Independence to Salt Lake City and expended much money for equipment and in establishing way stations. But their contract was suddenly suspended, probably through the machinations of Magraw, the previous mail contractor and the writer of the letter against the Mormons (reproduced in the Appendix to this volume).

has affected his throat and lungs, and thru these his midriff and stomach. I first gave him (yesterday) a bolus of garlic, and then a drench consisting of 2/3 of a tumbler of molasses, 2/3 of do of water, ½ do of vinegar and a heaped tablespoon of lard – stoppig his com at night.

Today I have applied a blister under his throat, and keep him blanketed. He cannot swallow and some of the above which I gave him is running from his nose.

Within the last few days I have noticed signs of rabbits. We have had no wood since leaving Ash Hollow, except what we have brought from there. The Cedar trees are seen in the distance. . .

THURSDAY AUG. 27. Marched 10 miles and then encamped at ½ past 9 a.m. at a beautiful site on the bank of the stream; a strip of fine grazing below us, wood and *argols* enough, and in view of the most picturesque features of the valley of the North Platte, such as Court House Rock, Chimney Rock, several Pyramids, and watch turrets. . .

We had a sharp frost last night. . . No animals but wolves, ducks, one fox, an antelope, and several rattlesnakes seen today. The buffalo have entirely disappeared; their bones everywhere strew the soil. . .

FRIDAY, AUG. 28. Marched 18 miles and then encamped on a fine grassy margin of the river just opposite Chimney Rock. . . Hardly a day passes but our route is marked out by old cast off pantaloons, shirts, shoes, etc. This road shows signs of having been traveled a great deal and for a great many years.[18] The fur trade

---

[18] Discarding of clothing and supplies had especially marked the California emigration. The previous year (1856) had witnessed the heavy Mormon handcart migration.

has rendered it a frequented thoroughfare to a certain class of people.

The flora of this region, I repeat, is interesting. The wild sage begins to be more common; the prickly pear is more frequently met with since we crossed the South Fork of the Platte, and today we passed through a whole congregation of Sunflowers, turning their honest faces in hearty worship towards the sun. . .

My horse breathes hard, eats little and desires to drink often. I have applied a blister at the intersection of his jaws and throat. . .

SATURDAY, AUG. 29. Commenced the march at 4 min. past 5, and ended it at 6 o'clock p.m. in which we accomplished 25 miles.

The manner in which we are deceived at this stage of the route as to distances is very remarkable. . .

We have seen but very little animal life to-day. We omitted to state that we have occasionally seen the buzzard, during the march. Military movements would be wanting in something without the presence of this bird. Tho the Eagle is the symbol of victory, the reverse of the medal is the buzzard hovering over deserted camps and carrion, seeking battlefields.

Mosquitoes have been numerous to-day, and they are now rather troublesome. . .

SUNDAY, AUG. 30. Commenced the march at 4.55 a.m. and ended it at 12.15 p.m. making 24 miles. Towards the close of our march we passed over a bluff or series of undulations . . . and from there descended to a rich tract of grass along the river a mile or more in width and two or three miles in length. The Infantry with their long train were seen coming along it to pitch their camp. They are now at the upper end.

My command is near the middle. A herd of several hundred beef cattle is between us, and below me at the lower end, an ox train which we had passed, has come up, parked its wagons, horses farther upon the slope of the bluff, and turned its numerous cattle down into the luxuriant grass. The train consists of 25 wagons, and as each wagon is drawn by six yoke of oxen, there are of course 300 oxen. There are at least the same number of beeves present; the animals of my command, horses and mules, number upwards of 200, and those of the Infantry about 500. Hence there are at least 1300 animals feeding upon this grass. On the other side of the river is a tract equal in extent, and on both sides are parties of mowers making hay for Ft. Laramie. . . Passed a small stream this morning running across the road called Horse Creek. Its water was very fine. . . Met another party of Californians with a drove of horses. The principal man seemed to be a Frenchman. They travel about 30 miles a day. . .

Soon after leaving camp this morning we saw three antelopes; subsequently three or four owls – such as intrude upon the prairie dog's hole, and finally one dove, and several crows. These crows appear to be large, fat and dignified; sharing somewhat perhaps in the stately reserve of the Rocky Mountains from which they may have come. . .

MONDAY, AUG. 31. Marched 18 miles. Mustered and inspected the company before commencing the march. After inspection, came into Battery by the command Action Front. Both the men and chiefs of piece were very awkward at it. Their attention has been so much devoted to grazing their animals and curing their galls that they have almost forgotten every thing else.

It is in fact not very easy to make cannoneers of drivers, or expect one set of men to perform both duties at the same time. . .

We are encamped upon the bank of the river, but there is only a very little grazing here. The land is parched up. There is a trading house[19] near by, and we are not far from where Lieut. Grattan and his men were killed by the Indians. A trader informs us that there were 1200 lodges here at the time of the massacre. Of these lodges we have seen several specimens to-day. One of them consisted of 22 buffalo skins, sewed together neatly, and covering numerous poles set up in the form of a cone. . .

Many of the traders among the Indians are descendants of the early French colonists of America. They are simple in their manners and habits, sensible in their conversation, and fond of a half Indian half civilized kind of life. We saw one to-day who had been in this region 20 years. He was just from the Arkansas River,[20] and knew a great deal of the Cheyennes – they are the bravest of the Indian tribes and could and did walk over all the other Indians of the plains. I bought a buffalo robe from him for 7 dollars. The common price for an ordinary one is 5 dollars, & this is the center of the trade. . .

At length, after a march of 600 miles we have seen to-day the first elevations of land that approach the character of mountains. They are spurs of the great chain that extends from Cape Horn to the Arctic Sea.

TUESDAY, SEPT. 1ST. Marched about 10 miles and encamped – near Fort Laramie – thus making the distance from Ft. Kearney 327 miles. An express passed

---

[19] This was probably Bordeau's post, about eight miles below Fort Laramie.
[20] Bent's Fort and Fort Pueblo were trading posts on the upper Arkansas.

us just before our arrival, nine days from Ft. Kearny. It brought me two private letters.   .   .

WEDNESDAY, SEPT. 2ND.   Remain in camp, greasing harness and cleaning arms, persons, clothing, etc., and at 5½ p.m. had a dress parade, inspection, and manual of the sabre and the pieces.   .   .   The appearance of the company was not bad.   .   .

THURSDAY, SEPT. 3RD.   Visited the Fort. Call on Col. Hoffman the Commanding officer and lady, get such articles as I want for the Battery, call at the camp of the 1st Infantry just beyond and near the fort; return, have parade, inspection, manual, etc.

There are several governmental parties at the Fort and in its vicinity at present. Among others is Magraw,[21] who has an appropriation of some 300,000 dollars for exploring the track from Fort Leavenworth, via Fort Laramie and Salt Lake to California. The party consists of a dozen officers, more or less, and a hundred men, and so far as the officers are concerned it is in a state of dissolution. They say that Magraw is an ignorant blackguard, totally unfit for the head of such an expedition, while the chief engineer of the party is.[22] It appears that Magraw's brother was a delegate to the convention that nominated Buchanan for the presidency, and hence, in the political logic of the present day, *must* be a party chief for a scientific exploring expedition.

But ever since Mr. Benton made such a noise about Fremont's journeys thro the country,[23] any other ex-

---

[21] Former mail contractor.

[22] This was F. W. Lander, a competent civilian engineer. Regarding his extensive services, see Jackson, *Wagon Roads West, op. cit.*

[23] Senator Thomas H. Benton, Fremont's father-in-law and supporter. See vol. VII of this *Series.*

travagance with regard to it is not so much to be wondered at. But folly, absurdity, and false pretensions must at length become exposed, . .

Another party present is that of Lieut. Warren's,[24] which is about to proceed toward the Blue Mountains and the L'eau-qui-court river[25] . . . with a view to ascertaining what timber can be found in that region. It is said to abound in pine.

This post is one of the prettiest outposts that I have seen. It has been furnished with a steam sawmill and enough lumber has in consequence been made to enable the commanding officer to put up passable quarters and store houses, . . But by far the neatest and most elegant and comfortable quarters are those which the commanding officer has designed and executed in adobes. There is a neatness, simplicity, and architectural effect about them that is really classical. . .[26]

FRIDAY, SEPT. 4TH. Remain in camp all day – cleaning the metal parts of harness, etc. The 5th Infantry arrived to-day and encamped just below us. The officers being mounted formed quite a cavalcade as they came in. They have 470 men and 100 wagons. . .

SATURDAY, SEPT. 5TH. The 10th Infantry left this morning, and a detachment of 65 dragoon recruits with horses arrived. They are for the two companies of Dragoons which are here, and have accompanied the ordnance train. This train will arrive tomorrow.

---

[24] G. K. Warren, graduate of West Point in 1850, served in the Corps of Topographical Engineers. He did surveys for wagon roads and railroads. He also prepared extensive maps of important western explorations. He died Aug. 8, 1882.

[25] The Running Water, or Niobrara River, of Nebraska.

[26] A number of the buildings of this historic post have been preserved or restored; the fort is now a National Monument.

The men were paid off. One of the fur traders brought 36 very indifferent robes for sale and tho they would not bear transportation to the States, he was paid for them by the men. Prices ran from 3 to 6 dollars apiece. . .

Sent my horse to the garrison to give him a chance for recovery, also two lame horses, one gravelled and the other corked, having been lame nearly a month.

SUNDAY, SEPT. 6TH. Left camp near Fort Laramie at 5:55 this morning and encamped on the North Platte at 10 a.m.— distance 11.71 miles. We are particular to give hundredths since we now have an odometer which was kindly loaned to us by Lieut. Warren. That promising young officer also politely supplied us with maps of the country and an almanack for getting the time of day. . .

The sage has a neat silvery look and is a pretty plant. . . The rose bush and the dwarf sumach with its little yellow burs are still also seen. . .

Laramie Peak, an elevation of some 7000 feet above the level of the sea, and the rest of the ridge in which it lies, blue and hazy in the S.W., have been seen more fully today than before. . . The camp is redolent with the fumes of argols, hempen sacks, tobacco, leather, and wild sage for such are the ingredients of fumigating torches which are held under the noses of the horses. Some 4 or 5 of them are suffering from colds with coughing and running at the nose. The object of the smoke is to act upon their lungs. . .

MONDAY, SEPT. 7. Commenced the march at 4:45 and ended it at 12:15 – distance 22.06 miles. The day is as hot as summer. . . The distance from Fort Laramie to Salt Lake City is about 500 miles. . .

We took a guide at Fort Laramie for the purpose of

disclosing to us the best grazing possible. His name is John S. Smith;[27] and he has been in this region and on the plains as a fur trader for a great many years. But he can certainly do more at talking than in finding grass. . .

TUESDAY, SEPT. 8. Another hot and dusty day.– the road good, not so hilly as yesterday. Distance made, 19.64 miles. We have touched the Platte twice to-day. . . For the first time we have noticed boulders of granite. . .

WEDNESDAY, SEPT. 9. Still another warm day. . . We are at last leaving Laramie Peak and the chain of Black Hills behind and to our left. Again our camp is close upon the bank of the river, the course of which is marked out by a few scattering tufts of small cotton-wood trees.

One of the Sergeants has invented a contrivance by which the horses are very much relieved of their galls. It consists of a pole five or six feet in length which passes over the limber chest and is made fast by ropes – to the pole at one end and to the stock at the other. The pole is not only thus kept from bearing upon the horses necks, but is made to partake of the motion of the after part of the carriage so that its movements are less sudden and jerky.

Saw, for the first time, a covey of sage hens. They appeared to be very fat. Saw also a little owl coming out of a [prairie] dog's hole. . . The dogs bark at us occasionally. They would seem to be squirrels rather than dogs. During the last three days we have seen several ducks and one flock of pigeons. . .

---

[27] John Simpson Smith was a noted Mountain Man and frontiersman. He has been identified as the original of Killbuck, lead character in G. F. Ruxton's *Life in the Far West* (Norman, University of Oklahoma Press, 1951), 240-44. He was one of the founders of Denver, Colorado.

THURSDAY, SEPT. 10.   Met with an accident to-day
– broke a pole of one of the wagons. It was done whilst
descending one of the worst pitches that we have seen
except that of Ash Hollow – though the Battery came
down without locking.   . .

We are encamped again upon the Platte – grazing
short and poor, having been eaten to the ground. Along
the stream nearby are found the fruit called Buffalo
berries. They are of the size and color of currants.   . .
They seem to partake in flavor of the apple, cherry,
and currant. The bush upon which they grow has a
leaf not unlike that of common sage, while the stalk
itself is somewhat like the cherry.   . .   Several flocks
of ducks seen today and a brace shot for dinner.

FRIDAY, SEPT. 11.   It rained last night, though not
a great deal. The wind died away and it became
warmer. Marched 19.16 miles, and encamped about a
mile from the Platte at the base of the hills where we
found a little grass.

Six or seven miles from our last night's camp we
crossed Deer Creek which is nearly dry. Coal is found
there tho it is not very good. There is a Trading house
there, a blacksmith's shop and several Indian lodges.
Two or three broad faced Indian women who came
out of the house to look at us, had each a half-white
little one strapped to her back. Half a dozen or more
large stalwart men were standing about. One of them
was a discharged sergeant of the 5th Infantry.   . .

SATURDAY, SEPT. 12.   Marched 5.82 miles and encamped about 121.7 miles from Fort Laramie, two
miles above the Infantry on the Platte. Grasses good
considering, but very scant.

This has been the worst day that we have passed. Our

camp last night was made muddy by the rain (for considerable rain fell during the night) and the boots were made unpleasantly heavy by it. . . A day of more suffering; the wind blowing away even thoughts.

SUNDAY, SEPT. 13. . . Our mess wagon was upset. The driver was the most hurt of all, and he only in his work as a teamster. He is a half breed Cherokee and a boy of great energy and force of character. . .

Six miles from camp we came near what is called "The Bridge."[28] It has been commenced across the Platte by someone as a speculation, the river being too high at certain seasons to be forded as it now is. The maker of the bridge, it is said, has made money and more than would have done by gold digging in California whither he was bound when the idea struck him. . . There is a trading establishment near the bridge, and also a coal mine. It is there that one route to Salt Lake finally leaves the Platte and strikes next for the Sweetwater, one of its tributaries.

One of the soldiers caught a large string of fish to-day – they appeared to be dace. The raven, which we have heretofore called the crow, is the only representative of wild animal life which we have seen to-day. . . This region, it is said, is noted for its wind at all seasons of the year.

MONDAY, SEPT. 14. Remain in camp, grazing, greasing, washing, etc. . . We have got a copy of the *Deseret News* of the 12th of August – which was found at the Bridge. It contains discourses from the prophet, brothers Kimball, Elias Smith and George A. Smith and a historical sketch of the founder of Mor-

---

[28] This was near the site of present Casper, Wyoming. The famous Platte Bridge Fight with the Indians took place here in 1865.

monism, Joseph Smith. Also, an editorial – all of which, except the sketch, allude to the force which is moving against Utah. The Saints evidently feel considerably honored by having become objects of importance enough to attract such notice from the United States. They are not very determined as to what they will do; tho' fighting is talked of considerably. Brigham says that his women bother him for new bonnets and such things. . .

TUESDAY, SEPT. 15. Marched as far as the Red Buttes – 10.61 miles – and encamped again and for the last time upon the Platte. . . We have at length approached quite near the ridge of mountains that has been running along on our left. The river runs thro it here, and the banks on both sides are red – hence the name of Red Buttes.

On our arrival here a man met us who said that he was a Californian, had been robbed in the Great Salt Lake Valley, had seen 700 Mormons at Green River and one hundred at Sweet water ready to defend the pass. He dismounted some distance from camp, borrowed cooking utensils from the wagon master; wanted a blanket and pair of shoes from the First Sergeant, cooked his meal of neat fresh looking provisions, and finally, in the course of some two hours, mounted and rode off down the River, having managed to see and count everything if he chose. . .

WEDNESDAY, SEPT. 16. Marched 13.42 miles. It is within a few days of two months since we left Fort Leavenworth, and this is the first time that it has rained while we were on the road.

We have finally taken leave of the Platte, . . The horses have to stand the long cold nights thro without

any long fodder or grass. Last night, they had a considerable allowance of long coarse grass. They have
four pounds of corn at night and four more in the
morning. . .

Our fires are made of wild sage and grease-wood.
The odor of this sage is very agreeable.

THURSDAY, SEPT. 17.   Marched 14.61 miles and encamped on a beautiful small but deep brook containing
fish. . .

An express arrived with pub. letters from Capt.
Simpson, the A Commissary of the Expedition, and
four private ones from the States for persons of the
10th Infantry. The Capt. says that the ox trains which
are to supply us with bread are behind us, so that if we
want hard bread we must look backwards instead of
forward for it. A pretty time – amidst cold barrenness
and short rations of corn, with wintering a long way
off, to be detained for provisions.

FRIDAY, SEPT. 18.   It is but two months since we left
Fort Leavenworth, during which time we have made
about 800 miles.

We marched 18.12 miles to-day and are encamped
about a mile below Devils Gate on the right bank of
the Sweet Water. Devils Gate is a narrow passage thro
a rocky hill thro which the river runs. The Sweet
Water, a fine large mountain brook, filled with fish, is
a tributary of the North fork of the Platte. . . We
reached the Sweet Water about four miles back at a
trading house and crossed on a toll bridge. Not long
afterwards we came up with Independence Rock,[29]
which is a rounded hill of naked granite looking like

[29] See R. S. Ellison's pamphlet, *Independence Rock, the Great Record of
the Desert* (1930), for a listing of names inscribed upon this rock.

one half of an immense boulder projecting above the soil. One can understand, when looking at this and other hills around, why the mountains which we are entering among are called Rocky Mountains. . .

Some four miles or more before arriving at the bridge over the Sweet Water we passed a region abounding in potash [alkalis]. Ponds in a clayey soil had become dessicated and the bottoms of them, like that of the potash kettle when fully boiled down, were covered with clots of potash. There were hundreds of tons of it.

We sent back a wagon this morning to the nearest ox train to get to-day additional hard bread.

While I write, a man rides up to my tent on a mule leading a horse with a pack on and says he is a returned Californian. He wants to stay in my camp all night and abuses the Mormons without stint. I tell him that I believe him to be a spy – that I detest spies – and advise him to go to the house at the bridge. He decides at once to do so, but still lingers and palavers a full hour. . .

SATURDAY, SEPT. 19.   Marched 19.31 miles and several of the horses gave out. The road most of the way very bad – muddy, white with potash as if frosted over & the ruts made by the trains which have gone before as hard almost as if frozen, making the draught very hard. . .

When about three hours out from camp this morning we met a man and woman on foot who said that they were English Mormons and that they had come away from Salt Lake in disgust.

We passed the Mormon trading house just above Devils Gate.[30] It was entirely abandoned and a flag staff

---

[30] This was also a former mail station. It was here that the Martin Company of Mormon handcart emigrants found some shelter in November, 1856, and then suffered such losses in nearby "Martin's Cove."

in the center of the establishment had been cut down, it is said by the 10th Infantry; a big house and a flag flying.

When near the close of our march we met a party of half a dozen of those who said that they were Californians and had come thru Salt Lake City three weeks ago. Brigham, they said, is all for war.

We are encamped upon the Sweet Water which has not one single tree or shrub upon its course. It is about 30 feet wide and its depth is such that our men cross it without wetting the tops of their boots.

MONDAY, SEPT. 20. Marched 14.09 miles. We are in a broad passway between mountains – those on our right are masses of granite while those on the left are covered with soil, wooded half way down from their summits. . .

MONDAY, SEPT. 21. Marched 25.98 miles. Met Capt. Van Vliet returning from Salt Lake City where he has been on some mission to Brigham Young. Mr. Bernsile [Bernhisel] the deputy to Congress from Utah, was in company with him. The Capt. says that we shall not enter the city this winter, and Brigham says if we ever enter it at all we shall find it a desolation. He and his people will render Deseret[31] as desert as it was before they went there. But where will they go? to British America? to the Amazon, perhaps?[32] There is evidently no place in Christendom for such extravagance as Mormonism. The experience of ages might teach them that the extreme of liberty ends in absolutism without the need of their giving a practical proof of it.

---

[31] Deseret was the name given to the government established by the Mormons in 1849.

[32] See the discussion of possible locations (in Nevada or in Central America) in Part x.

We have been in sight of Fremont's Peak during most of the day. It is covered with snow. . .

The 10th Infantry are encamped about a mile above us, we having overtaken them during the day. We have the best grazing here that we have had since our arrival at Fort Laramie. . .

9 p.m. The officers of the 10th sent an express tonight to overtake Capt. Van Vliet with letters, and politely call for our letters to go by it. . .

TUESDAY, SEPT. 22ND. Remain in camp enjoying our good grazing. The horses get so full that they frequently roll over for relief. It is a great pleasure to know that something is going in to help fill out some of their ribs which are beginning to look rather rebukeful of Mr. Buchanan and his administration. But it is their business to give *orders,* not to care for *horses.* Reflect for one moment how ill we compare with the English in that practical knowledge which is necessary to constitute Statesmanship! Most of our statesmen are born as such – and hence have not the ability in themselves or the confidence in each other to take or comprehend good advice when it is given. Only great measures in which details are overlooked are suitable to their genius – It is on the high horse and not the humble mule that *they* mount the Alps.

But that eternal slave question excuses everything, no matter however foolish, lavish criminal or absurd a statesman could do nothing but stumble under it whatever might be his ability.

The infantry got off with the sun this morning. The question of winter quarters begins to be interesting to us all for the season is pretty far advanced. Ice made last night half an inch thick. . .

Some one of our party shot an antelope yesterday, and to-day the doctor brought in a fine bunch of birds, viz: one sage hen and several varieties of ducks such as blue wing teal and summer duck. Who would ever look for ducks among the Rocky Mountains! Heard a wolf howl this morning – nothing uncommon; but his dismal howl heard amidst frost, barren and lone primeval stillness sounded peculiarly appropriate – as if it voiced forth the sentiment of the occasion. What a meeting of extremes is here – the cry of the wolf in the yet unbroken solitudes of nature, and that of the jackall amidst the desolate ruins of human grandeur! The cry is the same and yet how different the ideas which they excite!

WEDNESDAY, SEPT. 23RD.   Marched 12.63 miles and encamped on the Sweet Water, on the ground that was occupied by the Infantry last night. There are shrubs and stunted trees along the margin of the stream at this point. The grazing is pretty good for this region and the season. If we could have such all the way we should do well, but we have some hundred miles of desert grassless land to go over before reaching our rendezvous on Green River. . .

THURSDAY, SEPT. 24.   Marched 21.48 miles, and encamped upon the Sweet Water amidst good grazing. The Wind River Mountains, amidst which is Fremont's Peak, bears N.W. from us, and are apparently not far distant. They are only slightly dashed with snow. . .

FRIDAY, SEPT. 25.   Marched 19.65 miles. Passed the dividing ridge[33] at 10 o'clock a.m. and encamped at about 12 a.m. on a small brook, whose waters ultimately

---

[33] The summit of South Pass, hardly perceptible in this sage-covered plain. There are two historical markers here. The old emigrant crossing is about two miles south of the modern paved highway.

find their way into the Gulf of California. The head
water of this brook is called Pacific Spring, which takes
its rise not far below the ridge among bogs and marshes,
patches of grass. These patches are beautifully green
and inviting, but the white bones of cattle protruding
here and there as warning to other cattle not to enter,
for they would become mired. Hence we have had to
remain with the scant grass that is found along the
brook.   .   .

Passed a station or trading house of the Mormons
which was still smouldering in ruins. They themselves
set fire to it night before last. And last night several of
them stampeded the animals of the 10th Infantry. They
rushed into camp at about 2 o'clock in the morning, and
by yells and discharge of firearms, succeeded in scattering the mules. They were, however, all recovered. The
Adjutant and quartermaster of the 10th came back a
long distance to inform us of this fact.

Lost two horses to-day, one from inflammation or
disease of the lungs contracted during the cold storm
two days ago, and the other, it is believed, from inflamatory cholic.

The wind has been very fresh from the S.W., blowing
dust into our eyes, and rendering the latter part of the
march uncomfortable.   .   .   If cold storms will hold
off a week longer, our horses may possibly get through.
Captains Dickerson and Clark with their small train
are encamped with us again to-night.[34]

SATURDAY, SEPT. 26TH. Made a long fatiguing
march of 31.75 miles, many of the horses gave out. We
are encamped on the Big Sandy. The road is descending most of the way – the country sandy and barren,

---

[34] Both are of the quartermaster department; see their reports in Part v.

producing nothing but tufts of sage and greasewood. One covey of sage hens was seen.

The channel of the brook is very deep, and between the water and the steep banks there is a strip of poor grass – no grazing at all, some might say. Fortunately the sacks of grass which the men brought from the other side of the mountain have stood us in good stead now for two nights. . .

SUNDAY, SEPT. 27. Marched 16.09 miles, and encamped again on the Big Sandy where the grass is even less than it was last night. The country is exceedingly dry and barren. . .

In front of us to-day has appeared the Uintah chain of mountains running East and West, and distant sixty or seventy miles. Their northern flank being presented to us, is covered with snow, whilst the southern slopes Wind River Mountains are only slightly flecked with white – the difference being due merely to exposure, for the Uintah Mountains are more than a hundred miles south of the Wind River Range.

The Infantry were encamped at this point last night. They saw yesterday, we are informed, sixty men in one party and forty in another who approached within a mile of camp. Some officers went out to reconnoitre them, and found them to be white men armed and mounted. They may possibly be Mormons hovering between us and the numerous animals of Brigham in the various grass valleys that lie this side of Salt Lake City. . .

MONDAY, SEPT. 28TH. Marched 13.31 miles and encamped on the right bank of Green River – the route dusty with pulverized clay, and still leading thru a barren desolate country. At length at about 11 o'clock

we reached the brink of the left bank of the valley of
Green River, far down below us lay a broad valley, the
river meandering thru it, skirted with trees yellowed
by the frost. The strong illuminating effect of the yellow
color gave a distinctness and relief to the numerous
figures of Indians, traders and trappers, seen moving to
and fro; there were lodges here and there with the
smoke curling up from them in the distance among the
trees; a train of ox wagons corralled upon the bank of
the river directly under us, then cattle strolling off for
food while the drivers were lounging along the stream,
and the scene appeared so *warm* and animated to one
who has come suddenly upon it from the midst of a
desert that it seemed like a dream. There was Indian
life in all its fascination amidst the golden tinged
trees beside a clear stream of a warm spring day in
autumn. Not long after we had been in camp a chief in
the full dress uniform coat of a dragoon officer with
eapaulettes mingling with his black locks that fell from
under a hat came with a score of his people to see me.
Whilst he took a chair in front of my tent they seated
themselves on the ground facing us. The pipe of peace
was lighted and passed around and I treated them all
to such fare as I happened to have, hard bread, sugar
and water flavored with the essence of ginger. They
could muster 800 mounted warriors and were willing
to accompany us to fight against the Mormons and
Utah Indians. . .

The proprietor of the trading establishment, or fort
as it is called at this point, is one Baptiste. He came
here from St. Louis twenty-two years ago and has
remained here ever since.

It has been quite warm to-day, so much so as to be

uncomfortable in a closed tent. It has been nearly clear and calm. A few cumulus clouds. . . Water froze last night.

The 10th Infantry left here last night at 2 o'clock for Hams Fork in consequence of a reputed threatened attack of the Mormons upon some half a dozen ox trains then loaded with supplies.

TUESDAY, SEPT. 29TH. Marched 16.65 miles – as usual thru a barren country and over a dusty road. The hands, face, and especially the lips are unpleasantly affected by the potash which it contains. There was hardly any grass where we encamped last night – it might well be said that there was none, and not a green thing or a drop of water did we see to-day until our arrival at this point upon a stream which is called Black's Fork, a branch of Green River. Here we find a little grass, but it is all golden yellow by the frosts. Tho dry and scant the horses have been feeding upon it assiduously since they were let loose from the harness, and as the declining sun shines upon it, upon them, and upon the camp at this hour, half past five, the scene is bright and pleasant.

What from Indians and liquor combined, some of the command had quite a debauch last night, and in consequence the march to-day has been somewhat irregular. The wagons remained behind longer than they need have done, and finally when they came up they were without Q. Master, Wagon Master, and Q. Master Sergeant.

Mr. Ficklin, one of the party of Surveyors of the road from Leavenworth to the Pacific, came into our camp from the rear night before last, and again yesterday morning on Green River to offer us an opportunity of sending letters to the States. The animals and some of the men of the party are to winter in Wind River Valley, and the Superintendent and Mr. Lander after making the arrangements to this end, are going to Washington. Mr. Ficklin is now drawing in the men and animals in this quarter. He says that there are buffalo and elk on Wind River. That stream empties into the Yellowstone and thence into the Missouri. . .

The sun has been scorching and the warmth oppressive – a dry September warmth. We must have a storm soon. . .

[BOOK 17] WEDNESDAY, SEPT. 30. Marched to Hams Fork and then up the stream some eight miles to find grazing – distance 13.69 miles. The 10th Infantry and several Ox trains are about four miles below us. Some of the Ox trains have been here several weeks, and all the grass below is pretty well consumed by them. . . The valley of the stream where we are encamped is nearly a mile in width, and its banks are some hundred feet in height. Far in the south are seen the Uintah Mountains. Such is the place where we are to remain several days, await the arrival of the other troops and the General, and recuperate before resuming the march. . .[35]

---

[35] Along Ham's Fork, Phelps and most of the other advance troops are to spend some time, and here Col. Johnston is finally to come up with them. The story of his coming and of subsequent developments are to be presented in accounts that follow.

V
Colonel Johnston Takes Troops
into Winter Quarters

INTRODUCTION

General W. S. Harney, who was at first placed in command of the troops being sent to Utah, was given an assignment in Kansas; and direction of the Utah Expedition was transferred to Albert Sidney Johnston, Colonel of the Second Cavalry. He was an officer of proven and recognized ability.

Albert S. Johnston, born in Kentucky on February 2, 1803, was of Scottish stock in New England. After attendance at Transylvania University in Lexington, he went to West Point, where he graduated in 1826. After service in the Black Hawk War he went to Texas, where he served in the military and then as Secretary of War. He distinguished himself at the Battle of Monterey in the Mexican War, and in 1855 was made Colonel of the Second United States Cavalry. From this position he was called to head the Expedition to Utah. On November 18, 1857, he was brevetted Brigadier General.

His life after leaving Utah does not concern us here. He had a brilliant career in the Confederate army and was killed at the Battle of Shiloh, April 5, 1862.[1]

---

[1] A detailed biography of Gen. Johnston, written by his son William Preston Johnston is *The Life of Gen. Albert Sidney Johnston,* etc., (New York, D. Appleton & Co., 1878).

1. COLONEL JOHNSTON COMMANDS THE UTAH EXPEDITION [2]

WASHINGTON   August 28, 1857

COL. ALBERT S. JOHNSTON
2d Cavalry, Washington, D.C.

COLONEL: In anticipation of the orders to be issued placing you in command of the Utah expedition, the general-in-chief directs you to repair, without delay, to Fort Leavenworth, and apply to Brevet Brigadier General Harney for all the orders and instructions he has received as commander of that expedition, which you will consider addressed to yourself and by which you will be governed accordingly. You will make your arrangements to set out from Fort Leavenworth at as early a day as practicable. Six companies of the 2d dragoons will be detached by General Harney to escort you and the civil authorities to Utah,[3] to remain as part of your command instead of the companies of the 1st cavalry, as heretofore ordered. Brevet Major T. [F] J. Porter, assistant adjutant general,[4] will be ordered to report to you for duty before you leave Fort Leavenworth.

I have the honor to be, colonel, very respectfully, your most obedient servant,   IRVIN MCDOWELL,
Assistant Adjutant General.

2. COLONEL JOHNSTON ASSUMES COMMAND [5]

HEADQUARTERS, ARMY OF UTAH
Fort Leavenworth,   Sept. 11th 1857

ASST. ADJT GENERAL   HEADQUARTERS OF THE ARMY
West Point, N.Y.

MAJOR: I have the honor to report my arrival at this post, and that, in obediance to my orders I have

---

[2] *Document 71, op. cit.,* p. 13.

assumed command of the Army of Utah. The order assigning six companies of the 2d Dragoons for service in Utah, was received on the 8th inst. They are expected in today and will march for their destination as soon as the necessary preparations can be made to place them on the route. I will leave in a few days and expect to reach Utah in about thirty-five days.

With great respect,   Your obdt. servant,
ALBERT S. JOHNSTON
Colonel 2d Cavalry, Commanding

F.J.P.   A.A.G.

3. JOHNSTON AND COOKE PREPARE TO MARCH [6]

HEADQUARTERS ARMY OF UTAH,
Fort Leavenworth,   September 16, 1857
MAJOR IRVIN MCDOWELL,
ASSISTANT ADJUTANT GENERAL
Headquarters of the Army, New York.

MAJOR: Six companies of the 2d dragoons, under the command of Lieutenant Colonel Cooke,[7] have been prepared for the march to Utah, and provided with every requisite to make it successful by Brevet Brigadier General Harney, agreeably to his instructions from the

---

[3] The civil authorities were Alfred Cumming, Governor; D. R. Eckles, John Cradlebaugh, and C. E. Sinclair, Justices; John Hartnett, Secretary; P. K. Dotson, Marshal; Alexander Wilson, Attorney; and Jacob Forney, Supt. of Indian Affairs.

[4] Major Fitz John Porter was to serve as adjutant to Col. Johnston throughout the Colonel's march to Utah and his service in the Territory.

[5] This report, apparently, is not in the printed documents, but was found as no. 81 in the large volume of "Department of Utah; Letters Sent" (National Archives in Washington, D.C.) Hereafter referred to as Letters Sent.

[6] *Doc. 71*, pp. 21-22.

[7] Philip St. George Cooke's previous military assignments had included the command of the Mormon Battalion in the War with Mexico. For his career see Otis E Young, *The West of Philip St. George Cooke, 1809-1895* (Glendale, The Arthur H. Clark Co., 1955).

headquarters of the army, and have by him been transferred to my command today.

I have ordered Colonel Cooke to put his command immediately en route for Utah, and charged him with the duty of escorting the governor (Colonel Cumming) and the other civil officers of that Territory to Salt Lake City, (see order herewith,) of which Colonel Cumming has been officially notified. From the nature of the service to be performed, the exercise of great discretion has been necessarily allowed Colonel Cooke; but he is a cavalry officer of great experience and well acquainted with frontier service, and, I do not doubt, will conduct the march with skill and success. He may be expected to arrive in the valley of Utah by the 15th or 20th November. Transportation has been provided for a half ration of corn for all his animals to Fort Kearny, at which place he can renew his supply to Laramie, and thence through, to guard against the chance of the grass being covered with snow.

As soon as I see Colonel Cooke's command on the route, I will also leave for Salt Lake City, with an escort of 40 men detached from the dragoons. Arrangements have been made for transporting the men of the escort, their baggage and subsistence, and forage for the draught animals in light spring wagons, which will enable me to accomplish the journey in about thirty-five days; so that my arrival at the place of destination may be expected by the 20th of October proximo.

I beg leave here to request the attention of the general-in-chief to the necessity of an appropriation by Congress, at the next session, for the building of permanent barracks for the accommodation of the troops destined for service in Utah, should there be a peacable occupation by them of that Territory.

Only approximate estimates of the cost can be made at this time for that purpose; but I understand that, after glass, corks, hinges, nails, &c., shall have been furnished, other materials to be had in Utah, may be obtained at a rate of cost not greater than that for material for the building of Fort Riley. The appropriation should be made in the coming session, so that there may be an early prosecution of the work next spring, in order that suitable quarters can be provided for the troops by the ensuing winter.

With great respect, your obedient servant,

A. S. JOHNSTON
Colonel 2d Cavalry, Commanding Army of Utah

4. SECOND DRAGOONS ESCORT CUMMING [8]

HEADQUARTERS, ARMY OF UTAH
Fort Leavenworth,   September 16th 1857
HIS EXCELLENCY A. CUMMING [9]
Governor of Utah Terr.

SIR: I have the honor to inform you that the six companies of Dragoons, designated in Orders by the Secretary of War as an escort for yourself and the other civil officers of the Territory of Utah will march tomorrow under the command of Lieut. Col. Cooke, who has received instructions accordingly, they will march in the afternoon and will encamp five or six miles from here on the route to Fort Riley.

With great respect   Your obdt servt

A. S. JOHNSTON
Colonel 2d Cavalry,   Commanding, Army of Utah

Memo: Sept. 12th. In person Col Johnston offered

---

[8] Letters Sent, no. 88.

[9] Alfred Cumming, was appointed as the new Governor for Utah on July 11, 1857. A sketch of his career will be given below, in Part x, where his letters are published.

Gov. Cumming the choice of the 2d Dragoons as escort, or accompanying him to Utah. The Governor chose the former.[10]

5. COLONEL JOHNSTON REPORTS FROM FORT KEARNY [11]

HEAD QUARTERS, ARMY OF UTAH
Fort Kearney,   September 24th 1857
MAJOR IRVIN MCDOWELL
Asst. Adjt. Genl., Hd.Qrs. Army

MAJOR: I have the honor to report my arrival at this Post today, having made the journey from Fort Leavenworth in seven days. Our march was retarded during the first two or three days by bad roads, made so by frequent showers of rain during that time. Since it cleared off, there has been an unclouded sky and the weather is very fine, at 6 o'clock this morning the thermometer stood at 54°, at 11½ 83°, the grass is fresh and abundant on the route to this place and I am informed that it is excellent to Laramie. There is no indication of an early winter and I see no reason to apprehend it. Beyond Laramie Capt. Van Vliet writes from Red Buttes, 150 miles west of Laramie that the grass is bad beyond belief, this timely notice will prevent any delay in the march of the six companies of the 2d Dragoons under Col Cooke. I have directed twenty-five strong teams and wagons to be turned over to Col. Cooke from the supply train of Col. Sumner's command[12] at the junction of the road from this place to

---

[10] This choice may be the inception of the friction between the Governor and the Colonel, which was to become rather bitter.

[11] Letters Sent, no. 90. The report is printed in *Doc. 71, op. cit.*, pp. 22-23, with mispellings of Phelps' and Reno's names.

[12] Col. Edwin V. Sumner had been conducting a campaign against the Cheyenne Indians between the Platte and Arkansas rivers.

Fort Riley, and six wagons and teams at this point on his arrival, these thirty-one additional wagons will I think be sufficient to enable him to transport the corn for his horses to Utah, if not, I understand that more can be supplied at Fort Laramie. Everything thus far encourages the belief that there will be no failure of any portion of the troops destined for Utah in the accomplishment of the march.

The 10th Infantry I have heard was to leave Laramie on the 5th of Sept., the 5th Inf. reached Laramie on the 4th. Phelps' and Reno's batteries on the 6th and 7th, and Col. Smith with two companies of the 10th Inf. has probably arrived at Laramie by this time.

The Dragoons should be here by the 4th or 5th of October, and with the additional transportation and the means of replacing animals injured on the route, you may rely on a rapid march by them from this post to Laramie.

I will leave here tomorrow morning and suppose I will reach Laramie in eight days. I will as soon as possible join the troops in advance.

With great respect,   Your obdt. servt.

A. S. JOHNSTON
Colonel 2d Cavalry, Commanding, Army of Utah

6. COLONEL JOHNSTON REPORTS FROM SOUTH PLATTE [13]

HEAD QUARTERS, ARMY OF UTAH
North Bank of South fork of Platte
September 29th 1857

MAJOR: We have just crossed the South fork of the Platte and met here the express with Captain Van Vliet's report of the result of his journey to Salt Lake

---

[13] Letters Sent, no. 96.

City, which I forward for the information of the General-in-Chief.

When I reach the troops in advance I will proceed at once to execute the orders I have received unless prevented by the destruction of the grass on the route by cold, or the filling up of the passes by snow.

In either event a suitable position will be taken until it is practicable to advance. We are making our journey with more despatch than I expected – we will be at Laramie on the 2d of October. The 5th and 10th Infantry, with the Batteries marched from Laramie as was expected, with the exception of Reno's Battery, which left on the 8th inst., a day later.

The weather continues mild and there is abundance of grass on the route. I think there can be no doubt of Col. Cooke's arrival at Laramie by the 18th of October.

I will travel with all rapidity practicable till I reach the troops in advance – and will report everything material by any opportunity.

With great respect,   your obdt servt.

A. S. JOHNSTON
Colonel 2d Cavalry, Commanding, Army of Utah

7. JOHNSTON'S REPORT FROM FORT LARAMIE [14]

HEAD QUARTERS, ARMY OF UTAH
Fort Laramie – En route to Salt Lake City
October 5th 1857

MAJOR: I arrived at this post last night, making the journey from Fort Leavenworth in seventeen days and a half, our march since we reached Ash Hollow has been greatly retarded by the badness of the road, usually, from that point, heavy on account of sandiness,

---

[14] *Ibid.*, no. 101.

but at the time we passed made much worse by frequent showers of rain.

On my arrival I ordered the two companies of Dragoons, "E" and "H" and a detachment of 47 men, left by Col Smith to escort the Governor of Utah, to march immediately to join the troops in advance. I have made such arrangements for transportation of forage and subsistence as will insure their arrival without delay.

I am greatly disappointed in not finding an abundant supply of corn at this post. I shall, after taking all at the post, have no more than barely sufficient for the Dragoon horses and draught animals of the train of that command, and for my own train. Two trains loaded partly with corn, may, I think certainly be expected to reach here before the arrival of Col. Cooke. Should a sufficient supply for his march be found here on his arrival he will be instructed to continue his march until he joins the advance – unless the indications of the rapid approach of winter shall be such as to make the risk too great to attempt the passage of the South Pass. The practicability of doing so must be left to the judgement of the commander of the Dragoons.

At present the weather is mild and we anticipate a protracted autumn; should such anticipation be realized I do not doubt Col. Cooke will accomplish the march. The march of the Dragoons will be somewhat retarded by the state of the roads, perhaps they will be a few days longer than estimated in my letter from the South fork of the Platte.

The 10th Infantry, on the 21st ult., was in advance at Ice Springs, 5 miles above the 5th crossing of Sweetwater; Capt. Phelps' a few miles behind; the 5th Infantry on the 21st was seven miles below the 3rd cross-

ing of the same stream, and on the 22d Capt. Reno was
10 miles above the 1st crossing, as I learned from
Captain Van Vliet, who I met on his way to Washington under instructions from Genl. Harney.

I met yesterday, Col. Hoffman in command of Co.
"B" and "C", 6th Infantry, en route to Fort Leavenworth, to whom I gave instructions to return to this
place, with the two companies and assume command of
this post. He arrived this morning and is now in command of the post. I did not feel justified in the present
posture of the affairs of Utah, in allowing the withdrawal of his force to a point so remote from where
they may be needed, and besides the means of transportation he had with him is indispensable for the
advance of the two companies of Dragoons, and detachment of Infantry which (see order herewith) has been
ordered forward. If I had transportation and corn the
two companies of the 6th would go forward.

If possible the troops will enter the valley of Utah
this fall; this question must be determined by the facility
of concentrating the troops, and properly securing the
supplies for the Army.

With great respect,   Your obed. servt,

A. S. JOHNSTON
Colonel 2d Cavalry, Commanding the Army of Utah

8.   JOHNSTON'S ORDER TO COOKE [15]

HEAD QUARTERS, ARMY OF UTAH
Fort Laramie, En route to Salt Lake City
October 5th, 1857

SIR: The Colonel commanding directs me to express the hope that, on arriving at this post, you will be

---

[15] *Ibid.,* no. 103.

able to continue your march to join the troops in advance, but to effect this you must not rely upon finding corn beyond this point. Two trains loaded with corn will precede you to this depot. From this supply you will take all you can carry and push on through the South Pass, permitting nothing but the rapid approach of winter and an impracticable march delaying you. The weather continues fair, and indications of a long autumn give assurances that your energy will overcome the obstacles in your path; but if forced to halt and all probability of joining him is precluded, the Colonel commanding relies upon your judgment to establish the command in the vicinity of this post so as best to secure its comfort and safety.

I am, Sir, very respectfully   Your obedt servt.

F. J. PORTER
Asst. Adjt. Genl.

9. JOHNSTON'S REPORT FROM THREE CROSSINGS [16]

HEAD QUARTERS, ARMY OF UTAH
Camp on the three crossings of Sweetwater
October 13th 1857

MAJOR: Tonight two men who live at Fort Laramie, and who had been sent on express to Col. Alexander, arrived at our camp on their way back. From them I learn that the Mormons having interposed a force in rear of our troops, then encamped at Ham's Fork of Green River, succeeded in burning three supply trains, with their contents; a message from Col. Alexander was sent by them to Col. C. F. Smith instructing him to protect the trains in the rear, which contain the clothing, Sibley tents, Subsistence, &c. The

---
[16] *Ibid.*, no. 109.

orders with regard to the march of the Cavalry and companies of the 6th, having been countermanded, leaves Col Smith with only 22 men; 47 men of his command were left at Laramie as the Governor's escort. Lieut. Smith[17] of the Dragoons is four days march behind us with two companies of Dragoons and the forty-seven men of Col. Smith's command, and twenty-five Dragoons of my escort who were left at Laramie to come on with Lieut. Smith; his command will number about 200 men. I have ordered him to hasten forward and join Col. Smith's command; we will march in the morning and expect to encamp with Col. Smith at night. The express man says Col. Alexander would attempt to reach the Valley of Salt Lake by the Bear River. It is much farther than by the usual route and why he selects it I could not learn unless from the probability of the grass being burnt by the Mormons on the direct route. These men say that it is certain that they will burn the grass on the route they were about to pursue. Under these circumstances if I could communicate with Col. Alexander I would direct him to take up a good position for the winter at Ham's Fork.[18]

The road is beset between this and Ham's Fork with companies of Mormons so that it is doubtful whether I shall be able to communicate with Col. Alexander.

With great respect,   Your obedt servt.

A. S. JOHNSTON
Colonel 2d Cavalry, Commanding the Army of Utah

[17] Lieut. W. D. Smith, born in Georgia, graduated from the U.S. Military Academy in 1846. He resigned in Jan., 1861, and died Oct. 4, 1862.

[18] Col. Johnston was disappointed in Alexander's selection of route and soon ordered his return to Ham's Fork. Before receipt of the order, Alexander had already begun a retreat.

10.   COLONEL JOHNSTON TO MR. MAGRAW [19]

HEAD QUARTERS, ARMY OF UTAH
Camp 12 miles East of South Pass
En route to Salt Lake City, October 16, 1857
WM M. F. MAGRAW,[20]
Supt. South Pass Wagon road

SIR: The Colonel commanding, desirous of obtaining additional means of transportation for the supplies of this Army, requests from you, for the ensuing three months, or till such time as you will require them for the continuation of your labor, the services of the fifteen wagons and six mule teams which you offered to place at his disposal if required.

This means of transportation the Colonel wishes delivered to him in the vicinity of the Pacific Springs [21] as soon as practicable.   I am, Sir, very respectfully,
Your obedt. servt.   F. J. PORTER
Asst. Adjt. Genl.[22]

11.   COLONEL JOHNSTON TO COLONEL
ALEXANDER [23]

HEAD QUARTERS, ARMY OF UTAH
Camp 12 miles East of the South Pass
En route to Salt Lake City, October 16, 1857
COLONEL E. B. ALEXANDER
Comd'g the advance of the Army of Utah

SIR: Colonel Johnston wishes to concentrate the

---

[19] Letters Sent, no. 110.

[20] This is the man previously referred to as the former mail contractor. He was now in the South Pass area engaged in the selection and building of a wagon road.

[21] Pacific Springs was the first water (and meadow) west of South Pass; about two miles from the summit.

[22] In another letter of Oct. 16, Col. Johnston solicited the enlistment of Magraw's men into the military service. See Letters Sent, no. 111.

[23] Letters Sent, no. 112.

command with the view of wintering in an eligible spot already selected. To effect this, and not cause suspicion of the intention, he wishes you to proceed by slow marches moving your camp short distances, and gradually working your way by Sublette's road to or near the mouth of Fontenelle Creek, so that he can join you about eleven day's hence with this command and all the trains now in your rear. The route has been indicated to the bearer, DuFour.[24]

Although I enclose the order of Colonel Johnston assuming command he wishes you to give all necessary orders, and to treat as enemies all who oppose your march, molest your trains, appear in arms on your route, or in any manner annoy you.

I am, Sir, very respectfully, your obedt. servt,

F. J. PORTER
Asst. Adgt. Genl.

12. COLONEL JOHNSTON'S REPORT FROM SOUTH PASS [25]

HEAD QUARTERS, ARMY OF UTAH
South Pass, En route to Salt Lake City,
October 18th 1857

MAJOR: Accompanying this communication I send you two letters from Col. Alexander,[26] the commander at present of the main body of the Army of Utah. In his letter of the 8th Oct., Col. Alexander questions, by the hesitation with which he assumes them, his right to exercise fully all the duties of commander. His authority to exercise them without restriction is clearly granted

---

[24] Eli Dufor had come from Col. Alexander on Ham's Fork with Alexander's letter of Oct. 14th. The Col. Johnston letter of the 16th was acknowledged in Alexander's letter of Oct. 22; see Part III.

[25] Letters Sent, no. 113.

[26] These letters, of Oct. 8 and 14, are printed in Part III.

by the 62d Article of War – Moreover General Orders No. 12, Head Qrs. of the Army, specially directs who shall command in the absence of the Genl. Harney, or to be inferred, any other named commander and sufficiently explains the objects of the Expedition, and no question for the decision of the commander, beyond his ordinary military duties, could arise before the arrival of Governor Cumming.

Misapprehending the authority with which he is invested by law, and the orders of the General-in-chief, that portion of his letter respecting command would be, if he was correct in his view of his own position, a merited reflection upon his superior and it is therefore that I have adverted to it. Pursuing his design indicated in his letter of Oct. 8th has, you will learn from his letter of Oct. 14th (herewith) has advanced up Ham's Fork of Green River 35 miles above the crossing (see map herewith) and there directs the movements to be made by his own immediate command and the troops in his rear to form a junction, which from erroneous suppositions would be wholly impracticable. First he evidently believes that Col. *Smith,* escorting the remainder of the supply trains, (in all about nine, including three Sutler's trains) is advancing on the Kinney Road or Cut-off with the force named in Genl. Harney's order of Aug. 18th and of course he has not received the countermand of that order. He assumes that the command in rear is capable of a more rapid movement than his own and therefore after waiting one day at the point indicated will resume his march. In this also he would have been disappointed, as the trains in rear, suffering from fatigue and scarcity of sustenance and without rest, which the trains with him have had, could not, if where he supposed them, overtake him.

These are the facts and if known by Col. Alexander
his dispositions, as determined in his letter of Oct. 8th
would have been wholly different. Col. Smith is here
at this camp with fifty men of his regiment. I overtook
him the day before yesterday (16th inst.) about 20
miles east of this and have added my escort, 15 dismounted dragoons, to his force. Lieut. Smith in command of a squadron of Dragoons and fifty of the 10th
Infantry, a force of about two hundred men, may be
expected here in three or four days. He is aware of the
necessity of promptness and I am sure will lose no
time. Mr. Wm Magraw, Supt. South Pass Wagon road,
with a partiotism highly creditable to him, placed at
the disposition of the Government as many of his
employees as will volunteer. He thinks fifty or sixty
will organize and I have agreed to accept their service
and have them mustered in for three or six months as
they may elect, and he has also tendered fifteen good
teams of mules and wagons which I have also accepted
and directed them to be receipted for when delivered.
Four supply trains, containing clothing, (of which the
troops now in the advance, I am informed, begin to
need), Ordnance, Medical, and Subsistence stores are
still in the rear and may be expected in two or three
days. The storm of last night may have destroyed some
of their oxen and on that account there may be more
delay than I estimate. 11 mules of Col. Smith's train
perished from cold last night,[27] the thermometer this
morning at sun rise was at 16°. The sky is now clear and
the thermometer at one o'clock stands at 34 and the
small quantity of snow that fell during the night is

[27] This was the first serious cold spell, the one that had helped slow Col.
Alexander almost to a standstill in his march up Ham's Fork.

melting so that the animals can graze freely. I am thus minute that the reason for the order transmitted to Col. Alexander yesterday morning (herewith) [28] may be fully comprehended. His intended movement, if met with opposition would have so retarded his march as to have made it impracticable and would have so probably entangled him in the midst of the deep snow of the valley of Bear River, which I understand never fails to fall there and usually early in the season, as to place him beyond the means of extrication. Our most potent enemy at present is the snow and constitutes at present our chief embarrassment.

The movement of Col. Alexander if effected, (for the reasons I have mentioned and of which he could not be apprised) would have separated him from supplies indispensable to the comfort and safety of the Army and deprived him of the assistance of the force which will be concentrated here in a few days, which however small, being partly of cavalry, is of vital importance.

In ordering Col. Alexander to the mouth of Fontenelle Creek a position about 30 miles from his camp on Ham's Fork, I did so with the design of making a junction practicable.[29] It is about seventy miles hence [30] and he can reach it by a good road and without any danger of surprise. There is there abundance of grass and it is a point from which I can reach the region I intend to occupy this winter, without risking the loss of our animals. As soon as the snow falls sufficiently on

---

[28] The preceding letter, dated Oct. 16.

[29] Col. Alexander, in his letter of Oct. 22 (printed in Part III), pleads to be spared the thirty-mile eastward march, as he thinks it is more than his teams can stand. Johnston wisely permitted the order to be ignored.

[30] This is, westward from South Pass.

Green River to prevent the burning of the grass, I will march to Henry's Fork and occupy that valley during the winter.[31] It is a commanding position and accessible two months earlier for re-inforcement and supplies by Cheyenne Pass[32] than by any other, and will enable me to march by Fort Bridger and on the most direct route to Salt Lake City as soon as practicable in the spring. At this position also Col. Cooke can join, which I still entertain the hope he will be able to do.

I greatly regret that the impossibility of concentrating the troops destined for this service, and their supplies, will prevent a forward movement before spring. It is now manifest that before the force can be united that the autumn will be too far advanced to move with a probability of success, tho' not opposed by the Mormons.

You are already apprised, by the proclamation of Brigham Young and his letter to Col. Alexander, which I transmitted on the 15th inst., of the political attitude assumed by the Mormons and the resistance they meditate to the just authority the Government desires to exercise in that territory, and the General-in-chief no doubt has already considered the necessity of a conquest of these traitorous people and has estimated the force necessary to accomplish the object. With a full view of the whole subject before him, his great experience would not be benefitted by any sugges-

---

[31] Henry's Fork of Green River lies considerably south of the emigrant road. Johnston is subsequently to change plans, and not march to Henry's Fork; but he would winter most of his stock in that valley.

[32] Cheyenne Pass was near the head of Pole Creek (which enters the South Platte at present Sedgwick, Colorado), and on the Bridger Pass route which Capt. Howard Stansbury had explored in 1850. Bridger Pass had been crossed by the California-bound Cherokee gold-seeking parties of 1849 and 1850.

tions of mine. I will however mention that unless a large force is sent here – from the nature of the country – that a protracted war on their part is inevitable. The great distance from our source of supply makes it impracticable to operate with a small force. It, in fact, requires the employment of such force to guard numerous trains of supplies, leaving but a small portion, if any, for offensive operations. A movement of troops from California, Oregon, and by this route, would terminate a war with the Mormons, speedily and more economically than if attempted by insufficient means.

In five or six days I think we will have all the force available here for a forward movement, by that time the train will all be up; they should be here sooner. In twelve days from this time I expect to join Col. Alexander at or near Fontenelle Creek.

The General may be assured that no retrograde movement will be made by this force.

With great respect,   Your obedt. servt.

A. S. JOHNSTON
Colonel 2d Cavalry, Commanding the Army of Utah

13. JOHNSTON TO ALEXANDER [33]

HEAD QUARTERS, ARMY OF UTAH,
Camp on Green river, 3 miles below Trading houses
En route to Salt Lake City,   November 1st 1857

SIR: The Colonel Commanding directs me to inform you of his present position, and his intention to camp tomorrow evening on Black's Fork below the road, at some point which will furnish good or sufficient grazing for the animals of the command. If practicable he will be pleased to have you join him with your

---

[33] *Ibid.*, no. 146.

command – but if now in an eligible position for a halt
of two or three days, he desires you to inform him at an
early hour, that, if possible, the army may be united
tomorrow.

I am, Sir, very respectfully, Your obedt servt

F. J. PORTER, A.A. G.

14. COLONEL JOHNSTON TO ARMY HEADQUARTERS [34]

HEAD QUARTERS, ARMY OF UTAH
Black Fork, 3 miles below mouth of Hams Fork
En route to Salt Lake City,   November 5, 1857

MAJOR: I have the honor to inform you that I
arrived here on the 3rd inst – This place I designated
in a communication to Colonel Alexander,[35] subsequent
to my letter to you from the South Pass, of the 18th of
October, at which, the force, consisting of one Squadron
Dragoons, two companies 10th Infantry, one company
Volunteers, in all about 300 men under the command
of Col. C. F. Smith, charged with the duty of protect-
ing the trains of supplies for the Army could with the
most facility join the main body – Col. Smith with his
command and the numerous trains guarded by it
reached here on the 3rd inst.

The march was slow and tedious, and effected in
eight days, averaging eleven miles per day; although
the road was excellent and the weather fine, it was not
possible to make any more rapid progress, on account
of the broken down condition of the draught animals.
The trains including Sutlers and merchants destined
for Salt Lake City (which I would not allow to go on)
in as close order as they could be made to travel

---

[34] *Ibid.*, no. 155.
[35] The preceding letter, of November 1.

occupied a space of five or six miles – no molestation whatever was attempted by the Mormons, which may be attributed to the presence of the Cavalry and the judicious dispositions and vigilance of Colonel Smith. Yesterday and today have been occupied in making arrangements necessary for a forward movement, which my orders (herewith) will explain – Tomorrow I will march upon Fort Bridger and dislodge any force I may find there, and await the arrival of Col. Cooke, where, as the approach of winter is too near to attempt the passage of the Wasach range of mountains, with a probability of success, I will seize upon the district mentioned in my letter from South Pass,[36] and occupy it until an advance is practicable.

The communication of Brigham Young to Colonel Alexander and Elder Taylor's to Captain Marcy[37] and the orders of D. Wells, the commander of the Mormons (herewith)[38] and the act of the Legislative assembly at the last session show a matured and settled design on the part of the sect of Mormons to hold & occupy this territory independent of and irrespective of the authority of the United States. They have with premeditation placed themselves in rebellion against the Union and entertain the insane design of establishing a form of government thoroughly despotic and utterly repugnant to our institutions[39]– occupying as they do an attitude of rebellion and open defiance, connected with numerous overt acts of treason, see orders & commissions (herewith) issued by their leaders. I have ordered that

---

[36] Valley of Henry's Fork.

[37] Printed in *Doc. 71, op. cit.,* pp. 57-62.

[38] Printed at the end of this report.

[39] Here he is making a political judgment rather beyond his function as a military officer.

wherever they are met in arms that they be treated as enemies. In my letter from the South Pass I submitted to the consideration of the General-in-Chief the necessity on the part of the Government of prompt and vigorous action. That the time for any further argument is past, and in my opinion, the people of the United States must now act or submit to an usurpation of their territory and the engrafting upon our institutions, a social organization and political principle totally incompatible with our own. Lest that letter may not have been received I send herewith a copy.

The state of things now existing has not been brought about by the movement of troops in this direction; for this people understand the relation of the military to the civil power of the government, as well as any other portion of the inhabitants of this union, and that the arms of our soldiers are designed for the preservation of the peaceful conditions of society and not for its disturbance. Their conduct, as I have before stated as my opinion, results from a settled determination on their part not to submit to the authority of the United States, or any other, outside of their church.

Enclosed is a statement by the chief commissary of the amount of Subsistence destroyed under the orders of Brigham Young.[40] The loss although great is less than I apprehended, a supply early in the spring must be forwarded. It should reach here by the 1st of June. The supplies of the contractors, sutlers &c. for their employees have been exhausted, so long a detention with the Army, was not anticipated by them, it has thus become necessary to give them bread, as there is no other source from which they can obtain it. Should a

---

[40] Also printed following this report.

long interval intervene without hearing from me you need only attribute it to the difficulty of sending expresses across the mountains in the winter months. The officers and men are in fine health and animated with an ardent desire to discharge their duty faithfully.

With great respect   Your Obedient Servant

A. S. JOHNSTON
Colonel 2d Cavalry, Commanding.

P.S.   We have made one days march since the date of this and are now (Nov. 7th) waiting the arrival of the trains, delayed yesterday by a storm, our trains occupy, in as close order as they can travel, the road for 13 or 14 miles, therefore the rear cannot move until late in the day.   A.S.J.

[GENERAL D. H. WELLS' ORDERS TO MAJOR
JOSEPH TAYLOR (MORMON)] [41]

HEADQUARTERS EASTERN EXPEDITION'
Camp near Cache Cave,[42]   Oct. 4, 1857

You will proceed, with all possible despatch, without injuring your animals, to the Oregon road, near the bend of Bear River, north by east of this place. Take close and correct observations of the country on your route. When you approach the road, send scouts ahead, to ascertain if the invading troops have passed that way. Should they have passed, take a concealed route, and get ahead of them. Express to Colonel Benton [Burton] [43] who is now on that road and in the vicinity of the troops, and effect a junction with him, so as to operate in concert. On ascertaining the locality or route of the troops, proceed at once to annoy them in every possible way. Use every exertion to stampede their animals and set fire to their trains. Burn the whole country

---

[41] Printed in *Doc. 71,* pp. 56-57.

[42] Near the head of Echo Creek, which enters Weber River near Echo City, Utah.

[43] Col. R. T. Burton was in charge of one of the advance raiding parties of Mormons. See Part VII.

before them, and on their flanks. Keep them from sleeping by night surprises; blockade the road by felling trees or destroying river fords; where you can. Watch for opportunities to set fire to the grass on their windward, so as if possible to envelope their trains. Leave no grass before them that can be burned. Keep your men concealed as much as possible, and guard against surprise. Keep scouts out at all times, and communications open with Colonel Benton, Major McAllester [44] and O. P. Rockwell,[45] who are operating in the same way. Keep me advised daily of your movements, and every step the troops take, and in which direction.

God bless you, and give you success.

Your brother in Christ.

DANIEL U [H.] WELLS

Major Joseph Taylor.[46]

[PROPERTY DESTROYED BY THE MORMONS] [47]

List of subsistence stores in supply teams (Russell & Waddell's) Nos. 5, 9, and 10, burnt by the Mormons at Green River, Utah, in the night of October 4, 1857.

			No. of rations,	
2,720	pounds ham			
92,700	pounds bacon	. . .	No. of rations,	115,875
167,900	pounds flour .	. . .	" " "	149,244
270	bushels beans	. . .	" " "	108,000
8,580	pounds Rio coffee	. .	" " "	143,000
330	pounds Java coffee			
1,400	pounds crushed sugar			
2,970	gallons vinegar	. . .	" " "	297,000
800	pounds sperm candles	.	" " "	80,000
13,333	pounds soap .	. . .	" " "	333,325
84	gallons molasses			
134	bushels dried peaches			
68,832	rations dessicated vegetables			
705	pounds tea	. . . .	" " "	52,875

[44] J. D. T. McAllister, leader of some Utah troops and a prominent churchman.

[45] Orrin Porter Rockwell, famed scout.

[46] Captured by the U.S. troops, and on whom Gen. Wells' order was found.

[47] *Doc. 71,* p. 63.

COLONEL ALBERT SIDNEY JOHNSTON

FORT BRIDGER in 1858

7,781 pounds hard bread . . " " "   7,781
  6 lanterns.

H. F. CLARKE
Capt. and C's U.S.A.

Made from bills of lading, October 10, 1857

15. JOHNSTON TO HOFFMAN [48]

HEAD QUARTERS, ARMY OF UTAH
Camp, Junction of Smith & Hams Fork

En route to Salt Lake City,   November 13th 1857

SIR: The Colonel Commanding directs that you cause to be pushed forward to these Head Quarters at Fort Bridger, as soon as practicable, a train of 30 pack mules loaded with salt. Your knowledge of the country, and of the persons you will employ, will guide you in the route to be taken.

In making your preparations for moving in the spring, the Colonel wishes you to take into consideration the route up the Laramie River, with the view of reaching this force at the earliest moment with the supply trains, time being the principal element to consider in your movement. As soon as Col. Cooke arrives, Jeanise,[49] or some other reliable person, will be sent over that route to report to you the probabilities of success – the difficulties to be overcome, the advantages of grass, and to be a guide in case you deem it advisable to move in that direction. It is hoped that you may be able to arrive here a month earlier than by the Oregon and California Route, South Pass, sending some of your troops in advance to make or repair the road. It is inferred from present information that a practicable

---

[48] Letters Sent, no. 181.

[49] Antoine Janise (variously spelled) was an early trapper and Indian trader before being employed by the army as a scout. The following year he was to settle on the Cache la Poudre River, a few miles west of present Fort Collins, Colorado.

road exists, and that probably the principal difficulties to overcome will be the cutting down banks and making bridges. The guide who passes over it will examine the obstacles.

If you have sufficient information to decide you, this route is suggested as one for the pack train as the grass is very scarce on this, and on the other it has not been injured.

The Colonel Commanding also suggests that the animals be not loaded heavier than 100 pounds. There is no salt with this Army.

I am, Sir, very respectfully,   Your Obedient Servant,   F. J. PORTER, A.A.G.

P.S.   Whichever route you take will require boats or rafts to enable you to cross the principal streams, the Colonel Commanding therefore suggests, that you bring with you wagons with bodies of corrugated iron, if you have them or can procure them in time, if not, sufficient timber to make a boat of sufficient dimensions to cross your stores.[50]

16.   BRIGHAM YOUNG OFFERS SALT TO JOHNSTON'S ARMY [51]

EXECUTIVE DEPARTMENT
Great Salt Lake City, U.T.   November 26, 1857
COL. A. S. JOHNSTON, United States Army,
    If he has arrived on Black's Fork, or
COL. B. C. [E. B.] ALEXANDER, United States Army
    SIR: Being reliably informed that your command, and the men belonging to the merchant trains, are much

---

[50] A Circular was issued by Col. Johnston on Nov. 19, inviting all persons discharged from the freight trains to enlist in the army. Several companies were so formed.

[51] *Doc. 71*, pp. 110-11.

in need of salt, I have taken the liberty to at once forward you a load (some eight hundred pounds) by Messrs. Henry Woodard and Jesse J. Earl. You are perfectly welcome to the salt now sent; but should you prefer making any compensation therefor, I have to request that you inform me, under sealed envelope, of weight received and the amount and kind of compensation returned. There is no design or wish to spy out your position, movements, or intentions, through the men now sent to your camp; but should you entertain any dubiety upon that point, you are at perfect liberty to stop and detain them outside your encampment, during the short time necessary for the delivery of their loading, in readiness to start upon their return.

Should any in your command be suspicious that the salt now forwarded contains any deleterious ingredients other than those combined in its natural deposition on the shore of Great Salt Lake, Mr. Woodard or Mr. Earl, in charge of its transportation and delivery, or doubtless Mr. Livingston, Mr. Gerrish, Mr. Perry,[52] or any other person in your camp that is acquainted with us, will freely partake of it to dispel any groundless suspicions, or your doctors may be able to test it to your satisfaction.

I have to inform you that the demonstrations which have been made upon your animals and trains have been made solely with a view to let you emphatically understand that we are in earnest when we assert, freemen like, that we will not tamely submit to any longer having our constitutional and inalienable rights trampled under foot. And, if you now are within our borders by the order of the President of the United

---

[52] These men were conducting trains of freight to Salt Lake City.

States, (of which I have no official notification), I have further to inform you that, by ordering you here upon pretexts solely founded upon lies, all of which have long since been exploded, the President has no more regard for the Constitution and laws of the United States, and the welfare of her loyal citizens, than he has for the constitution, laws, and subjects of the kingdom of Belzebub.

Of the persons reported to be retained by you as prisoners, the two who are said to have hailed from Oregon are entire strangers to us; Mr. Grow, on his way here from the States, is probably treated by you in a reasonably humane manner, for which you have my thanks, as it saves us the expense of his board; and if you imagine that keeping, mistreating, or killing Mr. Stowell[53] will redound to your credit or advantage, future experience may add to the stock of your better judgment.

Colonel Alexander, I am informed that among the mules that have come into our settlements is a small white one belonging to you, and a favorite of yours. The mule in question arrived in poor condition, and, learning that it was a favorite with you, it gives me pleasure to inform you that I immediately caused the mule to be placed in my stables, where it is well fed and cared for, and is held subject to your order; but should you prefer leaving it in my care during the winter, it will probably be in better plight for your use upon your return to the east in the spring.

Trusting that the bearers of a welcome and frankly proffered gift will be courteously received, and permitted, with their animals and wagon, to peaceably

---

[53] For Stowell's experiences see Part VII, B.

start upon their immediate return, I have the honor to remain, very respectfully, your obedient servant,

BRIGHAM YOUNG
Governor of Utah Territory [54]

17. THE CALL UPON GENERAL GARLAND FOR REPLACEMENTS [55]

HEAD QUARTERS, ARMY OF UTAH
Camp Scott, near Fort Bridger,[56] Black's Fork
November 25th 1857

BRIG. GENL. JOHN GARLAND
Comdg. Dept. New Mexico, Santa Fee.

GENERAL: A large proportion of Cavalry and Battery horses as well as many draught animals of my command, have been starved by the unprecedented cold

[54] Col. Johnston apparently made no written response to Young's offer of salt. His reaction is reported in *Gove's Letters, op. cit.,* p. 103: "Brigham Young sent in to Col. Johnston some salt and an impudent letter; the Colonel told him to go back with his salt and tell Brigham not to attempt to hold any more communication with him or his emissaries would hang; that he could not treat with him only under a white flag, and he considered him as a traitor to his government and should treat him as such." Fitz John Porter, Johnston's adjutant, reports the Colonel as saying: "I will not accept of this salt sent by Brigham Young, not for the reason hinted in his letter, but I can accept of nothing from him so long as he and his people maintain a hostile position to my Government. I regret he has insinuated the probability of its refusal on account of its deleterious property. There is no portion of the American people who would be guilty of so base an act, and none to suspect it. So far as poison is concerned, I would freely partake of Brigham Young's hospitality, but I can accept of no present, nor interchange courtesies so long as he continues his present course. I have no answer to send. I can hold no intercourse with Brigham Young and his people. I have nothing to do with him or them." W. P. Johnston, *The Life of Gen. Albert Sidney Johnston, op. cit.,* p. 219.

[55] Letters Sent, *op. cit.* A terrible storm has occurred; it will be described in the following document, Johnston's report of Nov. 30.

[56] Camp Scott, set up by the army, was about two miles from Fort Bridger.

Fort Bridger, at the present town of Fort Bridger, Wyoming, was built by the famous early trapper, trader, and Mountain Man, James Bridger. See this *Far West and the Rockies Series,* III, pp. 107, 270.

The Mormons purchased the fort from Bridger and Louis Vasquez in

weather of the last month, and the great scarcity of grass on our route. I have therefore ordered Captain R. B. Marcy,[57] 5th U.S. Infantry, to proceed to New Mexico to purchase remount for the Dragoons and Batteries, and a sufficient number of draught animals to replace those which have died or been broken down on the march.

It is of the greatest importance that he should return to this place as early in the spring as he can, keeping in view the necessity of bringing on the animals in good condition assistance such as you have it in your power to give, for the promotion of the objects which it is so desirable that he should accomplish, would very greatly facilitate his speedy return.

I have also to request that a squadron of the Rifle Regiment, or such force as you may deem requisite, may be ordered to give him protection on his route back. Capt. Marcy will give you the particulars of our march &c.

With great respect,   Your Obedient Servant,

A. S. JOHNSTON [58]

F. J. PORTER,   A.A.G.

1855. See L. R. Hafen, "Mountain Men; Louis Vasquez," in the *Colorado Magazine,* x, p. 20. In 1856-57 the Mormons strengthened the fort considerably, building a stone wall; see the John Pulsipher diary published in Part VII. Upon the approach of the U.S. troops the Mormons burned the fort, but the stone wall remained, and was utilized by the army in providing storage for supplies.

[57] For an account of the expedition see "Affairs in Utah," *House Exec. Doc. 2,* 35 Cong., 2 sess., pp. 187-97; and R. B. Marcy, *Thirty Years of Army Life on the Border, op. cit.*

[58] On Nov. 22nd Quartermaster Dickerson wrote a report (*Doc. 71,* pp. 100-101) on the grazing in the vicinity of Camp Scott. He said there was not enough grass within ten miles to subsist the animals of the command for six weeks. He recommended that all the animals, except those immediately needed about camp, be sent to Henry's Fork for the winter. The number sent, including beef cattle, would be about 2400.

In a report two days later (*Doc. 71,* pp. 101-103) Dickerson said that 558 mules of the command had died since leaving Fort Leavenworth, over nine-

18. COLONEL JOHNSTON'S REPORT
TO ARMY HEADQUARTERS [59]

HEADQUARTERS, ARMY OF UTAH
Camp Scott near Fort Bridger
Black's Fork, Green River,   November 30, 1857

SIR: Since my last report the troops and all the supply trains have arrived at this place, and will remain here or in this district during the winter. In effecting the march from near the junction of Ham's and Black's Forks of Green River, a distance of only 35 miles, the loss of Battery horses, draught mules, oxen of the contractors has been very great in consequence of some storms which we were encountered on the route, and intense cold. Our marches each day were necessarily short on account of the extreme coldness and inclemency of the weather, and because of the great number of miles on the road occupied by the supply trains and others, and the failing condition of the draught animals starving from cold and hunger, were resumed from each camp as soon as the troops in the rear and trains could be brought up, allowing a day or more at each camp for rest and the grazing of the animals. Fifteen days were consumed in this tedious operation. Shelter for our thousands of animals seemed indispensable for the preservation of life, yet a more rapid advance to attain it would, we believe, be attended with immense loss. The snow storms raged with short intermissions after it commenced, for several days during which time it was exceedingly cold. The ther-

tenths of the loss having occurred during the last month. About half of the horses of the two batteries were dead and two-thirds of the dragoons were dismounted. Other animals would die during the winter. He recommended that more animals and some supplies be sent for in New Mexico. He estimated that 400 horses and 800 mules could be procured for $138,800.

[59] Letters Sent, *op. cit.*

mometer ranged from ten degrees above to sixteen degrees below zero.

If shelter could have been found, a halt till the storm subsided would have been ordered; but there was none. The country between this and the South Pass, with the exception of the narrow vallies of water courses, is a great desert, affording no shelter by its conformation or by woods, or even bushes from the furious blasts of these high regions; and no fuel, except the wild sage or willow bushes. There was no alternative but to press forward perseveringly, though slowly making our route by the frozen horses, mules and oxen.[60] A sufficient

---

[60] There are a number of accounts of the fury of the storm. Capt. Gove reports Nov. 6: "This morning it commenced to snow and was very cold. . . All day we plodded along with those villainous trains until about 10 o'clock at night, when I got in camp nearly frozen, a more disagreeable day's duty I never experienced. . .

[Nov. 8th] This morning was one of the severest as yet. The thermometer at daylight must have been far below zero; at 7½ I put mine out and it indicated 3 above only. Several of the mules died last night. . .

[Nov. 9th] Today is our 2d day's march. Made about 7 miles, animals lying along the road every rod, almost, and daily and hourly dying as they are driven along the road. Snow about 7 inches deep. Fort Bridger is our hope. If we once get there we shall be safe with our stores. Hundreds of animals die every twenty-four hours . . . we stayed without any shelter and anything to eat 24 hours. No fire except what we could make from the sage bushes. It was awful. Never was men more exposed or had a harder tour of duty. Some of the men were frost bitten. My dear Maria, it is quite Russian. You see our animals have no corn, and the grass, what little there is, is under the snow, and they having come some 1100 miles, poor as can be, hundreds dropping down in the harness for want of strength to stand up. . .

Today 10. . . Still in Camp No. 2. Animals died last night by fifties. Thermometer far below zero.

"Nov. 12. Thermometer 14. Horribly cold. . .

"Nov. 14. Thermometer 11. . .

"15th Nov. At 3 p.m. moved my camp to position for outpost duty. Left Michael with Dandy in wall tent. He cannot long survive, is very sick. . .

"Nov. 16 3 p.m. Just relieved from duty. Glad that it is so. Dandy died last night. I feel his loss very much. He was in splendid spirits when I missed him. Well, he has served me well so far. He was considered a great

number of oxen, though poor, have been saved to supply
the meat part of ration six days in the week, and we
have on hand bacon for one day in the week for seven
months, and also flour and small rations.– (See the

horse by everyone. Tell Charlie that he will never see Dandy again. . .

"Nov. 17 . . . Cattle have died so rapidly that they have to send back
oxen to draw one train at a time. . .

"Nov. 18 . . . We arrived at Ft. Bridger about 8 p.m."

Captain Phelps records in his diary (a large section of which is reproduced in Part IV):

"Nov. 6 . . . The snow is driving down (9 p.m.) in a perfect storm,
against which there is no shelter. The cries of bewildered geese are heard
in the air amidst the storm. . .

"Nov. 7 . . . We lost eight horses yesterday. . . They become so
weak that they reel, stagger and fall. It is a very unpleasant sight to witness
their decline – wild, haggard, and tremulous with hunger and cold. They
seem to eat today nothing but the sage brush, in which there is no sustenance. . .

"Nov. 12 . . . The thermometer fell last night to sixteen degrees
below zero. This temperature in a wall tent without fire is very uncomfortable, especially when one sleeps alone. . .

"Nov. 16 . . . The animals are still dying rapidly. They are seen
fallen in such attitudes as could only result from the last possible effort of
remaining strength to resist the effects of starvation and cold – bent crushed
down in every variety of posture by the stern cold hand of death. I noticed
particularly a dying horse today. He happened to be down in a natural
attitude, but he held his head up and bent backward. He ate languidly of the
little grass which I placed before him for a while, and then stopped with his
mouth full unchewed. A drowsiness seemed stealing over him, but his eye
shone with peculiar fire. His head would now and then jerk suddenly as if
from a doze till finally he laid back upon his side and died.

"Misery makes strange companionship. The honest, patient, long enduring
ox too, falls as if crushed down against his will, his cold death-eye glaring
up at the pitiless sky. We saw a poor hard-working ox today, lying down
close by a dead horse and apparently with hardly strength enough to chew
his cud. Horses, mules and oxen in some places all lie together. . .

"Nov. 18 . . . One of my horses fell down today and refused to stand
up, even when put upon his legs. At length I gave him a tumbler of whiskey,
& it acted like magic, he got up and went to eating right away."

See also the letter of Col. Johnston to his friend Eaton, written from Camp
Scott, Feb. 5, 1858, and found in the Johnston collection at Tulane University,
New Orleans.

report of the chief commissary of subsistence herewith.) [61]

Colonel Cooke, in command of six companies 2d dragoons, arrived on the 19th instant. You will learn from his report (herewith) that the storm dealt as roughly with his command as it did with the army in advance.[62] He lost nearly half of his horses, besides a number of mules. His march, from his report, appears to have been conducted with care and skill. If a further advance of the army were otherwise practicable and proper at this season of the year, the necessity of appropriating the remainder of the work oxen for food for the troops would now prevent.

The diminished number and reduced condition of the cavalry and battery horses and draught mules, makes a remount for the former and an additional number of mules for the quartermaster's department

---

[61] The report of Capt. H. F. Clarke, in charge of subsistence, is printed in *Doc. 71*, pp. 104-105. Clarke says that about 2400 men are dependent upon the present stock of government supplies for subsistence. He lists about 2000 head of cattle; and sufficient coffee and sugar. He recommends that bacon, including hams, be issued but once in seven days; 2 pounds of fresh beef per ration; 12 ounces of flour per ration; in every 10 days beans be issued thrice, rice five times and desiccated vegetables twice; half rations of vinegar, candles and soap; molasses to be issued twice and dried peaches once in fifteen days.

He reports subsistence items stored at Fort Bridger as: 46,800 lbs. of bacon, 5,000 lbs. of ham; 405,500 lbs. of flour; 375 bushels of beans; 26,100 lbs. of rice; 19,750 lbs. of coffee; 260 lbs. of tea; 62,500 lbs. of sugar; 3,300 gallons of vinegar; 4,480 lbs. of candles; 7,550 lbs. of soap; 1,000 gallons of molasses; 104 bushels of dried peaches.

Capt. J. H. Dickerson, Asst. Quartermaster, reported on Nov. 29 (*Doc. 71*, pp. 106-107) clothing and equipment that included: 560 caps and hats; 938 infantry coats; 3,162 uniform trousers; 3,905 flannel shirts; 3,290 pairs of drawers; 675 pairs of boots, 600 pairs of socks; 676 great coats, 723 blankets, 3,150 bed sacks; 39 Sibley tents; 31 hospital tents, 452 haversacks, etc.

[62] Cooke's diary of his march is published in *Doc. 71*, pp. 92-100. It is a record of hardihood and perseverance. Of his horses, he lost 134, and arrived with 144.

indispensable. A further advance cannot be made without them. I have, therefore, taken measures (see orders to Captain Marcy and estimates of the chief quartermasters' herewith) [63] to supply all deficiencies. Captain Marcy has been despatched, with a sufficient party suitably organized and equipped, to New Mexico, as the nearest and most accessible region from which they can be obtained early in the spring, with instructions to purchase the number required, and to return as soon in the spring as he can, having regard to the good condition of the horses and mules; and he is authorized to contract for a supply of salt, of which we have none, and forward it on his arrival. I respectfully request the sanction of the general-in-chief to my orders to Captain Marcy, and that he will give instructions to General Garland, or commanding officer of the Department of New Mexico, to furnish Captain Marcy a sufficient escort of the mounted rifles to protect him from predatory attacks of the Indians on the route back to this place. I enclose a copy of my letter to General Garland, making the request. The Mormons, before they retired, burnt the buildings in and about Fort Bridger, and also Fort Supply on Smith's fork, twelve miles hence, and destroyed the grain, and as far as they could, other crops at that place.[64] Fort Bridger, so called, is a high, well built, strong stone wall, enclosing a square of one hundred feet, and has been appropriated for the storage of the supplies for the army. The addition and the other on the northeast corner of a stone enclosure adjoining the main one, but not so high, will make it defensible by a small force, and a safe place of deposit

[63] Referred to and summarized above, in footnotes 64 and 65.
[64] See Pulsipher's diary, Part VII.

for the public property that may be left when the army advances. The herds of mules, battery horses, and cattle have been sent with herdsmen to Henry's Fork to graze during the winter, and six companies of the 2d dragoons, under the command of Colonel Cooke, have been ordered to encamp near them, and guard them and protect the herdsmen. He has with him about two hundred dragoon horses. Two companies of the same regiment are stationed here, and have about fifty horses, all feeble, for want of sufficient sustenance. In the spring the army, with the volunteer force included, about two thousand strong, will resume their march as soon as a supply of horses and mules arrive, and the grass on the mountains shall be found sufficient to sustain them.

Two full companies of volunteers have been mustered into the service for nine (9) months,[65] and I expect in a few days that two more companies will be mustered in. They are young, active, and hardy men, generally good shots, and with such instructions as they will receive, will make most excellent light troops. I have to request that the emolument of these men may be early made known to the Secretary of War, so that provision may be made, by an appropriation by Congress for their payment at the expiration of their term of service.

The troops have borne the hardships and privations of the march with patience and cheerfulness, and continue in fine health; some few of the different regiments are still suffering from frost bite.

Governor Cumming and family, Judge Eckel, the secretary, attorney general, and marshal of the Terri-

---

[65] From Magraw's wagon road men and from teamsters with the freighting outfits.

tory, and also Dr. Forney, superintendent of Indian affairs, and Dr. Hunt [Hurt], agent, are encamped within our lines, and have received every facility and means to make them comfortable, as much so as can be expected under canvas.

I enclose copies of all orders given by me which will fully acquaint you with any matter omitted in this communication.

With great respect, your obedient servant,

A. S. JOHNSTON
Colonel 2d Cavalry, Commanding

P.S. A field return is transmitted herewith. I beg leave to ask your attention to the absence of a great number of officers as exhibited by the return.

Respectfully, A. S. JOHNSTON
Colonel 2d Cavalry, Commanding

VI
Mormon Reactions to the Approach
of the Military Expedition

INTRODUCTION

One of the first indications of recent friction between the United States Government and the Mormons was given by Brigham Young in a speech at the Bowery, Salt Lake City, on June 7, 1857. He told the assembled people that trouble was brewing, and that some of the officers who had been sent to the Territory were circulating false rumors about the Latter-day Saints.[1] President Young accused William Smith, brother of Joseph Smith (founder of the Mormon Church), of writing articles in the newspapers and magazines of the East in which he defied "the United States to send a Governor here that can do anything with the 'Mormons,' except himself, . . and if you do not believe me, try me, and if you think I cannot, give me the right to go there with a good army."[2]

In a sermon at the Bowery on July 5, President Young said: "Persons who are as ignorant as jackasses pass through this city, and they are so prejudiced that

---

[1] *Deseret News* (Salt Lake City), June 17, 1857 (VII, pp. 116-117). The principal report, and doubtless the one here referred to, was that written by Judge W. W. Drummond on March 30, 1857, when resigning from the Supreme Court of Utah Territory. This Drummond letter is printed in the Appendix.

[2] Young's speech, printed in the *Deseret News,* June 17, 1857 (VII, p. 116, c. 2).

they cannot see and hear well enough to report things straight.   .   .

"I will say to all parties, if you come here and do not observe wholesome laws, we will introduce you to them. In regard to troops coming here, as has been rumored, should 1500 or 2000 come, what will you see? You will see that they will ask us to make their soldiers behave themselves, until they can get out of this place, which they will do as soon as possible. They are not coming here to fight us, though if they were to I should pray that the Lord would bring those here that mobbed us in days gone by, and just let us look at them."[3]

Again in a speech on July 19, Young reprimanded the people who were writing and speaking slander about the church. "Will troops come here and inquire into my just rebukes of such characters and conduct?" he asked. Troops had been among them many times, he said, and if the Saints would live their religion they need not fear.[4]

The above references to troops were based on rumors only. But on July 24, when some twenty-six hundred Mormons at the head of Big Cottonwood Canyon were celebrating the tenth anniversary of the entrance of the Saints into the valley of the Great Salt Lake, A. O. Smoot, Judson Stoddard, and Porter Rockwell brought word that an army was actually coming. These messengers, who had sped the five hundred miles from Fort Laramie in five days, arrived at the mountain resort scene of the festivities at noon. Brigham and

---

[3] *Ibid.,* July 15, 1857 (VII, p. 148, c. 3 and 4). Orders for the asembling of troops to march to Utah had been issued by General Scott on May 28, 1857 (see Part I), but the positive news had not reached Utah by July 5.

[4] *Ibid.,* July 29, 1857 (VII, p. 164, c. 4).

GOVERNOR BRIGHAM YOUNG

other leaders were apprised of what was happening in the States, but the news was not given to the crowd until evening, when the celebration was at an end. And then it was announced calmly, to prevent undue excitement.[5]

1. BRIGHAM YOUNG SPEAKING AT THE BOWERY IN SALT LAKE CITY, JULY 26, 1857 [6]

. . . I am a yankee guesser, and guess that James Buchanan has ordered this expedition to appease the wrath of the angry hounds who are howling around him. He did not design to start men on the 15th of July to cross these plains to this point on foot. Russell & Co. will, probably make from eight to ten hundred thousand dollars by freighting the baggage of the expedition. . .

But woe, woe to that man who comes here to unlawfully interfere with my affairs. Woe, woe to those men who come here to unlawfully meddle with me and this people. I swore in Nauvoo when my enemies were looking me in the face, that I would send them to hell across-lots, if they meddled with me; and I ask no more odds of all hell today. . .

2. HEBER C. KIMBALL, SPEAKING THE SAME DAY [7]

. . . Sending a man here with 2,500 troops! — they have no design in God Almighty's world only to raise a rookery with this people and bring us into

---

[5] See the extensive account of the celebration in the *Deseret News* of July 29 (VII, p. 165, c. 4). The coming of an army was given a very minor play in that news story. It was reported that 2587 persons, 464 carriages and wagons, 1028 horses and mules, 332 oxen and cows were at the head of Big Cottonwood Canyon.

[6] *Deseret News,* Aug. 5, 1857 (VII, p. 172, c. 4).

[7] *Ibid.,* Aug. 12, 1857 (VII, p. 179, c. 2; p. 182, c. 2). Kimball was First Counsellor to President Brigham Young in heading the Mormon Church.

collision with the United States, and when they come here, the first dab will be to take br. Brigham Young and Heber C. Kimball and others and they will slay us, that is their design, and if we will not yield to their meanness, they will say we have mutinied against the President of the United States, and then they will put us under martial law and massacre this people. That has been the design of the men that have been here. (Voice in the stand, "They can't come it.") No, they can't come it.

Drummond and those miserable scoundrels and some that are now in our midst, how do I feel towards them? pray for them, Yes, I pray that God Almighty would send them to hell, some say across lots, but I would like to have them take a round about road and be as long as they can be in going there. How do you suppose I feel?

I have been driven five times, been broken up and my goods robbed from me, and I have been afflicted almost to death. I am here with my wives and children and as good women as can be found in the United States. . .

Send 2500 troops here, our brethren, to make a desolation of this people! God Almighty helping me, I will fight until there is not a drop of blood in my veins. Good God! I have wives enough to whip out the United States, for they will whip themselves. AMEN.

3. HEBER C. KIMBALL'S SPEECH OF AUGUST 30,[8] 1857

. . . You all acknowledge brother Brigham as the President of the Church of Jesus Christ of Latter-

[8] *Journal of Discourses delivered by President Brigham Young, his two Counsellors, the Twelve Apostles, and others. Reported by G. D. Watt, J. V. Long, and others, and humbly dedicated to the Latter-Day Saints in all the World* (Liverpool, Edited and published by Asa Calkin, 42 Islington, 1858), v, pp. 160-65.

day Saints; then you acknowledge him as our Leader, Prophet, Seer, and Revelator; and then you acknowledge him in every capacity that pertains to his calling, both in Church and State, do you not? (Voices: "Yes.") Well, he is our Governor. What is Governor? One who presides or governs. Well, now, we have declared, in a legislative capacity, that we will not have poor, rotten-hearted curses come and rule over us, such as some they have been accustomed to send. We drafted a memorial, and the Council and the House of Representatives signed it, and we sent to them the names of men of our own choice – as many as from five to eight men for each office – men from our own midst, out of whom to appoint officers for this Territory. We sent that number for the President of the United States to make a selection from, and asked him to give us men of our own choice, in accordance with the rights constitutionally guaranteed to all American citizens.[9] We just told them right up and down, that if they sent any more such miserable curses as some they had sent were, we would send them home; and that is one reason why an army, or rather a mob, is on the way here, as reported. You did not know the reason before, did you?

Well, we did that in a legislative capacity; we did it as members of the Legislature – as your representatives; and now you have got to back us up. You sent us, just as we sent brother Bernhisel to seek for our rights and to stand in our defence at Washington.[10]

Well, here is brother Brigham: he is the man of our

---

[9] The various Territories of the United States were continually voicing the same sentiments, asking that officials be selected from local residents. But the powers in Washington seldom gave much heed to such requests; and of course the President was not by law required to do so.

[10] Dr. John M. Bernhisel was Delegate to Congress from Utah.

own choice; he is our Governor, in the capacity of a Territory, and also as Saints of the Most High.

Well, it is reported that they have another Governor on the way now, three Judges, a District Attorney, a Marshal, a Postmaster, and Secretary, and that they are coming here with twenty-five hundred men. The United States design to force those officers upon us by the point of the bayonet. . .

We are the people of Deseret,[11] and it is for us to say whether we will have brother Brigham for our Governor, or those poor, miserable devils they are reported to be trying to bring here. You must know they are miserable devils to have to come here under arms; but they shall not rule over us nor come into this Territory. What do you say about it? Are you willing, as a people, that they should come in here? You that say they shall not, raise your right hands. (All hands raised.) . . .

We never shall leave these valleys – till we get ready; no, never; no, never. We will live here till we go back to Jackson County,[12] Missouri. I prophesy that, in the name of Israel's God. (The congregation shouted "Amen," and President B. Young said, "It is true.")

If our enemies force us to destroy our orchards and our property, to destroy and lay waste our houses, fields, and everything else, we shall never build and plant again, till we do it in Jackson County. But our enemies are not here yet, and we have not yet thrown down our houses. . .

I mean just what I say, and this people say they will

---

[11] Deseret was the name of the proposed state set up by the Mormons in 1849.

[12] Jackson County, Missouri, had been proclaimed by Joseph Smith in 1831 as Zion, the gathering place of modern Israel (the Mormons). After expulsion from this area the Mormons continued to preach and talk of the early return to and occupancy of Jackson County (Independence was the County Seat).

not have any other Governor, and especially any one that has to come here under arms; for we consider that any man is a poor, damned curse that has to come here under arms to rule over us. These are my feelings; and if anybody votes against it, they are not of us: . .

When we reject brother Brigham Young, we reject the head; but we will not do it, for the body shall dwell together, and we are members of that body, and he shall be our Governor just as long as God Almighty will have him to be. Those who are in favour of it, raise your hands. (The vote was unanimous.). . .

4. BRIGHAM YOUNG'S SPEECH, SEPTEMBER 13 [13]

On the 24th of July last, a number of us went to Big Cottonwood Kanyon, to pass the anniversary of our arrival into this Valley. Ten years ago the 24th of July last, a few of the Elders arrived here and began to plough and to plant seeds, to raise food to sustain themselves. Whilst speaking to the brethren on that day, I said, inadvertently, If the people of the United States will let us alone for ten years, we will ask no odds of them; and ten years from that very day, we had a message by Brother Smoot, Stoddard, and Rockwell, that the Government had stopped the mail, and that they had ordered 2,500 troops to come here and hold the "Mormons" still, while priests, politicians, speculators, whoremongers, and every mean, filthy character that could be raked up should come here and kill off the "Mormons." I did not think about what I had said ten years ago, till I heard that the President of the

[13] *Journal of Discourses, op. cit.,* v, pp. 226-31. Capt. Stewart Van Vliet visited the Mormons in early September, 1857. See in Part II, the quoted conversations at Brigham Young's office on September 9. On Sunday, the 13th, the Captain attended the general Mormon service, was seated on the stand, and listened to the speech here printed. Also published in the *Deseret News,* September 23, 1857.

United States had so unjustly ordered troops here; and then I said, when my former expression came to my mind, In the name of Israel's God we ask no odds of them.   .   .

The officer in command of the United States' Army, on its way to Utah, detailed one of his staff, Captain Van Vliet, who is now on the stand, to come here and learn whether he could procure the necessary supplies for the army.   .   .[14]

Well, the enquiry is, "What is the news? What is the conclusion?" It is this – We have to trust in God. I am not in the least concerned as to the result, if we put our trust in God. The administrators of our Government have issued orders for marching troops and expending much treasure, and all predicated upon falsehoods, while every honorable man would have first made an economical and peaceful enquiry into the circumstances.   .   .   We have got to protect ourselves by the strength of our God.

If you do your duty in this respect, you need not be afraid of mobs, nor of forces sent out in violation of the very genius of our free institutions, holding you till mobs kill you. Mobs? Yes; for where is there the least particle of authority, either in our Constitution or laws for sending troops here, or even for appointing civil officers contrary to the voluntary consent of the governed? We came here without any help from our enemies, and we intend to stay as long as we please.

They say that their army is legal, and I say that such a statement is as false as hell and that they are as rotten as an old pumpkin that has been frozen seven times and then melted in a harvest sun. Come on with your

---

[14] The rest of the reference to the Captain is given above, in Part II, fn. 3.

thousands of illegally-ordered troops, and I will promise you, in the name of Israel's God that you shall melt away as the snow before a July sun. . .

We are not to be persecuted as we have been. We can say "Come as a mob, and we can sweeten you up right suddenly." They never did anything against Joseph till they had ostensibly legalized a mob; and I shall treat every army and every armed company that attempts to come here as a mob. (The congregation responded, "Amen"). You might as well tell me that you can make hell into a powder-house as to tell me that you could let an army in here and have peace; and I intend to tell them and show them this, if they do not keep away. By taking this course, you will find that every man and woman feels happy, and they say, "All is right, all is well;" and I say that our enemies shall not slip the bow on "Old Bright's neck" again.

God bless you. AMEN.

5. PRESIDENT YOUNG'S AFTERNOON SPEECH [15]

I would like very well to hear some of the rest of the brethren speak, if I had entirely got over being angry and had patience to sit and hear. I think, however, that I shall be able to calm and control my feelings, though I do not expect to become entirely settled until the affairs around me are settled.

It is a pretty bold stand for this people to take, to say that they will not be controlled by the corrupt administrations of our General Government. We will be controlled by them, if they will be controlled by the Constitution and laws; but they will not. . .

I do not lift my voice against the great and glorious Government guaranteed to every citizen by our Constitution, but against those corrupt administrators, who trample the Constitution and just laws under their feet.   .   .

I have said that if the brethren will have faith, the Lord will fight our battles, and we will have the privilege of living here in peace. I have counted the cost to this people of a collision with our enemies; but I cannot begin to count the cost it will be to them.

I have told you that if this people will live their religion, all will be well; and I have told you that if there is any man or woman that is not willing to destroy anything and everything of their property that would be of use to an enemy, if left, I wanted them to go out of the Territory; and I again say so today; for when the time comes to burn and lay waste our improvements, if any man undertakes to shield his, he will be sheared down; for "judgment will be laid to the line and righteousness to the plummet." Now the faint-hearted can go in peace; but should that time come, they must not interfere. Before I will suffer what I have in times gone by, there shall not be one building, nor one foot of lumber, nor a stick, nor a tree, nor a particle of grass and hay, that will burn, left in reach of our enemies. I am sworn, if driven to extremity, to utterly lay waste, in the name of Israel's god.   .   .

If the troops are now this side of Laramie, remember that the Sweetwater is this side of that place. They must have some place to winter, for they cannot come through here this season. We could go out and use them up, and it would not require fifty men to do it. But probably we shall not have occasion to take that course, for we do not want to kill men. They may winter in peace at some place east of us; but when spring comes, they must go back to the States, or, at any rate, they must leave the mountains.[16]

6. *DESERET NEWS* EDITORIAL, SEPTEMBER 23 [17]

The Government could do nothing for us, but left no stone unturned to do everything against us, to the utmost stretch that priests, politicians, and their clans could bring the popular opinion to bear. And now, after a large class of its citizens have been ruthlessly thrust from State after State and forced to seek an asylum from religious persecution amid the rocks and deserts of a then foreign power, and after those citizens have furnished an unjustly required and immensely disproportionate quota of troops for the conquest of the country they now occupy, and after they have turned dreary wastes into the smiling abodes of free men, the very Government that "could do nothing for them" though their cause was just, has bowed down, like an ass beneath a burthen of rotteness, beneath the clamors of sectarian, political and speculating selfishness, and is openly striving to exterminate the Saints of God and banish His Priesthood from the Earth. . .

Neither is it to be supposed that the large majority of American-born citizens in Utah, reared in the schools, academies and colleges of the States, do not know the rights guaranteed to them, and that they have not enough of the spirit of '76 and of the Anglo-Saxon blood of their Revolutionary sires, to maintain those rights inviolate to the utmost of the power which the Almighty may see fit to vouchsafe. . .

---

[16] On September 15 Young issued his Proclamation of martial law. This is printed in Part III.

[17] Albert Carrington, Editor of the News, first recounted the trials of the Saints throughout their history and how the Government had maintained, "Your cause is just, but we can do nothing for you."

It is most readily obvious to all that the administration of our Government is becoming rotten even to loathing, when anonymous liars and a whoring, lying, venomous late associate justice[18] can incite the expenditure of millions of public treasure in an unjust, outrageously wicked and illegal movement against a peaceful and known zealously loyal people inhabiting a region they had reclaimed and which no other ever had desired, or would now occupy were it laid waste for their entrance. Dear Uncle Sam, we were reared and taught under the broad folds of the "Star-Spangled Banner," and notwithstanding you have deprived us of our Eastern mail, we are perfectly aware of the designs of those who are eating your very vitals, and forewarn you that Utah alone cannot avert your speedy dissolution, unless you shake yourself of the vampires now praying upon you, cease your ungodly crusade against an innocent people, and return to the old landmarks of meteing even-handed justice to all.

7. YOUNG'S REPORT AND MESSAGE OF OCTOBER 18 [19]

I purpose to have read to you this morning some of the communications that have passed between our enemies and ourselves, for the people are . . . very anxious to learn the news. I am perfectly willing that they should know all. . .

If the Government of the United States have sent soldiers to this Territory, I do not know it; for I have had no official notice of such a circumstance, and you will perceive that I treat them accordingly. If they are

---

[18] Referring to Justice Drummond and his accusations printed below, in the Appendix.

[19] Given in the newly completed Tabernacle in Salt Lake City. Printed in the *Journal of Discourses,* v, pp. 336-43.

sent by Government, they are sent expressly to destroy this people . . . therefore I shall treat them, as I have informed the officers in command, the same as though they were an avowed mob – not as I would those that have heretofore mobbed us, but as parties have come to mob us now.

I have informed Colonel Alexander that had his command been the men who have heretofore mobbed us, and the lying scribblers, and the wicked rabble, who have all the day long been trying to incite mobs against us, they never would have seen the South Pass.

You will perceive from the communication which brother John T. Caine will read, the feelings of the two parties. . .

[Caine then reads the correspondence with army officials.] [20]

When the mob in Missouri commenced burning our habitations we frequently sent to the Governor, petitioning him to stop mobbings; but instead of doing that, he rendered them assistance, by ordering about 3,500 men to go and lay waste the city of Far West, and destroy men, women, and children. Those orders General Clark had, though at their close the Governor said to him, "I shall leave it discretionary with you whether you kill all the Mormons or not." We saw them coming, and some thought they were sent to disperse the mob, in answer to our petition; but the mob were expecting them and seemed to understand the movement. . .

It is pretty hard for us to come here with nothing; and we have come as near coming here with nothing as the Lord did to creating the heavens and the earth out

---

[20] Caine read an unofficial letter from Young to Alexander, dated Oct. 14; one from Lieut. Gen. Wells to Young, dated Oct. 15; one from Alexander to Young, dated Oct. 12; and one from Young to Alexander, of Oct. 16.

of nothing; and I have frequently thought a little nigher. . .

We have sought for peace all the day long; and I have sought for peace with the army now on our borders, and have warned them that we all most firmly believe that they are sent here solely with a view to destroy this people, though they may be ignorant of that fact. And though we may believe that they are sent by the Government of the United States, yet I, as Governor of this Territory, have no business to know any such thing until I am notified by proper authority at Washington. I have a right to treat them as a mob, just as though they had been raised and officered in Missouri and sent here expressly to destroy this people. We have been merciful and very lenient to them. . .

I would just as soon tell them as to tell you my mode of warfare. As the Lord God lives, we will waste our enemies by millions, if they send them here to destroy us, and not a man of us be hurt. That is the method I intend to pursue. Do you want to know what is going to be done with the enemies now on our borders? If they come here, I will tell you what will be done. As soon as they start to come into our settlements, let sleep depart from their eyes and slumber from their eyelids until they sleep in death, for they have been warned and forewarned that we will not tamely submit to being destroyed. Men shall be secreted here and there and shall waste away our enemies, in the name of Israel's God. . .

I intend to publish the communication between the Army and myself; for I wish the whole United States to understand it. . .

VII
Mormon Operations Against the United States Army

INTRODUCTION

Upon receipt of definite news of the dispatch of an army toward Utah, the Mormon leaders began to plan for defense. Eight days after the couriers delivered their message to the celebrating Saints at Big Cottonwood Canyon, the following order was issued to the Utah militia, still known as the "Nauvoo Legion:"

HEADQUARTERS NAUVOO LEGION,
Adjt. General's Office,   G.S.L. City,   Aug. 1, 1857

SIR: Reports, tolerably well authenticated, have reached this office that an army from the Eastern States is now *en route* to invade this Territory.

The people of this Territory have lived in strict obedience to the laws of the parent and home governments, and are ever zealous for the supremacy of the Constitution and the rights guaranteed thereby. In such time, when anarchy takes the place of orderly government and mobocratic tyranny usurps the power of rulers, they have left the inalienable right to defend themselves against all aggression upon their constitutional privileges. It is enough that for successive years they have witnessed the desolation of their homes; the barbarous wrath of mobs poured upon their unoffending brethren and sisters; their leaders arrested, incarcerated and slain, and themselves driven to cull life from the hospitality of the desert and the savage. They are not willing to endure longer these unceasing outrages; but if an exterminating war be purposed against them and blood alone can cleanse pollution from the Nation's bulwarks, to the God of our fathers let the appeal be made.

You are instructed to hold your command in readiness to march at the shortest possible notice to any part of the Territory. See that the law is strictly enforced in regard to arms and ammunition, and as far as practicable that each Ten be provided with a good wagon and four horses or mules, as well as the necessary clothing, etc., for a winter campaign. Particularly let your influence be used for the preservation of the grain. Avoid all excitement, but be ready.

DANIEL H. WELLS,
Lieut. General Commanding
By JAMES FERGUSON, Adjt. Gen.[1]

Copies of this letter were sent to militia leaders throughout the Territory. Soon there was much activity in the cleaning and repair of firearms, equipping of horses, and the preparation of camping outfits.

On August 13 the first order was issued for movement of troops. It directed Colonel Robert T. Burton[2] to take men of the first regiment and march east along the main road to the States. He was to aid the incoming emigrants and supply trains and to learn the strength and equipment of the armed forces headed for Utah. Colonel Burton reported:

We arrived at Fort Bridger August 21st, and met the first company of immigrants at Pacific Springs on the 26th. On the following day we met Moody's company from Texas, also several large supply trains, entirely unprotected by any escort. On the 29th I left my wagons and half of the men and animals on the

---

[1] Quoted in "The Echo Canyon War," in *The Contributor* (Salt Lake City), III, p. 177. This account of the conflict between Utah and the nation ran serially in 1882-83. Wells and Ferguson have been identified in previous footnotes.

[2] Burton, born in Canada in 1821, had previously fought Indian campaigns in Utah. He was to hold various civil, military, and ecclesiastical positions in the state. He died Nov. 11, 1907. Andrew Jenson, *Latter-Day Saint Biographical Encyclopedia* (Salt Lake City, Andrew Jenson History Co., 1901), I, pp. 238-41; III, p. 746. Hereafter cited as Jenson, *Bio. Ency.* Burton's diary of his operations from Oct. 21 to Dec. 5 (31 pages in a small book) are in the Mormon Church Historian's Office, Salt Lake City.

Sweetwater, proceeding with pack animals. On the 30th I arrived at Devil's Gate, with Kimball, Cummings and Decker's command coming up the next day; here on the 31st we met Jones, Stringam and others on their way from Deer Creek to Salt Lake City, and on the day after Capt. John R. Murdock, from the States. The latter brought word of the intense bitterness expressed all over the Union against the Mormons, and of the expectations that many entertained that the people of Utah were about to be annihilated by the strong arm of the military power.

[Col. Burton cached provisions for future use and then sent men to the Platte to do scouting. Information was frequently expressed to General Wells and President Young. On the 21st Burton, with three men] moved east to the vicinity of Devil's Gate, and camped, Sept. 22nd, within half a mile of Col. E. B. Alexander's command. Here they first met the advance of the Utah army, and from that time were its immediate neighbors until it arrived at Ham's Fork. . . Scouts and spies were with them continually, examining their camps, arms, equipments, etc., and reporting to headquarters.[3]

On September 29, General D. H. Wells left Salt Lake City and proceeded on the main road to Echo Canyon, where he established headquarters at the "narrows" of the canyon, some 65 miles east of Salt Lake City. Companies of the Nauvoo Legion from the various military districts of the Territory, totaling about 1250 men, were ordered to report at Echo with provisions for thirty days. Here troops were soon employed in digging trenches across the canyon, throwing up breastworks, and loosening on the heights above, stones that could be rolled down upon a force attempting to push through the canyon.

The accounts of Mormon military activity which have been chosen for presentation here are: (A) the diary of a soldier, John Pulsipher; and (B) the narration of the most famous raider, Lot Smith.

---

[3] *The Contributor*, III, p. 178.

A. DIARY OF JOHN PULSIPHER[4]

On 27 (MAY) 1857, George Boyd and Joshua Terry returned from the journey to States carrying the mail, had a cold rough time going – & returned with the mail for this month; They say the people are terribly wicked – have no peace there & are determined to make war on us. So that we can have no peace.

ON SATURDAY, THE 13 OF JUNE we organized a battalion of military men & boys, 7 tens filled up, & room for more captains of 10's, 50's, & 100.[5] Isaac Bullock captain of 100 or majority of Green River Battalion of Nauvoo Legion. . .

JUNE 28 while we were in meeting today, 40 Arapahoe Indians rode up to the gate of the Fort & were invited in, unsaddled & turned out horses & sat down on the floor. An Indian interpreter, said his name was Friday,[6] told who they were and that they came 500 miles – from Platte River in the Black Hills[7]– had been on case [chase] of a band of thieving Utes & had came over the mountains from the south to see us &

---

[4] This diary was made available to us by the diarist's grandson and our friend, Lewis Pulsipher of Mesquite, Nevada. A typewritten copy of the diary is in the library of Brigham Young University. Accompanying it is a biographical sketch of Pulsipher.

John Pulsipher was born in Spafford, Onendago County, New York, on July 17, 1827. He was reared in the Mormon Church, his father Zerah having joined the new sect in January, 1832, before it was two years old. In 1856-57 John, as a young married man, was living at the new town of Fort Supply, twelve miles south of Fort Bridger.

Pulsipher's diary gives first an interesting account of conditions and reactions at this Mormon frontier outpost area. Then it records the service of a soldier in the Mormon troops.

[5] The Mormon system of organizing emigrating companies and military companies was in the Biblical pattern of tens, fifties, and hundreds.

[6] The Arapaho rescued as a boy in 1831 by Thomas Fitzpatrick. See the account of him in this *Series,* v, pp. 300-308; and in L. R. Hafen and W. J. Ghent, *Broken Hand,* etc. (Denver, Old West Publishing Co., 1931), 269-82.

[7] These were the Black Hills near Fort Laramie.

get on the Mormon wagon road on the return journey.
. . They were tall noble looking men – well dressed
in skins & good buffalo robes for blankets. . . The
chief named Wattoma which in our language is Black
Bear.

JULY 26 . . . The News from the States is –
That Hell is boiling over, the Devil is mad – The U.S.
mail is stopped & an army is coming to kill us. Parley
Pratt is murdered [8] & etc.

Three bands of Ute Indians made us a visit, led by
Lowe-ett, Soldier & Tintic. The last named seemed to
be a surly ill-tempered fellow. . .

AUGUST 12   Bro. Robinson [9] made feast and dance,
invited us all to celebrate the completion of the new
Fort Bridger – Strong stone walls 16 feet high & five
feet thick [10] Is church property & a good job our men
worked considerable at it. We sawed the lumber.

Elder S. W. Richards [11] & others past as swift messengers to call the Elders home from the States. [12]

AUGUST 16   Pres. Young sent us a letter which was
read in meeting giving instructions to prepare for coming events. Br. Bullock was advised to gather up all the
people, the stoke [stock], provisions & everything valuable & move carefully to the [Salt Lake] Valley.

This looks like former times when we have had to

---

[8] Parley P. Pratt, one of the Twelve Apostles and an outstanding leader
of the Mormon Church, was killed in Arkansas on May 13, 1857.

[9] Lewis Robinson, soon to become quartermaster of the Mormon troops.
Probably the same person as Jack Robinson; see this *Series,* III, 60.

[10] The Mormons were soon to burn Fort Bridger; but these stone walls
remained standing and were to be very helpful in providing shelter for the
army supplies.

[11] We shall hear of Richards again as he writes a letter to Thomas L.
Kane, friend of the Mormons.

[12] The Mormon leaders not only called home their missionaries, but also
the far flung colonists in San Bernardino, California, and Carson Valley,
present Nevada.

leave our homes & hard earned possessions – but we all are very willing to prepare for safety – for we have no confidence in the Government officials. Knowing that their design has been all the time to destroy us – have never given us our constitutional rights – & after the many times they have robbed, mobbed & driven us – the many murders they have committed & no redress – & protection for us in any of these States & after coming away to the Mountain out of everybodies way – the government is extended over us & their poor devilish wicked officers are sent to rule over us, & on their false charges & his, this move is made against us – I suppose they thot by stopping the U.S. mail we would not know what was going on & the army come on us unawares but we have friends that will bring us word & the Lord is our friend and we need not fear.

AUGUST 17   I wrote to John Alger on the charges of business & etc.

THURSDAY 20   Bro. Charles with a few minute men came this morning – stayed till next morning – fine time good news from Valley – We gave supplies of grain & vegetables etc. & they went on as spies.

AUGUST 21, 1857   We made a feast for 115 Indians led by Teaboointoetsy came into the Fort dancing, making their own music, on instrunts of their own make. . .[13]

A few days ago Washakee[14] & a band of Shoshones made us a visit & had a feast & presents to take away. This is quite a tax on us – but we are on their land & wish to be at peace & give them no cause of complaiant against us. Government having never bought their land

---

[13] These were doubtless Shoshone Indians.

[14] For a biography of this famous chief, see Grace R. Hebard, *Washakie* (Glendale, The Arthur H. Clark Company, 1930).

– we wish to do right by them. . . They came by the mill where I was sawing, I showed them the different parts & how it worked. They thot that was wonderful.

Busy harvesting & saving crops, which are good. have had a warm summer with exception of occasional frosts – not to kill much – & we have been blest with a number of warm showers of rain so this is by far the best crop raised here & we wish to have it all saved for future use.

SEPTEMBER 3   Lewis Huffaker going to meet his father called, rested, & visited a few days. . .

Bro. T. S. Terry[15] arrived in the night & we all had a good time together not much time to sleep – next day self & wife went with them to camp near Bridger. took Potatoes & etc. & treated the company. had introduction to many of their traveling companions.

We also saw the company of our brethren who have spent the summer making a farm and mail station at Deer Creek 400 miles from Valley – labor lost, as Government has taken away the mail contract & etc.[16]

Father & mother returned to Fort Supply with us & stayed another night made us some presents & we gave them Potatoes & etc. & our thanks. Much pleased to see our emigration coming in, in good time this year.[17]

SEPTEMBER 20   today we received the Proclamation

---

[15] Thomas Searles Terry, born Oct. 3, 1825, migrated to Utah in 1847. He was married to two sisters of John Pulsipher. He was just returning from a mission to the Eastern states. See his biography in Jenson, *Bio. Ency.*, III, pp. 261-62.

[16] This farm on the Deer Creek branch of the North Platte was to have been a station on the B.Y. Express Company line.

[17] The early arrival of emigrants was especially gratifying because of the terrible suffering and loss of life in the late handcart companies of the preceding year.

of the Governor of Utah, Brigham Young; dated 15 September 1857 forbidding all armed forces coming into the Territory under any pretence whatever. Calls on all the Militia to be in readiness at a moments warning. Also, declares martial law to exist after publication of this document.

Good, we received it with joy.

September 20, President Bullock received a letter from Bro. Brigham of the 16th giving us further instructions in regard to carrying into effect the foregoing Proclamation. Altho the invading army is approaching – but this martial law must be carried out. Be careful of the lives of people. See that there are no more killed than is absolutely necessary to carry out these orders.

Mentions in this that it would be well to move the families in from Fort Supply as that is a hard place to live.

SUNDAY SEPTEMBER 27 Bro. Bullock went to Fort Bridger to learn how things are going on the road. We supposed it would be best to move soon if we did not get all our crops secured. Bro. Edson Whipple & myself went with the stock here today to be sure that they were safe. When we came in at night with the herd Bro. Bullock had returned, and it was time to go. So we fixed and loaded wagons in the night for a start in the morning. Bro. Charles came to see us.

MONDAY 28 right from the enemy's camps where he & his company & others have been watching the movements & etc. said they will not stop by any fare means – are taking any of our boys prisoners that they can catch – When the Government Proclamation was presented to them, they hooted & wanted to know who was Brigham Young – & force marched harder than before. So our boys commenced giving some hints that they might understand that we meant what we said. These plain hints consisted of taking the Herds of beef stock to the Valley where they will winter well – & of burning the heavy freight trains of supplies – These things were done in day time & some of it right in sight of the main army[18]– & when persued our boys could easily keep out of their way among these ragged rockey mountains.

SEPTEMBER 28   Bro. Charles also thot it was best for us to move our families soon & helped me hitch up the team which consisted of 3 cows & one steer. Our company being ready – a few single men being selected to stay & finish the harvest & keep the Fort, we started in order. Bro. Charles went a mile & helped to steady my rude team & visit still more with us, when we parted wishing the blessing of the Lord to attend each other. I to take my family to safe Quarters so I can return – & he to stay as a Scout in Defence of the Saints who have endured so much persecution.

Our company now was only about 30 families – as some had gone to the Valley before – we traveled night & day so that we might not fall into the hands of enemies 'til we heard they had made a halt on Ham's Fork. Then we went more leisurely with our slow teams & old wagons & in 7 days were safe in the Valley among friends. Then we separated & went to the different wards or settlements where our former homes had been.

Lord bless that noble band of brethren & sisters that have labored so to build up the Kingdom by making peace with the natives & form a settlement in that cold dreary place in Green River County. We worked hard

---

[18] The burning of the wagon trains did not occur until Oct. 5; so this may have been written later.

& by the Lords blessing on our work were quite comfortably situated to live.

Besides public work, traveling, missionary, making water ditches, building meeting House, Public coral & etc. I have cleared land of its timber – Grubed out willow thickets, for plow & hay land & got some of it fenced all round by it self share of mill, lumber on hand – which at a low rate is upwards of a *thousand dollars,* of my individual property left – a total loss to me, because of this cruel persecution that Government allows against us. The crops we wish used by our guards.

I went to Father Pulsiphers place Sunday Evening October 4. They were almost over joyed to see us safe in the Valley once more.

Father said he wished me to stay with him when I was not needed away for the public good – he was tired, aged & feeble & could not hire help that was of much use, Wm. was young & etc. Father had married two other wives besides my mother. Had a number of Poor old country people[19] depending on him for support & did not know much of the ways of this new country. A good portion of his time was occupied in council with the 70's[20] or the City Council – & besides his City home he had a large farm three miles out.

This request was all right with me willing now as ever to do all I can for his comfort – glad I am here to help – the old folks look tired & worn with care.

I went & enlisted into the ranks of the 16th Ward Battalion of Nauvoo Legion so as to be ready for the

---

[19] Recent emigrants from the "Old Country" (Europe).

[20] The "Seventies" was a special group of the priesthood, especially "called" to do missionary work.

public Defence. I then went on with the work & found plenty to do.

I attended Conference on the 6 & 7 of October. The church business was done in good order. Much valuable instruction was given. Bro. Brigham felt sorry that our enemies were so anxious to make war on an innocent people – But he was firm, that, if government does sustain this approaching hostile force, & will not let us have peace then the thread is cut that bound us to them & we will be free. Many predictions in regard to the Triumph of Israel.[21]

The people feel first rate & seem to have no fears knowing the Lord is able to help us thru.

OCTOBER 20   received letter from Bro. Charles of 17th says the U.S. Army as they call themselves are determined to come in – & say they are fully able to do so – yet he says we are whipping them without killing a man having taken their stock burned their freight trains – & now have burned Fort Supply & Bridger to save them from falling into their hands.

OCTOBER 24   Sunday before meeting I wrote to Bro. Charles folks, well comfortably fixed to live – have good meetings & instruction. The prophets speak good for Israel. On Monday, went with my family & visited Charles folks & Thos. at Union 12 miles south. Also made Father Huffaker a visit – He gave us a new cook stove that he brot from the states for us – a nice present, Lord bless them. Mother was feeling sorrowful for the loss of her little ones in her absence – we tried to comfort her – not mourn as the wicked do without hope, but be faithful & look forward to the time which is not far distant when they will be restored to life again.   .   .

---

21 The Mormons considered themselves as modern Israel.

NOVEMBER 8   Sunday evening an express from the East brot word that the army had left Ham's Fork of Green River & made a start for the Valley. Bro. Wm. Pulsipher took the word thro the South settlements of the country – about 15 miles an hour on his own pony.

ON TUESDAY THE 10TH   upwards of 2,000 men were on the move to stop the invading army. A regular Mountain snow-storm set in, which made it rather hard for men that had been used to good beds in warm houses. A baggage wagon was taken for each ten men, but snow was so deep not much load could be taken, & climbing the mountains – men had to carry the baggage up & go back & help the teams with the empty wagon – truly this was work.

To see the long train climbing the snowy mountains made me think of Bonaparts army crossing the Alps in winter.[22]

When we got the wagons up it was dark & an awful cold night & we on the summit of the big Mountain[23] in deep snow. We had to go two miles further to place where dry wood could be got for camp. A few of us went ahead with axes & cut & carried wood for fires, as it was some distance up the mountain & snow to our arms – made the fires on the snow, as it was too deep to allow us to get to the ground either for the fires or for our beds. This was the third night – three days hard work to get 20 miles. Wm. & myself were on guard part of the night; clear & fearful cold – when we went

[22] This was the same general storm through which Johnston's army was struggling, as described above.

[23] Big Mountain was immediately east of the headwaters of Emigration Creek, and about eighteen miles east of Salt Lake City. This is the highest mountain on the road, with an elevation of 7,245 feet, according to W. Clayton, *The Latter-day Saints' Emigrants' Guide* (St. Louis, Mo., Republican Steam Power Press – Chambers & Knapp, 1848), 19.

to bed spread our blankets on snow & could scarcely keep from freezing. Some were up walking, up and down the snow path & some, more brave were fetching wood & trying to make fires. Well, it was a long night.

Wm. Riley Judd & others camped with us, as they were coming in with a herd of stock taken from the mob.

NOVEMBER 13   started at daylight, went down the mountain & down East Kanyon to lower ford, 3 miles today & camped before sunset – found land & slept well – next day went 14 miles & crossed Weber River, foot men on the ice. Our Regiment stopped at Col. Harmons station on Weber.

SUNDAY 15   was spent chopping & hauling firewood – a number of men were sent home – were so badly frozen – Some were sent back with frozen feet before we got over the big Mountain. I could not get a pair of new boots in the City so I came with the old shoes I made of some old boot legs.

MONDAY 16   our Battalion worked on the Fortifications, Digging trenches, Rifle pits.

TUESDAY 17   Orders came for our regiment to move to Echo Kanyon so we gathered up teams & moved three miles & joined the largest camp under the command of Col. N. V. Jones – 1600 men now at this place.

Here we worked on the fortifications & getting fire wood & etc. to be comfortable while we stay & ready to meet the enemy when they come.[24]

Wm. & myself made a house by odd jobs without neglecting our public work, & had a comfortable place to cook & eat. We dry in a leveled place by a steep bank which formed two sides, closed up the other sides

---

[24] Here in Echo Canyon the principal Mormon fortifications were constructed.

with poles, willows & grass, cane, or flags & thatched the roof with same & covered with dirt so as to protect it from fire – we dug a good fire place in the bank – had bed in one corner on some coarse dry grass & bunk bedstead of poles & willows.

We were so comfortable, we had many visitors – & finally our whole 10th company that we belonged to joined us. We were so comfortable, sheltered from storm and wind, by a good fire – that many others done likewise & this camp, before we left it – became quite a city of Wickeups. Tents scarce & not so warm, so our style of building suited best.

NOVEMBER 23 Brother Charles who had been to the Valley with a band of horses that he & others had taken from the enemy – now returned with a small herd of beef cattle sent for the use of our camps. we gave him dinner in our new house – a visit & chat of one hour, on business, news & etc. then he went on business to General Wells station 12 miles further.

NOVEMBER 25, after our days work – we assembled in a general evening meeting & listened to a Legal Discourse from Elder Taylor who lives here with us – one of the boys proved the legality of our position – & that it is lawful for us to defend ourselves against all such mobs & our Governor Brigham Young is acting in his office according to the Constitution of the U.S. in forbidding that army to come in to this Territory.

NOVEMBER 26, 1857 Having a little leisure time today I made an oven to bake our bread in – dug in the clay bank near the fire place in our house – which proved to be a valuable improvement. We could now have light bread baked just right – Ever so much better than the burnt dough that is so common in camp life. Our rations were now too big – could not eat a pound

& quarter of flour per day in good light bread. When our friends and neighbors saw how we lived they were very neighborly & patronized our oven & kept it hot much of the time.

Our captain of 10 – J. W. Phippen – called on me to take charge of our ten in hauling fire wood. not having feed for teams, we took the wagon & soon had a nice pile of wood – got 2 or 3 loads a day – & ten men not balky could get a better load than any team in our town.

SATURDAY 28   today made wickeup for our Major Kesler head Quarters for our Battalion – had a tent but wanted something better – to follow a comfortable fashion – made of poles, brush, & long grass – round, sharp at top cost 30 days work.

After dark tonight we were called out on the parade ground & informed that we were all disbanded. But as it happens, this order comes from a source that we do not acknowledge. An express has arrived from the East brought the news that the Mob has settled on the ruins of Fort Bridger for the winter, & a person calling himself Governor A. Coming, has arrived direct from the States says he is Governor of Utah & he commands us to disperse & go home.[25]

He shows no authority, & we have no knowledge that the U.S. President has sent or appointed any Governor for Utah but Brigham Young. Maybe he is sent to govern us, & maybe not. Who could not write such a letter – but who would believe, or obey it? It was directed to Brigham Young, Esq. Ex-governor of Utah & the Mormon army said to be under arms.

SUNDAY 29, NOVEMBER   I was on guard today – at 6 in evening attended meeting. Elder Taylor preached good discourse & closing refered to the person calling

---

[25] See Gov. Cumming's Proclamation, in Part x.

himself Governor A. Cuming – said he & his party may be good looking but can't come in.

MONDAY 30   General Wells moved down today so head quarters will be here now. About 2,500 men are camped along this Kanyon within a few miles.[26] Weather cold – has commenced snowing again. We have our fortifications well made so a few men can defend, or guard this road without much danger of being hurt.

Snow is deep East of us & the invading Army have settled for the winter.

TUESDAY DECEMBER 1   General Wells gave order to pack up & go home – except a small number that were to stay as guards & a few that are on picket duty further out. A few of us went & brot the animals from the warm side of the Mountain 3 or 4 miles south, where they lived on grass – it winter day – more snow coming. arrived with the herd about noon. soon hitched up & were on the move. While we were after the stock the camp was in meeting.

General Wells preached, said the Lord had accepted our offering & confused and stopped our enemies & we have no fighting to do at present – advised all young men to quit using tobacco, if they use it. Profit by this campaign & be valiant for the kingdom of God.

At half past 12 we bid farewell to our much loved camp & were on the move all in order – baggage wagons in place. Travelled 11 miles crossed water & camped at Col. Littles station. Bro. Charles was here. I slept with him. had a good visit, he was to stay awhile.

DECEMBER 2, 1857.   The army of men were on the move two hours before daylight. Very slippery walking – went 20 miles over big Mountain – camped in deep snow with very little fire – not much to eat went to bed on snow cold, wet & tired.

THURSDAY 3   We arose from our wet blankets & beds of snow so cold we could not sleep so packed up & started eating a bit of frozen bread as we walked along the icy path – making ten miles before daylight over little Mountain & so on into town passing the Governors office about 11 o'clock. The governor Bro. Brigham came out & viewed us as we past looking very clever and good. We were halted on the Temple Block – after a short speech & the Lords blessing on us we were dismissed to the hands of majors who marched the battalions to the wards where they lived – When we were dismissed, took baggage from wagon & were soon at home & found folks well.

The Lord has accepted our offering has confused & stopped our enemies & we have not had to kill them or even fire a gun at them but we have showed them that we would stand for our rights, & would not submit to such unlawful & unjust demands as they were determined to force upon us.

Brother Brigham has written to them showing the unjust & unconstitutional course government is taking in making war on us without a cause – yet it was of no effect – they were determined we would not let them in with their present hostile feelings to kill or drive us from our homes as in the past.

I went right to work on Fathers farm repairing fences getting out manure & etc. & hauling fire wood from the Mountains.

By the first week in March I had about 20 acres of wheat oats & barley put in Bro. Wm. was with me some of the time.

About this time, Bro. Brigham proclaimed to the

people that it was the will of the Lord that we should move Southward. All the Settlements north of Utah Valley.

The policy was to get the people nearer together so they could be defended & the cuntry could be desolated behind us & we then are ready if U.S. does reenforce the army & determine on a big war.

I had made my calculations to go into farming quite largely for one of my size but with me as with others – individual plans must change when the public good requires it. So we are very willing to leave our homes – & to our tents again.   .   .

The U.S. army East of us have wintered very well, & are threatening to come upon us & make a final end of all that will not join them. Truly this is a trying time – Destruction stares us in the face which ever way we turn – They that have not the holy Ghost the comforter in them, are beginning to tremble. The prophet Brigham is as calm as if there was no danger – says *move South & see the Salvation of God*. And almost the entire people say Amen to it & are as happy as were the children of Israel led by Moses, anciently when they passed thru the red Sea.

APRIL 6   This is the birthday of the Church.[27] The U.S. Army are preparing to make a start for the Valley so it is necessary for us to be ready to stop them. I met with the Nauvoo Legion at 8 :O'clock – attended Drill & inspection of arms, & at 11 :O'clock the Legion marched into the Tabernacle where the women & children & a few men were holding Conference – When we were seated Bro. Brigham arose & spoke about an

---

[27] The Church of Jesus Christ of Latter-Day Saints (Mormon) was organized April 6, 1830, in New York state.

hour – felt first rate – perfectly satisfied as to the triumph of Israel.

Said it is all I can do to hold back from killing those Infernal scoundrels out yonder at Bridger, sent by Government to destroy this people. Pres. Buchanan has violated his oath of office in sending that army against us, as peaceable citizens as are in the union.

They are determined not to pay us one dime of what they owe us – But are paying thousands & hundreds of thousands of dollars to hire the Indians to kill us.

I need a breeching as strong as that of Dutch harness to enable me to hold back from killing every Devil of that army – But it is best to hold back & let them whip themselves. It is the will of the Lord that we leave this city & the north country – Move south – & if our enemies come upon us, when we are doing all we can to get away we will send them to hell across lots – & if they hire the Indians to help them, we are good for all of them. AMEN.

At 12 o'clock the Legion Paraded again & men were selected to go to the Mountains & keep the army from coming upon us before we could get the families moved away – I was one of the number chosen to go.

Ten men have been between us & the enemy thru the winter – relieved once in two weeks now as spring has come & the enemy are preparing to come – a stronger guard is needed.

We have to go on foot as the snow is too deep to get teams over the Mountains yet our packs were of considerable size – arms – ammunition – blankets & provisions – my bundle weighed fifty 50 pounds.

APRIL 7   I left my wife on the farm alone to take care of two little children, four horses, a few head of cattle & four cows to milk.

I leave them in care of the Lord & shouldered my pack & started thru mud then climbing over Mountains wallowing thro deep snow – then mud again – then wading the rushing streams of cold water or crawling along the brushey steeps to avoid the crossing of the crooked stream.

We were two days and nights going 48 miles – stormed most of the time. Did not spend much time in sleep our blankets were wet & too much snow for good sleeping.

On arriving at the fortifications in Echo Kanyon, with what force was there we numbered about 175 men, under command of Col. Callister Bro. Wm. was here and well, came out 9 days before me. I joined the company with Bro. Wm. he was sergeant John Jones captain of 10. Wm. Scott captain of 50 & Harrison Burgess, major or captain of 100.

More men keep coming from the Valley & there are about 300 out now. I was chosen by the officers & voted for by the men, to be the captain of a 50 & to go up to the head of Echo Kanyon to the furtherest station of our army.

MONDAY 12 APRIL   I chose Ira K. Hillman an old friend born & raised with me, to be my adjutant. We started on foot a part of our company with us – the others were at the station we were going to, 24 miles where we arrived about one o'clock.

Here we found men enough with those that came with us to make 100 under command of major Dan McArthur another old friend that I traveled 1,000 miles with 20 years ago. My adjutant & myself were invited to the majors tent to mess with the officers of the Battalion. Israel Ivins was comissary & Sam Carnes cook.

Gove

Cumming

Outpost of spies on the
Southeast—

GOVERNOR CUMMING'S TENT, CAMP SCOTT
From a sketch by Albert Tracy

Fort Bridger from North East – with Camp beyond
June 5th 1858.

FORT BRIDGER, JUNE 5, 1858
From a sketch by Albert Tracy

This station is 70 miles from the valley & 4 miles north of the road – hid up, with guards on the highlands to see all that is passing & not be seen.

It is expected that the army will try to force their way in to the Valley & if they do, we are determined to stop them. If they can't do without Salt Lake City they must wait 'til we can move our families away – or, by the help of the Lord we will make them wait.

Captain Thomas Todd & myself take turns in acting as officer of the day putting out guards – camp & etc. I take particular pleasure to be out looking around to see what is going on & if the guards do their duty.

There are now about 600 men out, guarding the different passes, 200 in Echo, 200 on an Indian trail leading thro last Creek Kanyon. Captain Lot Smith with 100 mounted guards & our 100 – we keep Uncle Sams army in their same old camp where they wintered.

Sometimes we get pretty hungry before our supplies arrive from the Valley, as the road is so bad – but our brother Soldiers don't complain as hired soldiers do, on short rations.

As our enemies have gave up the idea of trying at present to come in one half of us are invited home. Captain Conger with 50 men that have no families, are to take our place, & arrived here on Tuesday night.

APRIL 20 & next morning we started for home on foot made 24 miles in six hours.

I stayed 4 hours & visited Bro. Wm. in camp at Echo & played ball with them officers & privates all boys together. I offered to stay in Williams place as he had been out longer than I had, but he would not, as he had no family – so I bid him farewell & went on & overtook my company at Weber River camped for the night.

Next morning at daylight we were on the march, anxious to get home & see to moving our families southward.

My feet were blistered in many places like many of my mess mates. We had to carry our baggage on our backs as the snow is yet so deep that there is no passing with wagons yet. A hard journey indeed – men tired lame & sore – climbing mountains & wading streams. I was glad I was able to help some by carrying their loads & encouraging them along. We travelled the 70 miles in two days bad as the road was & carried our guns ammunition, beding, & etc. on about one days rations. Found my folks well & still living on farm west of Jordan.

APRIL 25   I helped father load his wagons & start his family southward, I was chosen as one of the guards of Salt Lake company. There is a continual crowd, or living stream on all the roads leading south.

The Saints are leaving their homes, beautiful habitations, farms & gardens, shade & fruit trees & go joyfully to the toils & hardships of camp life. I kept my family until the teams returned – we were happy working in our home, made butter & cheese put in considerable crops of small grain.

ON THE 12TH MAY   I sent my family South in care of George M. Burgess, my sisters boy, who had been with father & returned with teams. I got Bro. John Alger to drive one team & Bro. Charles Pulsipher to drive the loose stock. From this time on, I, like my Bro. Soldiers, keep bachelors hall – live at our own houses – take care of the property & be ready to burn the buildings & fences & improvements & desolate the country if necessary to prepare for the reception of the enemy provided that it be necessary. I have a good time for meditation & not much talk, being alone night & day – but have plenty to do to keep me from being lonesome putting in & taking care of crops – I have about four miles of fence to keep in repair that is left in my care. Some have not moved their stock yet.

I have plenty to do to keep things safe I meet twice a week with the guards of the City & attend roll call & hear the news.

Bro. Wm. is yet in Echo Kanyon with that noble band of boys, to keep the U.S. Army from coming up on us unawares.

Col. Thos. L. Kane an old friend of this people – seeing the situation of things came in haste from Washington to this place & then to the army. He finally got Governor Cuming to leave the army & come to Salt Lake City And when we found that he would come in peaceably without an army & that he really was sent to be the Governor of Utah we were willing to receive & acknowledge him as such.   .   .

General Johnson the commander of the army also issued a proclamation & promised to keep the peace & neither molest persons nor property, said he wished to pass thro the city to some out of the way place, where he could locate & wait for future orders.

As their feelings are so changed that they are not the hostile army now, that they were when we stopped them – so when they were humbled enough & promised so well. Our boys guarding the road were invited home & the great U.S. Army allowed to come in.

B. NARRATIVE OF LOT SMITH[1]

When I returned to camp, I was invited to take dinner with the commanding-general and his aids. During the meal, General Wells, looking at me as straight as possible, asked if I could take a few men and turn back the trains that were on the road or *burn* them. I replied that I thought I could do just what he told me to. The answer appeared to please him, and he accepted it, telling me that he could furnish only a few men, but that they would be sufficient, for they would appear many more to our enemies. As for provisions, none would be supplied, as we were expected to board at the expense of Uncle Sam. As this seemed to be an open order, I did not complain, and at 4 o'clock, October 3d,[2] we started, numbering forty-four men, rank and file, Major Lot Smith in command, Captain H. D. Haight,[3] Lieutenants Thomas Abbott and John Vance, officers. We rode nearly all night, and early the next morning came in sight of an ox train headed westward. I left half of my men to get breakfast, and with the

---

[1] This account, given from memory, was taken by Junius F. Wells and was published by him serially in *The Contributor* (Salt Lake City, 1882-83), III, pp. 271-74, IV, 27-29, 47-50, 167-69, and 224-26.

Lot Smith was born May 15, 1830, in Oswego County, New York. At the age of sixteen he marched to California in the Mormon Battalion of the Mexican War. After arrival in Utah he served in campaigns against the Indians. Later he moved to Arizona, where he became prominent in church and civic affairs. He was killed by the Indians at Tuba City, Arizona, June 21, 1892. Jenson, *Biog. Ency.*, I, 803-06.

Lot Smith's daring service in the Utah War is celebrated. He helped deliver Gov. Young's message of Sept. 29 to Col. Alexander. When the Colonel declined to forsake his movement into Utah, the Mormon military leaders decided upon overt action. Lot Smith takes up the story at this point.

[2] This date tallies with George A. Smith's Journal, found in the L.D.S. Church Historian's Office, Salt Lake City. George A. Smith was then the official Mormon Church Historian.

[3] Horton David Haight, born in New York state in 1832, came to Utah in 1847. He was an experienced man in overland freighting and emigrant travel. His later years were spent in Idaho, where he died Jan. 19, 1920. Jenson, *op. cit.*, I, pp. 302-03.

others proceeded to interview the bull-whackers. On calling for the captain, a large fine-looking man stepped forward and gave his name as Rankin. I informed him that we wanted him to turn his train and go the other way, until he reached the States. He wanted to know by what authority I presumed to issue such orders. I replied, pointing to my men, that *there* was a part of it, and the remainder was a little further on concealed in the brush. He swore pretty strongly, and thought that was good in a free country like this; however, he faced about and started to go east, but as soon as out of sight would turn again towards the mountains. The troops met him that day and took out his lading, leaving the wagons and teams standing. I camped near these troops on that night on the banks of Green River.

Losing the opportunity to make much impression on Rankin's train, I thought something must be done speedily to carry out the instructions received, so I sent Captain Haight with twenty men to see if he could get the mules of the tenth Regiment on any terms. With the remaining twenty-three men I started for Sandy Fork to intercept trains that might be approaching in that direction. On the road, seeing a large cloud of dust at a distance up the river, on the old Mormon road, I sent scouts to see what caused it. They returned, overtaking me at Sandy, and reported a train of twenty-six large freight wagons. We took supper and started at dark. After traveling fourteen miles, we came up to the train, but discovered that the teamsters were drunk, and knowing that drunken men were easily excited and always ready to fight, and remembering my positive orders not to hurt anyone except in self-defense, we remained in ambush until after midnight. I then sent scouts to thoroughly examine the appearance of their camp, to note the number of wagons and men and to report all they discovered. When they returned and reported twenty-six wagons in two lines a short distance apart, I concluded that counting one teamster to each wagon and throwing in eight or ten extra men would make their force about forty. I thought we would be a match for them, and so advanced to their camp.

On nearing the wagons, I found I had misunderstood the scouts, for instead of one train of twenty-six wagons there were two, doubling the number of men, and putting quite another phaze on our relative strength and situation. There was a large camp-fire burning, and a number of men were standing around it smoking. It was expected by my men that on finding out the real number of wagons and men, I would not go farther than to make some inquiries and passing our sortie upon the trains as a joke would go on until some more favorable time. But it seemed to me that it was no time for joking. I arranged my men, and we advanced until our horses' heads came into the light of the fire then I discovered that we had the advantage, for looking back into the darkness, I could not see where my line of troops ended, and could imagine my twenty followers stringing out to a hundred or more as well as not. I inquired for the captain of the train. Mr. Dawson stepped out and said he was the man.[4] I told him that I had a little business with him. He inquired the nature of it, and I replied by requesting him to get all of his men and their private property as quickly as possible out of the wagons for I meant to put a little fire into them. He exclaimed: "For God's sake, don't burn the trains." I said it was for His sake that I was going to burn them, and pointed out a place for his men to stack their arms, and another where they were to stand in a group,

---

[4] John M. Dawson, wagon master for the freighting firm of Russell, Majors, and Waddell, according to Settle, *Empire on Wheels, op. cit.,* p. 19.

placing a guard over both. I then sent a scout down towards Little Mountaineer Fork, failing to put one out towards Ham's Fork on the army. While I was busy with the train a messenger from the latter surprised us by coming into camp. I asked him if he had dispatches and to hand them to me. He said he had, but they were verbal. I told him if he lied to me his life was not worth a straw. He became terrified, in fact I never saw a man more frightened. The weather was a little cool but his jaws fairly clattered. I took his mule and arms and told him where to stand, at the same time placing a large Irish Gentile [5] I had with me as guard over him, with instructions to shoot him if he moved. He plead piteously for his life; but I indicated that soldiers' lives were not worth much, it was only the bull-whackers who could expect to get off easy. He said afterwards that he expected every moment to be killed. His orders to the train men were from the commander at Camp Winfield, and were to the effect that the Mormons were in the field and that they must not go to sleep but keep night guard on their trains, and that four companies of cavalry and two pieces of artillery would come over in the morning to escort them to camp.

While I was engaged with the first train a guard of the second came down to see what was going on. I told him to go back and not move and that I would be up soon and attend to them. My scout said, afterwards, that when the guard returned he squatted down by a wagon wheel and never moved until I came up. Captain Dawson and I shortly after went up to the second train. Dawson shaking the wagon in which the wagon-master slept called loudly for Bill. "Bill" seemed considerably dazed and grumbled at being called up so early. Daw-

---

[5] With the Mormons, any person who was not a member of their church was a gentile.

son exclaimed with peculiar emphasis. "Damn it man, get up, or you'll be burned to a cinder in five minutes!" Bill suddenly displayed remarkable activity.[6] I introduced the same programme to him that we had carried out with the first train, having them come out man by man, stack their arms and huddle together under guard. By the time I had my men scattered out, guarding the different interests, they appeared to have dwindled to a very small body to me, but the sixty or seventy prisoners, for with extras the teamsters numbered that many, never discovered it. Having got them disposed of I inquired of Dawson what kind of loading he had, as I was much in need of overcoats for my boys, the season getting late and weather cold. I also asked if they had much powder on board for if so it would be convenient when I fired the wagons to take him with me. He was much frightened at that proposition and hastily produced his bills of lading. I told him to hunt himself as I had no time. He searched diligently for powder and my boys for overcoats and clothing. Dawson announced that there were large quantities of saltpetre and sulphur in the wagons and said they were nearly as dangerous as powder. I told him we would have to take the risk of injury from them. He begged me not to make him fire the train, saying: "For the good Lord's sake don't take me, I've been sick and am not well yet, and don't want to be hurt." There were many such laughable incidents connected with the adventures of the night, if we had dared to laugh. One old man, shaking with St. Anthony's dance or something else, came up to me and wanted to know why we had driven up the oxen so early. Learning that our business was of a different nature, he tremblingly said he thought we would have come sooner and not waited until they were in bed and

6 This was R. W. Barrett. Settle, *ibid.*

some of them liable to be burned up. My big Irishman told him we were so busy that we nearly left him without calling him up at all, at all.

When all was ready, I made a torch, instructing my Gentile follower, known as Big James, to do the same, as I thought it was proper for the "Gentiles to spoil the Gentiles." At this stage of our proceedings an Indian came from the Mountaineer Fork and seeing how the thing was going asked for some presents. He wanted two wagon covers for a lodge, some flour and soap. I filled his order and he went away much elated. Out of respect to the candor poor Dawson had showed, I released him from going with me when we fired the trains, taking Big James instead, he not being afraid of saltpetre or sulphur either.

While riding from wagon to wagon, with torch in hand and the wind blowing, the covers seemed to me to catch very slowly. I so stated it to James. He replied, swinging his long torch over his head: "By St. Patrick, ain't it beautiful! I never saw anything go better in all my life." About this time I had Dawson send in his men to the wagons, not yet fired, to get us some provisions, enough to thoroughly furnish us, telling him to get plenty of sugar and coffee for though I never used the latter myself, some of my men below, intimating that I had a force down there, were fond of it. On completing this task I told him that we were going just a little way off and that if he or his men molested the trains or undertook to put the fire out, they would be instantly killed. We rode away leaving the wagons all ablaze.

After our encounter with the two trains on the old Mormon road, which we left in a blaze, we proceeded to the bluffs of Green River. From there I started an express to General Wells with details of our maneuvres up to date. I told the man selected to carry these dispatches that he must go alone as I could not spare any one to go with him, and that he must look out for the troops, which by this time would be on the alert to capture or kill any of our men they might meet. He said they were welcome to him if they caught him, and started away. He got through all right.

We camped on the banks of the Sandy that night, getting a little sleep, which, considering the night work of the previous week, was very grateful to us all. On the morning following we met another train at a place that has ever since been known as Simpson's Hollow. I asked for the captain and being told that he was out after cattle, we disarmed the teamsters, and I rode out and met him about half a mile away. I told him that I came on business. He inquired the nature of it when I demanded his pistols. He replied: "By G – d, sir, no man ever took them yet, and if you think you can, without killing me, try it." We were all the time riding towards the train, with our noses about as close together as two Scotch terriers would have held theirs – his eyes flashing fire; I couldn't see mine – I told him that I admired a brave man, but that I didn't like blood – you insist on my killing you, which will only take a minute, but I don't want to do it. We had by this time reached the train. He, seeing that his men were under guard, surrendered, saying: "I see you have me at a disadvantage my men being disarmed." I replied that I didn't need the advantage, and asked him what he would do if we should give them their arms. "I'll fight you!" "Then," says I, "we know something about that too – take up your arms!" His men exclaimed, "Not by a d – n sight! We came out here to whack bulls, not to fight." "What do you say to that, Simpson?" I asked. "Damnation," he replied, grinding his teeth in the most violent manner, "if I had been here before and they had refused to fight, I would have killed every man of them."

Captain Simpson[7] was the bravest man I met during the campaign. He was a son-in-law of Mr. Majors,[8] a large contractor for government freighting. He was terribly exercised over the capture of his train, and wanted to know what kind of report he could make to the commander, and what he could do with his crowd of cowardly teamsters left on the plains to starve. I told him that I would give him a wagon loaded with provisions. "You will give me two, I know it by your looks!" I told them to hurry up and get their things out, and take their two wagons for we wanted to go on. Simpson begged me not to burn the train while he was in sight, and said that it would ruin his reputation as a wagon master. I told him not to be squeamish, that the trains burned very nicely, I had seen them before, and that we hadn't time to be ceremonious. We then supplied ourselves with provisions, set the wagons afire and rode on about two miles from the stream to rest. I expected any moment to be overtaken by troops from the camp, and fired my pistol to call in our picket guard.

They hurriedly came to the place where we were resting, a place that will always be remembered as the scene of the most distressing event which occurred on the expedition. While I was reloading my pistol, and as the guards came in from picket duty, one of the guns – a United States yauger – was discharged. The heavy ball passed through Orson P. Arnold's thigh, breaking

[7] Lewis Simpson, say our friends the Settles, *ibid.*, 20, 152.

[8] Alexander Majors was an outstanding western freighter and pioneer. His portrait in a stained glass window is one of sixteen in the dome of the Colorado State Capitol. Majors' career is recounted in his *Seventy Years on the Frontier* (New York, 1893). His old home in present Kansas City, Missouri, has been proposed for utilization as a transportation museum.

the bone in a fearful manner, struck Philo Dibble in the side of the head, and went through Samuel Bateman's hat just missing his head and pulling his hair. I sprang up and caught young Arnold, straightening him out, for he fell with his leg under him, the jagged points of the broken bone sticking out, while the blood streamed from the awful wound. It looked as though he would bleed to death in five minutes. We laid our hands upon him according to the order of the Church, and asked our Father to preserve him for we knew that we could not.

I immediately sent two men to the Sandy for poles with which to make a litter. We calculated that the distance to a safe place on Green River was not less than thirty miles, and that we must carry our wounded comrade there as soon and as comfortably as possible. While engaged setting the broken bone, a picket guard came running into camp and reported two hundred cavalry close upon us. Under the circumstances nothing could have produced greater consternation. One of the men moved that we surrender. I told them that I would say when to do that. He then proposed that we *run*. I replied that I would kill the man that made that motion, myself, if he dared to try it. Then I made my first war speech. I told the men that we were not out here of our own choice, on our own business. Our people and their rights were being assailed. It was the Lord's work that they were engaged in, and we were called by Him to protect our homes and our religion. If he suffered those troops to come near us, we would trust in Him and whip them, no matter about their numbers. The boys gathered around me and said that I had spoken right, that they would stand by me if I would stand. I was well repaid for stiffening my knees, for poor Orson looked up and said he knew I wouldn't run away and leave him to die. Poor boy! The first words he spoke were: "I shall always be a cripple, and will never be able to fight soldiers any more."

Then came the tug of war! We took up our wounded man and carried him on poles for thirty miles. Talk about mules with sore shoulders! ours equaled anything of that kind ever heard of. Our way lay across a trackless desert the whole distance, with no water on the road but what we carried in our canteens, and a wounded man burning with fever and inflammation constantly wants water.

A curious incident happened during the journey across this desert plane. By night we ran short of water, the men were tired out and I advised all to stop and lie down to rest until morning. But some of the men proposed, if I would consent, that they go on for water, and that the rest carry the litter until they returned and overtook us. The proposition was agreed to and they started, but the carrying party failed in less than a mile. One of the poles broke and we nearly let the other fall to the ground. Orson had slept during most of the night, and when this accident happened made the first sign of pain. He must have suffered fearfully. I told the rest of the boys they would have to go now for water; that it was at least eight miles and to hurry back. They went and thought it fully that far, but they came back making the journey in the dark, and met us in the plain, without fire, road or any land mark to guide them. I only know of one way to account for the incident. We had to have the water or the boy would die, and a Power greater than we *knew* it. When we, at last, all gave out the men lopped over, one by one, and were fast asleep as soon as they touched the ground. I went around and took off the saddles, arms, etc., and watched the horses until feeling too tired to remain awake longer, I thought of a little fellow, who being too short to carry the litter, was fresh compared to the rest of us. I woke him up, and asked him to look after the horses. In a moment I was asleep, and unable to rouse myself, though conscious that the short fellow I had called, had only turned over and had not got up. The next time I wanted him up to stand guard I had him on his feet before leaving him.

Before daylight we were again on the march. When we came in sight of the river, the same man that had reported the two hundred cavalry, came back and said there were soldiers on the banks and advised us to make a circuit of about five miles to strike the river below. I told him that I was in no mood to prolong our journey. That all could do so who wished, but that I was going to a small grove of cottonwoods on the river bottom, to which I pointed, and that it would take a right smart lot of soldiers to get me out of it. We left the wounded boy in charge of two men on the bluffs, but they took him down in a ravine where he came near suffocating. He begged them to take him on the hill and let him die, to leave him and look out for themselves. When we reached the river I sent out scouts to look up the soldiers that had been seen, at the same time climbing a large tree to survey the situation myself. A man soon rushed into the grove saying that two of our men were running this way, chased by two soldiers. Without thought I sprang down, caught up my gun and ran; my men following me. In a minute or two I stopped short, and asked him if he said that two of our men were being chased by *two* soldiers. He said "yes." "Then I hope they will catch them. I don't want any two men that any other two can chase." They all laughed. We soon found out the truth. Two of our men were after a couple of mountaineers. When they overtook them the latter slung off their canteens in double quick time and offered the boys a drink. We made arrangements with these mountaineers to take charge of our helpless comrade, and they kept him ten days, doing the best they could for him, until General Wells sent a team to convey him home. He however suffered extremely, but we were told by the surgeon that no one could have set the broken leg better, under the circumstances, than we had done. When we came upon the soldiers that our picket guard, who was a good man but with eyes that would magnify, had reported, we found them to consist of Captain Haight and company, and were very glad to meet friends again instead of enemies.

The express sent from the bluffs of Green River, reporting progress of my labors, was carried by Edwin Booth. It was a hazardous undertaking for a single horseman, liable to run upon the enemy at any hour, but he was courageous and discreet, and meant every word of it when he said they were welcome to him if they caught him. He reached headquarters all right and delivered the dispatch. The following communication was received in response:

HEADQUARTERS EASTERN EXPEDITION,
Camp Yellow Creek,   Oct. 14, 1857

MAJOR LOT SMITH: I am glad to hear so good an account of your success on your mission, and trust you will continue to be blessed in carrying out instructions given. I wish you to keep a good look out on your rear as well as ahead, so as not to be surprised by any fresh arrival of troops. Furnish your men and as many others as you conveniently can with supplies of clothing and food from any of the trains when you have a good chance. Remain in the rear of the enemy's camp till you receive further orders, not neglecting every opportunity to burn their trains, stampede their stock, and keep them under arms by night surprises, so that they will be worn out. I have sent a spring wagon to Bridger for the wounded man. Draw on Callister for supplies as you may need. Keep up communication with Major Mc-Allister, who has gone out on the Oregon road. May the Lord God of Israel bless you and help you to hedge up the way of our enemies, and cause them to leave our Territory. If we could learn of a surety that they purposed making winter quarters at Fort Hall, we would cease molesting them. Your brother in Christ,

(Signed)   Daniel H. Wells

p.s.   Let Livingston & Kinkead's and Gilbert & Gerrish's trains, with goods intended for the city, pass. Treat Perry's as any other government train, unless they turn and go back. Make no difference in your operations because of any prisoners the troops may have.   D.H.W.

After meeting Captain Haight and company, W. H. Hickman came to me and reported that a large herd of cattle was located near Mountaineer Fort, where we had burned the first trains. We went up there and found the teamsters of the three trains which had been destroyed. They asked me if we had come to take the cattle. I told them we wanted a few, and gathering up about a hundred and fifty head, Hickman took them into the valley. He was accompanied by several of the train men, who said they had enough government bull-whacking to last them for the rest of their lives. I was glad to find my brave friend Simpson again, for we had run short of supplies, and I could reasonably expect that he would treat us generously, as we had given him a fair show when we burnt his train. He said they were going to run short of flour and bacon, but for us to help ourselves. We took such supplies as we needed, but left them all the flour but ten sacks, and we only took two of bacon. Here I met a man who was a prisoner at Bridger when I left there. He reminded me of the fact, and said that he saw me and my command there, and that we were a fine lot of men. I asked him how many.

Lot Smith

He replied that he would estimate them at five hundred. General Wells had told us that our numbers would be magnified in the eyes of the enemy, and it proved to be so. We passed during all the fall for from five hundred to a thousand men, while in fact the whole number never exceeded at any time one hundred, and generally was not half that many.

I suppose that after we left them the teamsters took all the stock remaining to Ham's Fork. We returned to the Sandy to see if other trains were coming, but fortunately for them and for us also we met no more trains. Our success had warmed our blood and the boys were only too eager for an encounter. President Young said it was providential for all parties, for if we had burned another train we would have been compelled before the end of winter to feed the enemy to keep them from starving.

From Sandy we started toward their main camp but stopped on Black's Fork. I proposed to my bed-fellow, Mark Bigler, that we go early in the morning to a neighboring high peak known as "the look out" to take observations. The morning was foggy and we got within three hundred yards of the summit when we discovered some men there before us. We took them for the enemy, for their action indicated that they were not as composed as Saints ought to be, and we started to retreat. The distance to camp, three miles, was too far to run, so we concluded to make the best of it and walk. We were soon overtaken, but found that instead of troops the early risers were O. P. Rockwell and Thomas Rich [9] with about thirty men. This reinforcement increased my command to nearly eighty men. With these we felt ready to proceed on up the river to Ham's Fork and

---

[9] Thomas Rich, a native of Indiana, migrated to Utah in 1850. He died Jan. 26, 1884. Porter Rockwell has been referred to previously.

reconnoitre the situation of the army and see what the troops were doing. Rockwell and I were good friends, on the following basis: I did as I pleased and he, regularly, damned me for it. When we arrived within sight of the camp, I discovered a herd of cattle numbering about fourteen hundred head on the bottom lands below. We were on the bluff. I told Porter we would take those cattle. He said that was just like me. The stock was left there as a trap laid on purpose to catch me. The troops had found out what a damphool I was, and that I didn't know any better than to put my foot into that kind of a trap. The willows were full of artillery, and the minute I exposed myself among the stock they would blow me and my command higher than Gilderoy's kite. I told him to sit down and I would go and take the cattle myself. He replied very roughly that he would see me in "limbo" first, and said that he had waited forty years for such a chance, and now I wanted to spoil it. While he stopped to survey the situation with his glass, I started down the bluff, only about one-third of the men being able to keep up as we rushed down the steep descent. Porter came on in a terrible rage, swearing at me for going so fast, and at the men for being so slow. He wanted me to wait for them all to catch up. There was, however, no time to wait. We had to run about two miles to reach the cattle, and by the time we got to them the guards had yoked up teams to three wagons and started with the herd at double quick pace for camp. We intercepted them, unyoked the cattle and turned their heads the other way, so that the poor cattle which had been in the rear were now in front. The boys then gave a shout, such as imported steers never heard before, and the latter started away pell mell, trodding many of the poorer under their feet and killing half a dozen of them. The guards were frightened as badly as the cattle and looked as pale as death. They came to me and asked me if we were going to take the stock. I replied that it looked a little as if we would. Captain Roupe, the head wagon master (the same man that had sworn the teamsters should have no pay because they would not fight when the trains were burned) was with this company of guards and appeared to be as badly scared as any of them. When he recovered a little from his fright, he asked me to let him have enough cattle with which to take his wagons to camp. We followed the stock and found the poorer ones were all in the rear again. I gave him about twenty head, and when we returned to where his men were, they made what appeared to me at the time a most singular request. They wanted to know if I would give them their arms back. As we hadn't seen their arms, this request led to an inquiry, when we found that on seeing us coming down the bluff, so much like a lot of wild men, they threw their guns away, some one saying if we found them unarmed we would spare their lives. I told the men they could go and get their guns as we had all we wanted. They did so, and several of them fired their weapons off to see if they were all right. In less time than it takes to tell it, about fifteen of our men came back over the bluff where they were following the cattle, as if they had been greased, thinking that Porter and I had got into a fight. When they found us all right they returned about as fast. Rockwell told Roupe to tell the Colonel when he got to camp that we had commenced in earnest, and would kill every man of them if he didn't liberate his prisoners, there being three of our men in his custody at that time. The guards then started for camp. They were the worst frightened men I ever saw. They ran the three teams until some of the cattle dropped dead, but they never stopped until they got within the lines.

We rode on and soon overtook our men with the stock. We divided the cattle into suitable herds and drove all night, Porter and I piloting the way. As we rode along in the darkness together, he thoroughly enjoyed reflecting upon the events of the day. He would repeat what he had said to the guards and chuckle to himself over their discomfiture until his sides ached. I reminded him of what he had said about attacking the herd, but he didn't care to hear anything about that. All was well with him that turned out well.

During the whole of the time while we were engaged driving off this herd and fitting out the guards, a company of two or three hundred soldiers was visible on the bluff. I have never been able to account for their inactivity. They appeared to be interested in our movements, but they made no attempt to interrupt or help us. In the drove were several hundred head of good beef cattle which had been bought of mountaineers. Nothing could have been more acceptable, and I believe we were all thankful for it, even if we had borrowed them from Uncle Sam. Rockwell went in with the cattle, very much to my regret. I never found many men like him. I think our officers were afraid that he and I could not get along together. But we could.

After Rockwell went into the valley with the cattle we had taken, I returned to the vicinity of the last camp of the army on Ham's Fork. As it was getting late in the season and no evidence of intention to retreat being manifested by the army, it appeared to me that something ought to be done to show them that we were at least determined that they should go no farther, and that their present location was too near our forces to be pleasant. Having Rockwell's men left with me, I felt that my command was pretty strong, and began maneuvering accordingly. We soon struck the trail of a detachment of troops and following it found ourselves unexpectedly in close quarters with quite a large force. I was mounted on a government mule at the time, and seeing that we were nearer the enemy than we were willing to be, I felt a little out of place. We, however, tried our old dodge of riding away over rough ground, and soon disappeared, leaving the impression that our numbers were far greater than they really were. In the evening, we returned to within half a mile of the main encampment, determined to take the troops' animals early on the following morning.

We attempted to remain up all night, but found the cold so intense, that I ordered the boys to sleep until two hours before daylight. They, however, couldn't be kept quiet, but long before that time, were jumping up and down in the effort to keep warm. Whether attracted by the sound made by our stamping or not I did not know, but suddenly we heard the tramping of animals, and the picket guard reported a hundred or more horsemen on the march. I left our packs in charge of Captain Haight and a squad of men, and followed the troops with the remainder. A few miles distant we overtook them, coming up quite close before being discovered. We found them to consist of Captain Marcy and company of about one hundred men. When they saw us right at their heels there was some lively scampering for a few moments and the enemy was brought into line. We halted about forty yards from them and I advanced and met Captain Marcy about twenty paces from his line of battle. He introduced himself, saying he supposed I was Captain Smith. I replied in the affirmative. He then said that the soldiers he commanded were United States troops, and asked me what armed force it was I had. I told him they were from Utah. "What is your business out here?" he inquired. "Watching you. What's your business?" I asked. He said they were looking out a way into Utah. "Nonsense," said I, "you have left the main road to the valley long ago. It passes through Echo Canyon. I have been that way myself many a time." The sneering way in which I said this caused him to smile. It was the only expression except the utmost coolness and civility I got out of him that morning. I afterwards regretted the rough manner I assumed toward him, for he remained perfectly calm, and was very gentlemanly during the whole of our interview. While we were engaged talking, his men were knocking the powder down in their guns and getting ready for the expected encounter. I knew all the time that Marcy was out hunting for me, and that he had been up the river on that business. He was now going down the stream on the same errand, but had found us before he expected to. He evidently did not want to fight, talking about almost everything but our present position. He at last said he regretted the difficulty that seemed imminent, and that the officers did not want to come to blows with us. I told him the Administration seemed to want them to, and that their coming here, put us in the position of a man holding off the hand that clutched a knife with which to cut his throat. We had a good hold of that arm raised against us, and would keep it. He said that he had letters of introduction to parties in Salt Lake, among others to President John Taylor. I told him he had better send them in, as he would not be able to go in himself that winter. He asked me if I would take them. I replied that the probabilities were that I should not go in either, and, observing that time was passing, we separated. I went directly towards his men, and he followed some distance after. My men skirted around to the right and we struck off to find our packs in charge of Captain Haight. As soon as Marcy returned to his troops, he sent out scouts to watch us. I told the boys that though we came for mules, we had no time to stop and catch them or anything else, that we would have all we could do to keep from getting caught; and that in three minutes we might expect the devil turned loose. Within that time, they came with beating drums, and fife, and bugle calls, shouting, etc. The whole force were out to meet us. We paid little attention to them, but were eagerly looking for our comrades. We soon came upon them, but by that time were nearly surrounded by Marcy's command, the trooops forming a long line below us. There was no apparent way of escape but up a steep mountain or to cut through the line. I rode into the river, and found the bank on the other side very steep. I sent my horse for it, and he went up with difficulty; I knew the rest could not do it. Matters then looked pretty blue for a few moments, as we could hear the troops thundering on as they drew in their circle around us. I ran up the river some distance, and found the bank cut by a ravine. Just as we all got across and had safely clambered up the bank, the cavalry came upon us and commanded us to halt. The boys sent back their compliments, more expressive than elegant, and the main body gave up the chase, as we leisurely rode up the hill. I sat down on the hillside, and looking across the river at them, imagined how chagrined they must feel, having let us slip through their fingers after having their hands fairly upon us. I had just started down the hill and observed to our men that if fighting had commenced, we would not have left those rocks, when Lieutenant Abbott came riding down like Tam O'Shanter, exclaiming, "The troops are upon us!" I could not believe it; but sure enough there they were within range. They jumped off their horses, took good aim, and sent forty shots among us before we could count ten. If ever I was mad, that was the time. Luckily for us they were in short range and over shot the mark – except Mark Hall, of Ogden, who got a bullet through his hat. Two horses were shot; a gray one falling near me. The troops thought I had fallen and shouted exultantly. I felt happy to know that they were mistaken.

When the troops came up so unexpectedly and fired upon us, I got mad. For three-quarters of an hour we had stood face to face with them without a sign of war, and now to be taken advantage of and caught just after leaving the rocks, made me righteously mad. I felt willing now to take a brush with them, and for this purpose sent all my men but twelve forward, and with the latter, tried as David did to get them to come down; but not like him, I declined to go up. If I could have induced them to come down out of the rocks, we would have whipped them if they had been the last troops Uncle Sam had. I knew that if I kept all my men they would not come, as they could see us and all our movements, we being upon a level plain. However, even after sending the main command on, the enemy refused to take up the gauntlet, and we were compelled to ride slowly away without an encounter. We fell back on Fort Supply, eating the beef we had borrowed and sampling some half-cooked government beans. This experiment developed, as never before conceived in my imagination, the enormous pressure the human stomach is capable of sustaining without damage, and came very near developing the necessity for some one else to write this sketch.

While at Bridger I caught a violent cold, and was so near being sick that I detailed Lieutenant Abbott and a platoon to go to the front and see what movements the troops were making. I felt, after his departure, that I ought to have warned him against an ambush, but he had gone. A few miles from their camp he discovered a lone horseman who allowed him to come near, when he spurred up and rode on towards camp. Had I been there I would have been too great a coward to risk chasing in that direction; but not so with Abbott, who was brave and fearless. Remarking that if he allowed them to get so close again he would repent it; he ordered his men to follow, and dashed on after the retreating soldier, who led them to an ambush of forty men, who, rising on the sides of a ravine, fired at thirty yards. Abbott and his men rolled off on the sides of their horses, and, as usual, the shots, in such cases always aimed too sure, missed every man, whizzing over their heads. Our little band felt glad to get off so easily. After this skirmish the troops retired to their camp on Ham's Fork, and we received orders not to molest them if they wished to go into Winter Quarters.

I made a trip to General Wells' camp on Black's Fork, being at the time suffering from severe cold and sickness. Fort Bridger was at this time burned after the supplies of grain and vegetables had been cached, and instructions were issued to let the troops winter in the ruins if they wished to. After remaining a few days at these quarters, being nursed as well as could be under the circumstances, I was again ordered to the front. I started with twenty-six men and one baggage wagon on the coldest day that I ever experienced. While making up the detachment, a number of young men volunteered and insisted on going with us. They were Brigham Young, Jr., Joseph C. Rich, Howard Spencer, Stephen Taylor, and several others. The General thought them too young to take so severe a trip, and it was decided that Joseph Rich and Howard Spencer remain in camp. The latter had a fever sore on his leg, and to show his indifference to a little hardship and express his disgust at being kept in camp, he remarked to his comrades: "Boys, if you want to get out of doing anything, just scratch your leg a little." He then rolled up his pants and filled the gaping wound with hot embers. I thought him then the right kind of stuff to make a soldier.[10] His future career proved it, for he has the reputation of being a man entirely without fear and indifferent to hardship. We had a terrible day. The men froze faces, ears and feet. I saw that all would perish if we remained with the baggage wagon, so I told the teamsters they could shelter themselves with the blankets, and we would push on to Colonel Burton's camp on Bear River. I was mounted on a magnificent horse, but the snow was deep and the wind blew fiercely. I ordered Captain Thomas Rich to the rear, with instructions to not allow any of our men to stop on any pretext whatever. It became so cold that one could not tell if his hat was on without feeling for it. I feared the night more than all the troops we had seen during the campaign. My horse proved himself a good man's best friend. I shall never forget how he plowed his way through the drifts, breaking the track and leading the company safely to camp. When we arrived, John Woolley said my nose was frozen. I told him I

---

[10] Howard O. Spencer, a son of Orson Spencer, first Chancellor of the University of Deseret (Utah), was born June 16, 1838, in Massachusetts.

didn't think it possible, for it was so short. He was not satisfied until he pinched it. But some of the boys had to be careful how they handled their ears, as they were stiff as sticks and discolored to blackness. We bound them in snow and did all that was possible to save them. The men with the wagon had their feet frozen, though they had the blankets of twenty-six men to cover them. The day is remembered throughout Utah as one of uncommon severity. After our baggage arrived, we made easy journeys to Bridger Buttes, west of the fort, where we took our stand, receiving deserters from the enemy daily, and sending them to the Valley.

When General Johnston turned towards Salt Lake, after going up Ham's Fork, one would have thought that he would go right through in a few days, but when he finally started, he made seventeen miles in one day, and it took two weeks to fetch up the rear; then the General began to see how far off Salt Lake really was.

Our duty was to watch the troops as they slowly came up to the ruins of Bridger and went into winter quarters. I suppose that it was this position, which the London *Punch* so graphically pictured in a cartoon in which the flower of the American army is being herded by ten Mormons. It soon became evident that the army would settle for the winter. The snow fell and covered the ground a great depth, but it was not so deep as our chaplain prayed for. He asked for twenty feet. One of our men, a little fearful that his prayer would be answered, wanted to know what would become of him and the rest of us. The chaplain's prayer was the echo of thousands of others offered at the Throne of Grace by a people whose homes were threatened and who looked to God alone for deliverance and safety. The word came to us to leave ten men on the Yellow Creek

Mountains to guard the army. The detail of this illustrious little band was made, and the rest of us turned towards home. When crossing the two mountain ranges, I felt satisfied that Uncle Sam would not attempt to follow.

I shall never forget my feelings on that homeward march; I had been "keyed up" to a higher tension for ten weeks than I ever thought a human frame could stand. I could ride night and day for weeks and not feel fatigued, but now when turning my back upon the scenes of such absorbing interest, the weariness of months seemed to overpower me, and I was as weak as a child. I think I had never disobeyed an order of my superiors until at this time, when I neglected some request of Colonel Burton. This feeling remained, stupifying me, until we reached President Young's office. He came out to the steps and spoke about ten words; I did not remember one of them, but they had the effect to dispel every sense of weakness or weariness. I was ready that moment to return to the mountains. I would like to know the words he uttered, though it was not the words but the spirit which dictated them that touched the keynote of my heart. I don't know how many men could have done it; he could.

To my comrades of 1857: You doubtless will have discovered a number of inaccuracies in the relation of this narrative. All has been written from memory and the editor has done well to get it in as good shape as it is.

VIII
Congressional Reactions
to the Utah Expedition

INTRODUCTION

The Mormon resistance to the entry of United States troops into Salt Lake Valley convinced the administration in Washington that additional military forces should be made available for reenforcements.

On January 21, 1858, Jefferson Davis, of the Senate Committee on Military Affairs, reported a bill (Senate no. 79) to increase the military establishment of the nation. He stated that the existing army consisted of over 17,000 and that the proposed increase was for over 6,000. The bill was brought up on the 26th, and during the ensuing month was to elicit a great deal of debate. Much of the controversy was upon the question whether to increase the army by raising volunteer regiments, or through enlistments in the regular army. There was also considerable debate in Congress about conditions in Utah and upon the best methods of dealing with the Mormons. The most pertinent discussions upon the latter topics have been extracted from the long debates and are presented below:

1. SENATOR ROBERT TOOMBS OF GEORGIA, JANUARY 26:[1]

As to the Mormon war, it is not yet a fact. Congress,

---

[1] *The Congressional Globe: Containing the Debates and Proceedings of the First Session of the Thirty-fifth Congress; also of the Special Session of the Senate* (Washington, Printed at the Office of John C. Rives, 1858), 407.

which alone has the power to make war, has not spoken; and it is very certain, unless our country has undergone a silent revolution, that the President cannot make that war. It is very certain, that unless the Senate and House of Representatives intend to go on in the downward path of vesting all the powers of government confided to the legislative department in the executive, this war does not exist in contemplation of law. Therefore, I say, Congress has not yet acted, and when that question shall come up, there may be gentlemen who may believe such a war to be unnecessary; who may believe it to be unnecessary to carry vast bodies of troops over the Rocky Mountains, in order to murder those people who are called Mormons. It may be that we may suppose that no such necessity may exist. These are my present impressions on the case, though I give no judgment. I am not prepared to declare such a war, nor to wage it; but if we do declare it, if we do wage it, it is very clear that it must be exceedingly brief and temporary. . .

2. SENATOR WILLIAM H. SEWARD OF NEW YORK, JANUARY 26 [2]

SIR, we are entering on a new experiment in the government of a Territory. The Territory of Utah stands out entirely distinct from the whole line of our past experience. . . Here we find a lodgment of a band of men which has been expelled from the heart of our country – cast out and rejected by its civilization – equally intolerant of us and intolerable by ourselves – men who have been driven to hate, and not yet instructed by all their calamities and experience to fear us. This body of the settlers of Utah are men who have

---

[2] *Ibid.,* p. 413.

set up for themselves another and peculiar religion. They have gone back two thousand five hundred years, and have set up a religion based upon the principles of Judaism – a system repudiated not only by ourselves, but repellent to the religious and moral sense of all Christendom. This community, thus made to fly before us, has taken refuge in passes of the Rocky Mountains, or in a region encircled by the mountains, which secures to them fortifications such as military science never yet has devised, or military art been able to construct. I look at that band, and see the perpetual increase of it by emigration from amongst ourselves, and by emigration from European and South American States; and I see in their religious and political constitution two martial elements – the elements of resistance to law and to authority such as have never yet been successfully overcome when combined: the one a lust of independence, of power, and dominion; and the other a religious license to the base passions of mankind.

This is the internal enemy which is lodged within a Territory across the path which leads from our Atlantic to our Pacific settlements. I trust in God that the difficulties in which we are placed with regard to these people will pass away as easily and lightly as Senators seem to think. I do not believe it. . .

I cannot be content that disaster shall happen to that small band of men who are now representing the United States, and hemmed in in winter quarters, distant from every part of our civilized country, in danger, and wasting away by disease, for aught I know, or by Indian or Mormon depredations deprived of their cattle and of their forage. I cannot endure the thought that I may possibly hear, at some not distant day, that disaster has overtaken that small band.

Then I come back to the question. It must be a military demonstration that shall be made. Why shall it not be a force of volunteers?

3. SENATOR JOHN BELL OF TENNESSEE, JANUARY 27:[3]

If five or ten regiments were necessary to rescue those gallant officers and soldiers from the conditions in which they are now placed, I should feel myself constrained to vote them. Whatever I might think of the indiscretion and the imprudence of the Government in precipitating those men into these difficulties, ordering them to enter upon the expedition at a season of the year when it was known to be almost impossible that they could pass the gorges of the Rocky Mountains until next spring, thus, of course, in the meantime exposing them to all the hardships, and privations, and severities of a Rocky Mountain winter, I would vote for the force demanded, if it was necessary, to rescue them. . .

But from the debate yesterday I am led to believe that no such exigency exists, and that there is an adequate and all-sufficient force ready to be sent in aid of that command. . .

Why, then, should we wish to exterminate the Mormons and drive them out mercilessly? If their women may be considered as not entitled to our sympathy, what do you say as to their children. Are they to be driven into the gorges of the mountains to perish in the snows, or by starvation upon the plains? Are they to be driven out to seek new climes and new homes? Where will they go? Sir, I know of no sect of men, no class of

---

[3] *Ibid.,* pp. 430, 432.

men in the world, however they may differ with men in sentiment or doctrine, even upon questions that I regard as vital, whom I would pursue with such relentless and indiscriminate vengeance. . . They cannot war upon us on equal terms of advantage in any respect. They can only resist us by retreating into the gorges of the mountains, putting their women and children in caves during the winter and summer. Notwithstanding what is alleged to be their numbers, I think this is the only mode in which they can carry on any warfare against us. They may, as bandits, range the mountains, annoying us, cutting off the supplies for our troops, harassing our troops in every way, but we know that they have not sufficient force to meet them on an open battle-field.

I did not intend, however, to go into these considerations, and I shall not extend my remarks further. I believe there is no necessity for this increase of the Army at the present time.

4. SENATOR ALFRED IVERSON OF GEORGIA, JANUARY 27 [4]

I believe there ought to be an increase in the regular force, not only to answer the present exigencies of the service, but for permanent employment hereafter. The present exigency is the Utah war. It is not a war in the technical sense of the term; it is a rebellion on the part of the Mormon people, which it becomes necessary and proper on the part of the Government of the United States to crush. . .

I am one of those who believe that this rebellion, or insurrection, or whatever else you may term it, in Utah,

---

[4] *Ibid.*, p. 433.

should be crushed; and crushed effectually, if it shall be necessary to sacrifice every individual in that country.

What is the condition of the Mormon war? What is the condition of the Mormon country? What force will it be necessary to send against them in order to effect this important object? I consider that the Mormon force is by no means one to be slighted. We have authentic information, such as I think every Senator will believe, that a force can be mustered into service in Utah under the command of Brigham Young, to the extent at least of four or five thousand efficient troops. We are informed, I think, by Captain Van Vliet, who was sent into that country for the purpose of spying out the land, that Brigham Young has an organized, well-equipped force of not less than four or five thousand men. We are informed upon reliable authority – upon authority on which I rely at least – that he has formed alliances with neighboring tribes, and that those Indians, incensed as they are against the people of the United States, and ready to strike a blow whenever they have an opportunity to do it, will readily join Brigham Young in his operations against the United States. Combine these two elements together, and I think the opposition power of Mormonism is by no means to be despised by this Government. Four or five thousand effective troops, well armed and equipped as we understand they are, fighting on their own soil, with a full knowledge of all the passways and the topography of the country, fighting for their hearthstones, and as they believe fighting for their religion, infuriated by their fanaticism, is not a force that is to be despised by this Government. With all the advantages which they will possess of a full knowledge of the country, standing behind the defiles and gorges of the mountains, I think it will require a large force to put them down.

What is the force that has been sent against them? We are told that there are only four or five regiments, the effective extent of which cannot exceed two thousand men. The probability is that the effective force of the army under Colonel Johnston, which is now in the mountains of Utah, does not exceed fifteen hundred men. . .

I am opposed to the use of volunteers in this Utah war. The very consideration of humanity is enough to prevent the calling out of the volunteer force. Send volunteers to Utah to suppress this insurrection! Why, sir, you know that volunteers, when they are once set in motion, are unrestrained by any order. Send volunteers to Utah, and every man, woman, and child in that Territory will be exposed to the danger of sacrifice. No, sir; let us send disciplined troops; let us send the regular Army; let us send troops who are disinterested, who are subject to the control of their officers, and will be regulated and directed by the dictates of humanity.

5. REPRESENTATIVE JOHN THOMPSON OF NEW YORK, JANUARY 27 [5]

As by a common impulse they [the Mormons] have come together from all parts of the world – from Germany, Sweden, Denmark, Scotland, England, Australia, and the United States. They have become a nation in a day. They have trade, industry, manufacturing and mechanical skill; they have law, government, and a religion. They are a homogeneous people; act by a common impulse upon definite and fixed principles.

[5] *Ibid.*, pp. 449-52.

[Brigham Young] has at length grown desperate enough to declare openly his defiance of the General Government; and emboldened by distance and long success, gathered from the supineness of the executive power that had employment nearer home for all its energies, comes out by proclamation declaring military law, usurps all the functions of territorial government in his person, and is training and marshaling his battalions for resistance and encounter. Three thousand brave men – our brothers and our sons – have in obedience to the executive mandate, crossed the plains and rest in their tents near the mountain passes that girdle that Territory. . .

Why they were ordered off at a season which compelled this inevitable exposure, contrary to all prudent foresight, and against the advice of wise and experienced councils, let those who did it explain and justify to the people and the country, if they can. . .

The General Government has superseded Young as Territorial Governor. His successor (Cumming) has issued his proclamation, exhorting the people to lay down their arms and refrain from all disorderly and treasonable projects. The idle wind that sweeps those plains is not more idle and ineffective than these proclamations upon that people. Their imperial priest, despot, and dictator, from his dual throne, as potentate of the Saints and vice regent of the Almighty, laughs them to scorn. . .

Clad in the sacerdotal robes of the priest, over which are drawn the vestments of the soldier, this unscrupulous and traitorous warrior-ecclestiastic rings out the blended war cry of the chieftain with the imperial edict of the Pope! From the sacred seclusion of the cloister, he emerges with mailed glove and plumed helmet. The will of the Almighty comes from his mouth, and His direst wrath foams on his hissing lip. . .

I would send an army there sufficient to apprehend Young and all his co-conspirators against the authority of the General Government – who will be found to include every lord of the seraglio – try them for treason, and hang every one, without distinction, who should be found guilty; excluding every Mormon from any participation in the legal processes of the court. . .

This religious fanaticism has now assumed the form of a civil polity, and this civil polity is anti-republican and despotic; and this despotism has committed overt treason against the Government of the United States. The authority of every Federal officer is denied, or a reign of terror instituted over all their acts. War is proclaimed in fact. Forces are levied and trained for action. Slaughter is threatened. Our troops are defied, our courts closed, our officers insulted; the savages incited to plunder and ravage. . .

Did General Washington hesitate and temporize and count the cost, when a part of Pennsylvania rebelled on the whisky tax? No, sir; he sent fifteen thousand men into the field, and this promptitude, energy, manliness, itself quelled the storm, without shedding a drop of blood. The Saints of Utah may be as wise as the whisky dealers of the land of Penn, if they find the Government are equally in earnest. If they choose to risk a battle, I trust it will be such a battle as has not been seen on this continent – overwhelming, decisive, complete; such as our brave Army will fight, even if fanaticism provokes to feats of superhuman valor.

6. SENATOR WILLIAM M. GWIN OF CALIFORNIA, FEBRUARY 18, 1858 [6]

It is well known that we have a large force in Utah already. There certainly is an emergency to relieve that force. It is not of sufficient strength to meet the Mormons if they intend war. They cannot be conquered with such a force. It is utterly impossible for the United States to retreat from its position; and that is to bring the Mormons to subordination to the laws of the United States. The latest intelligence we have is, that they are in open collision with the authorities of this Government, and it is impossible for the President to retreat from his present position without disgrace and dishonor. The emergency exists. We have a portion of our Army there, and they must be relieved. The President must go on, unless Congress, by refusing to give him the proper aid, puts it out of his power to progress in bringing the Mormons to subordination.

I am in favor of giving the President this aid . . . we ought to relieve Colonel Johnston in the speediest manner that is possible. I know that we cannot get soldiers to enlist in the regular Army in the State I represent. The people of that State will not enlist, but they will respond to a call for volunteers. The President ought to have power to call out a force of either volunteers or regulars. We ought to give him the power, or censure him for sending that portion of the Army now in Utah to that Territory. I think a volunteer force would be more efficient, for the reason that if you intend to relieve Colonel Johnston, you must do it in the most speedy manner; and I believe by raising volunteers nearest to the country where those troops are, and marching them expeditiously, you will sooner bring the war to a conclusion.

---

[6] *Ibid.*, p. 759.

I have made some examinations in regard to the manner of approaching this Utah Territory, and I have made comparisons from official documents to show that you can get from the Pacific Coast to Salt Lake forty-five days sooner than you can by starting from Fort Leavenworth.

7. SENATOR ALBERT G. BROWN OF MISSISSIPPI, FEBRUARY 25 [7]

. . . if you send volunteers there, you will have war. If you send volunteers from Missouri and Illinois, from which two States they are more likely to come than anywhere else, as I said then, and I tried to impress that idea on the Senate . . . they will go to wreak vengeance on the Mormons, and they will bring on a war. If you send regular troops, and make a proper demonstration, I have never believed, and do not now believe that Brigham Young will fight; . . These Mormons are all wrong. That they must be required to obey the laws of the country, I am as ready to admit as anybody else; but I would send no volunteer force there, that would go to wreak vengeance for past wrongs, and thus precipitate you into a conflict whether you would or not.

8. SENATOR SAM HOUSTON OF TEXAS, FEBRUARY 25 [8]

I am opposed to the increase of the regular Army; and if it is intended for the Mormons, I tell you that we cannot wait two years to raise troops to subdue them. If they have to be subdued – and God forfend us

---

[7] *Ibid.,* p. 867.

[8] *Ibid.,* pp. 873-74. The Senate bill was finally reported as amended, on February 25. It authorized the President to call for and accept volunteers, not to exceed 3,000 officers and men, to serve for twelve months, unless sooner discharged. The bill was then voted upon and was defeated by a vote of 35 to 16 (p. 876).

from such a result – and the valley of Salt Lake is to be ensanguined with the blood of American citizens, I think it will be one of the most fearful calamities that has befallen this country, from its inception to the present moment. I deprecate it as an intolerable evil. I am satisfied that the Executive has not had the information he ought to have had on this subject before making such a movement as he has directed to be made. I am convinced that facts have been concealed from him. I think his wisdom and patriotism should have dictated the propriety of ascertaining, in the first place, whether the people of Utah were willing to submit to the authority of the United States. Why not send to them men to whom they could unbosom themselves, and see whether they would say, "we are ready to submit to the authorities of the United States, if you send to us honest men and gentlemen, whose morals, whose wisdom, and whose character, comport with the high station they fill. . .

But, sir, there is never a pretext wanting here when it is proposed to increase the regular Army, . .

The more men you send to the Mormon war the more you increase the difficulty. They have to be fed. For some sixteen hundred miles you have to transport provisions. The regiments sent there have found Fort Bridger and other places, as they approached them, heaps of ashes. They will find Salt Lake, if they ever reach it, a heap of ashes. They will find that they will have to fight against Russia and the Russians. Whoever goes there will meet the fate of Napoleon's army when he went to Moscow. Just as sure as we are now standing in the Senate, these people, if they fight at all, will fight desperately. They are defending their homes.

They are fighting to prevent the execution of threats that have been made, which touch their hearths and their families; and depend upon it they will fight until every man perishes before he surrenders. That is not all. If they do not choose to go into conflict immediately, they will secure their women and children in the fastnesses of the mountains; they have provisions for two years; and they will carry on a guerilla warfare which will be most terrific to the troops you send there. They will get no supplies there. You will have to transport them all from Independence, in Missouri. When the fire will consume it, there will not be a spear of grass left that will not be burnt. . .

I know not what course will be taken on this subject. I hope it will be one of conciliation. . . Mr. President, in my opinion, whether we are to have a war with the Mormons or not, will depend on the fact whether our troops advance or not. If they do not advance; if negotiations be opened; if we understand what the Mormons are really willing to do; that they are ready to acquiesce in the mandates of the Government, and render obedience to the Constitution; if you will take time to ascertain that, and not repudiate all idea of peace, we may have peace. But so sure as the troops advance, so sure they will be annihilated. You may treble them, and you will only add to the catastrophe, not diminish human suffering. These people expect nothing but extermination, or abuse more intolerable than even extermination would be, from your troops, and they will oppose them. . .

An act of civility was tendered by Brigham Young, and you might, if you please, construe it, under the circumstances, rather as an act of submission on his part. He sent salt to the troops, understanding that it was scarce there, and was selling at seven dollars a pint. As an act of humanity, thinking at least that it would not be regarded as discourteous, he sent a supply of salt requisite for the relief of the encampment, intimating to the commander that he could pay for it, if he would not accept of it as a present. What was the message the military officer sent him back? I believe the substance of it was that he would have no inter-course with a rebel, and that when they met they would fight. They will fight; and if they fight, he will get miserably whipped. That was a time to make peace with Brigham Young, because there is something potent in salt.

9. REPRESENTATIVE WILLIAM W. BOYCE OF SOUTH CAROLINA, MARCH 11 [9]

There are two modes of solving the Mormon ques-tion – first by peaceful means; second, by force. There can be no doubt that the first mode is infinitely the best, if it can be made efficacious. The peaceful mode is more congenial to the spirit of our institutions.   .   .

Peaceful solution costs nothing; whereas war will entail an expenditure of the most astonishing amount. It will be the most expensive military expedition, to the force employed, ever set on foot in modern times. Utah is eleven hundred miles from the Missouri; a land passage through an uncultivated wilderness; a portion of the way through deserts and difficult moun-tains. Subsistence will have to be carried by wagons from the Missouri; even the animals with the army cannot be sustained at all seasons along the route by the native grasses.   .   .

---

[9] *Ibid.*, pp. 1085-86.

The peaceful solution of the question, besides the advantages I have already mentioned, is also by far the most efficacious. If we can restore order in Utah without bloodshed, then we will have accomplished all we desire. . .

Let us go to the utmost verge of moderation; let us manifest our intentions of peace, of kindness, and generosity, in the most unmistakable manner to these people; let us before a gun is fired, gain a moral victory over Brigham Young. That moral victory may supersede the necessity of resorting to force. . .

This Mormon question is a great question. It is not one of those common-place matters which you can summarily dispose of. It is not a question of partisanship, but a question of statesmanship. You may turn from it, but there is Utah; there are the Mormons; there is the cancer on your body-politic. How will you get rid of it? Will you strike at it with the sword? Those rough remedies sometimes aggravate the disease. It needs, in my opinion, to be dealt with gently, and with consummate wisdom.

IX
Thomas L. Kane's Mission of Reconciliation

INTRODUCTION

On August 13, 1857, the day on which the first order was issued for Mormon troops to reconnoiter the movements of military forces headed for Utah, Samuel W. Richards left Salt Lake City with a message from Brigham Young for Thomas L. Kane.

Colonel Kane, philanthropist and humanitarian of Philadelphia, was a proven friend of the Mormons.[1] At the time of the expulsion of the Saints from Nauvoo, Illinois, Kane had become interested in this people and journeyed west in 1847 to make a personal investigation. On the trip he became seriously ill and was nursed with solicitous care through his sickness by the Mormons. Kane wrote good objective reports of the conditions he found, and sent various letters soliciting protection and aid for the Mormons. In March, 1850, he gave, before the Pennsylvania Historical Society, a

---

[1] Thomas Leiper Kane was born Jan. 27, 1822, in Philadelphia. He was the son of John K. Kane, a prominent federal judge, and a brother of Elisha K. Kane, arctic explorer. As a young man, Thomas Kane traveled in Europe. He studied law, and was admitted to the bar in 1846. In addition to his solicitude for the Mormons, Kane's humanitarianism was exemplified by his interest in and aid to the movement for abolition of slavery, and to other social and philanthropic causes. He served with distinction in the Civil War, reaching the rank of Brigadier-General. He died, Dec. 26, 1883. For further information see Oscar O. Winther, *The Private Papers and Diary of Thomas Leiper Kane, a Friend of the Mormons* (San Francisco, Gelber-Lilienthal, Inc., 1937).

talk upon the Mormons, which address appeared afterward in book form. Some contact was maintained thereafter between Kane and members of the sect, and the Mormons continued to look upon him as their friend.

So it was natural that when Brigham Young saw his people about to become embroiled in a serious difficulty that he would think of Kane and hope that the generous Colonel might be able to give advice or help.

Colonel Kane responded magnanimously. He went to President Buchanan and offered to go to the Mormons as a mediator. The President was glad for intervention, but unwilling to initiate the matter or give Kane official designation. So the Colonel went as a private citizen and at his own expense.

Kane left New York on January 5, 1858, going by steamboat to Panama, across the isthmus by railroad, and up the coast to California by boat. From Los Angeles he traveled on horseback to Salt Lake City, arriving on February 25. He traveled under the name of Dr. Osborne.[2]

After conferences with Brigham Young and the Mormon leaders he journeyed eastward and arrived at Camp Scott on March 12. He asked Governor Cumming to go with him back to Salt Lake City, on assurances that the Mormons would accept him as Governor. Colonel Johnston opposed this procedure, but the Governor finally acceded. Upon arrival in Salt Lake City, Cumming was acknowledged as the chief executive of the Territory.

---

[2] The Journal History (L.D.S. Church Historian's Office Library) under date of Feb. 25, reports the arrival of Dr. Osborne in Salt Lake City in company with Amasa M. Lyman and others. They had left Cedar City, Utah, on Feb. 20.

Colonel Kane was ill on the trip, but he heroically endured suffering and abuse to do what his heart dictated. His mission was highly successful; he performed a great service to the Mormons and to the nation. Much of importance that occurred during his negotiations was not put into writing, but the pertinent documents available are quoted below.

1. S. W. RICHARDS TAKES MESSAGE TO KANE [3]

NEW YORK CITY   Sept. 16th 1857

T. L. KANE   ESQ.

DEAR COL.   I beg you will excuse the liberty I take in addressing you.

Having just arrived from Utah I took the liberty of calling at your office in Philadelphia at the instance of Gov. B. Young to communicate to you such items as you might be pleased to learn relative to the state of things in Utah the intentions of the Authorities there, etc., and also to learn of you anything that you might have in your possession and be pleased to communicate, relating to the present movements of Government and their designs against us in that Territory.   .   .

I left G.S.L. City on the 13th ult. arrived at Florence on the 1st inst.   .   .

Gov. Young was quite willing I should tell you of his full intentions relative to the Government and the course he should pursue, esteeming you as a warm friend, and worthy of that confidence of course I should not feel to commit to paper with the same freedom that I would speak.   .   .

My mission is to the Churches in the States and Europe.

---

[3] This letter is copied into the Journal History, *op. cit.*

Messrs. Kimball, Wells and others wished a very warm remembrance to you.

Praying God to increase your power and influence in the earth, I am with much esteem,   Yours sincerely,

SAML W. RICHARDS

2. LETTER OF PRESIDENT BUCHANAN TO COLONEL KANE [4]

WASHINGTON CITY,   December 31, 1857

COLONEL THOMAS L. KANE

MY DEAR SIR: You furnish the strongest evidence of your desire to serve the Mormons by abandoning the comforts of friends, family, and home, and voluntarily encountering the perils and dangers of a journey to Utah at the present inclement season of the year, at your own expense, and without official position. Your only reward must be a consciousness that you are doing your duty. Nothing but pure philanthropy and a strong desire to serve the Mormon people could have dictated a course so much at war with your private interests.

You express a strong conviction, in which however I do not participate, that a large portion of the Mormons labor under a mistake as to the intentions of the federal government towards them. If this be so, my late message [5] will disabuse their minds. My views therein expressed, as I have already informed you, have undergone no change. These sentiments were expressed in sincerity and truth, and I trust that your representations of them may meet with the success you anticipate. I hope that the people of Utah may be convinced, ere

---

[4] This letter was written, apparently, for presentation to Brigham Young. It is printed in *House Ex. Doc. 2,* 35 Cong., 2 Sess., pp. 162-63 (Ser. no. 998). Hereafter referred to as *Doc. 2.*

[5] This would be the President's Annual Message to Congress of December, 1857.

it is to late, that there exist no duties of higher obligation than those which they owe to their country. They cannot doubt your friendship, and the services which you have rendered to them in times past will conciliate their regard.

At the same time I deem it my duty to say that, whilst reposing entire confidence in the purity and patriotism of your motives, and entertaining a warm personal regard for yourself, I would not at the present moment, in view of the hostile attitude they have assumed against the United States, send any agent to visit them on behalf of the government. If the case were otherwise, however, I know no person to whom I should more cheerfully confide such a mission than yourself.

With every sentiment of personal regard, I remain truly your friend,

JAMES BUCHANAN

3. PRESIDENT BUCHANAN TO COLONEL KANE[6]

Dec. 31, 1857

COLONEL THOMAS L. KANE

MY DEAR SIR: As you have been impelled by your own sense of duty to visit Utah, and having informed me that nothing can divert you from this purpose, it affords me pleasure to commend you to the favorable regard of all officers of the United States whom you may meet in the course of your travels. Possessed as you are of my confidence, and being well informed as to passing events, you may have it in your power to impart to them useful information from this side of the continent. I do not doubt that they will, in the exercise of whatever discretion their instructions may

---

[6] This was intended for presentation to military and civil officials of the government.

permit, render you all the aid and facilities in their power in expediting you on your journey, undertaken of your own accord, to accomplish the pacific and philanthropic objects you have in view.

Heartily wishing you success, I remain, very respectfully, your friend,

JAMES BUCHANAN

4. COLONEL KANE TO BRIGHAM YOUNG AND MORMON LEADERS, FEBRUARY 25, 1858 [7]

GOVERNOR YOUNG AND GENTLEMEN: I come as an ambassador from the chief executive of our nation, and am fully prepared and authorized to lay before you, most fully and definitely, the feelings and views of the citizens of our common country and the feelings of the executive towards you, relating to the present position of officers of this territory, and the army of the United States now upon your borders, and after giving you the most satisfactory evidence in relation to the matter concerning you now pending, I shall then call your attention and wish to enlist your sympathies in behalf of the poor soldiers, who are now suffering in the cold and snow of the mountains, and request you to render them aid and comfort, and to assist them to come here and to bid them a hearty welcome into your hospitable valley.

[Kane is reported to have then turned to Brigham Young and requested an interview with him alone.[8] On the following Sunday President Young, in the course of his address to the congregation, referred to the presence in the city of a "gentleman from

---

[7] This statement is given as reported in the Wilford Woodruff Journal of Feb. 25. The original Journal is in the Church Historian's Library, L.D.S. (Mormon) Church, Salt Lake City.

[8] B. H. Roberts in his *History of the Mormon Church* (Americana), VIII, p. 933.

Washington," a "Doctor Osborne," whose "errand was of no particular moment to the people or himself; that he had come on his own responsibility and at his own expense to see and learn the situation of affairs here." [9]

We have found no written report of the negotiations between Kane and Young, but Kane must have obtained assurances from the Mormon leader that his people would accept Cumming as Governor, if he would come in to Salt Lake City without the army. Also, it appears, Kane induced President Young to offer beef and flour to the army, in accordance with the above request. Kane was escorted by Mormon scouts to the vicinity of Camp Scott and with him carried Young's offer, as embodied in the following document:]

5. BRIGHAM YOUNG OFFERS SUPPLIES [10]

GREAT SALT LAKE CITY,
March 9, 1858 – Tuesday, 8 o'clock p.m.
COLONEL THOMAS L. KANE

DEAR SIR: We have just learned, through the southern Indians, that the troops are very destitute of provisions.

Mr. Gerrish, a merchant, formerly of this place, and who is now supposed to be detained in Colonel Johnston's camp, has quite a herd of cattle here, and for which he would doubtless like a market. We know of none that would be equal to the army of the United States, now encamped within our borders. We have, therefore, concluded to send this herd, consisting of nearly two hundred head of cattle, a portion of which are tolerable good beef. In addition to the foregoing, we shall send out fifteen or twenty thousand pounds of flour to the army, to which they will be made perfectly welcome, or pay for, just as they choose. All of which will be forwarded in a few days, so soon as the neces-

---

[9] *Deseret News.*
[10] Addressed to Col. Kane and printed in *Doc. 2, op. cit.,* pp. 87-88.

sary arrangements can be made and the snow will admit. If, after your arrival, you learn that Colonel Johnston will not receive the flour, we will be obliged if you will be at the trouble of communicating the fact to those who attend you, that we may be saved the trouble.

I send this by my son, Joseph A., and George Stringham.

Trusting that you are rapidly regaining your health, and that success may attend you, I remain, most respectfully, BRIGHAM YOUNG

6. CAPTAIN JESSE GOVE REPORTS ARRIVAL OF KANE [11]

BRIDGER'S FORT, U.T., March 14, 1858

. . . [FRIDAY, MARCH 12th] About retreat a man came in from the Salt Lake direction with a pack mule, splendidly mounted, so much fatigued that he could not apparently speak. He saw nothing of Ross and his Indians. He is very reserved, says he came from California to Salt Lake City, remained there 9 days, and then came here under a Mormon escort till within a few miles. His whole outfit is new and well made up. Says he has despatches for Gov. Cumming.[12] My men want to hang him. Say he is a Mormon. Half persuaded that they are right from recent developments. Yesterday, 13th, he went to the upper camp and is now with Gov. Cumming. What his business is no one yet knows.

12 O'CLOCK NOON, SUNDAY. Reports are many and varied this morning. Some trouble had already arisen

11 O. G. Hammond (ed.), *The Utah Expedition, 1857-1858; Letters of Capt. Jesse A. Gove*, etc. (Concord, New Hampshire Historical Society, 1928), 134. Hereafter cited as *Gove's Letters*.

12 Part of his offense was that he went first to the civil rather than to the military leader.

between the civil and military authorities relative to this man. He says his name is Kane, from Philadelphia, brother to the late Dr. Kane, that he left New York the 5th of January. He has not as yet delivered any despatches to Col. Johnston, though he told him he had some for him.

7. COLONEL KANE TO COLONEL JOHNSTON [13]

CAMP SCOTT, GREEN RIVER COUNTY
Utah Territory, March 14, 1858

SIR: I have learned, I hope incorrectly, that since my arrival at this place a horseman, or a group of horsemen, discerned at a considerable distance from camp were approached by a party of the soldiery under your command, and, without notice or question addressed them, fired upon. If you were not apprised of the fact before, permit me to state that there may be, at this time, a person or persons in waiting for your answer to the proposal of Brigham Young, of Great Salt Lake City, to furnish this army with provisions. I most respectfully pray, therefore, that you will be pleased to issue such orders as will prevent unnecessary bloodshed. I trust I am not indiscreet in adding that I regard this as of extreme importance at the present exigency.

Your very obedient servant, THOMAS L. KANE
of Philadelphia

8. JOHNSTON'S REPLY TO KANE [14]

HEADQUARTERS DEPARTMENT OF UTAH
Camp Scott, Utah Territory, March 15, 1858

SIR: I have just received your note of this morning, informing me that a party of horsemen have been fired

---

[13] Printed in *Doc. 2*, p. 89.
[14] *Ibid.*, p. 90.

upon by a party of soldiers. I regret that the party in question, if a portion of your escort, did not come in with you, or was not reported to me. In that case, their safety would have been assured to them; and I now have say to you, if the person or persons alluded to can be communicated with by you, or you can inform me where they can be found, I will give such orders as will insure their protection, and take care that they suffer no molestation. My orders are strict, and armed parties should be careful, in approaching, to make known, by signals or otherwise, that they desire to communicate on business.

I am, sir, with great respect, your obedient servant,

A. S. JOHNSTON,
Colonel 2d Cavalry, Commanding

9. COLONEL KANE TO COLONEL JOHNSTON [15]

ECKELSVILLE, March 15, 1858

SIR: With respect to the person or persons who may at this time be exposing themselves through a desire to communicate on business, etc., I am only able to state that the guide who accompanied me as far as the vicinity of what is called Muddy Creek, a distance of, I fancy, eleven or twelve miles from Fort Bridger, was a slightly built man of swarthy complexion, with dark eyes, and mounted upon a black Indian pony, slow of foot. His name given me was Lewis Robinson, and he is or was the reputed owner and late occupant of the premises at and around Bridger, for which reason I selected him to point me out my way. If this person, either alone or in the company of others, has been driven off from the vicinity of the Salt Lake road west of this by being fired upon, I have little hope that the

---

[15] *Ibid.,* pp. 89-90.

effort which I am about to make to look him up will prove successful. But that it would be out of place on my part, I would express my regret at the strictness of your orders. I presume that I can only request, conformably to the offer contained in your letter of this morning, that you will give such orders as will insure protection to any one small party or single individual not plainly seen to be armed, discovered at a considerable distance beyond your furthest outpost in the neighborhood of the high road west, and not observed to be approaching, or otherwise conducting himself or themselves in what may be deemed a suspicious and exceptionable manner.

I have been informed that I need a "countersign," to enable me to pass sentinels, &c., when desirous to "communicate," as proposed. Will you be good enough to give me what you think I should be provided with?

With great respect, your obedient servant,

THOMAS L. KANE

10. JOHNSTON'S REPLY TO YOUNG'S OFFER OF SUPPLIES [16]

HEADQUARTERS, DEPARTMENT OF UTAH
Camp Scott, Utah Ter., Mar. 15, 1858

COLONEL THOMAS L. KANE
Eckelsville, Utah Territory

SIR: President Brigham Young is not correctly informed with regard to the state of the supply of provisions of this army. There has been no deficiency, nor is there any now. We have abundance to last until the government can renew the supply. Whatever might be the need of the army under my command for food, we would neither ask, nor receive from President Young

---

[16] *Ibid.*, p. 88.

and his confederates any supplies while they continue to be enemies of the government. If Mr. Gerrish desires to have his cattle sent to him I will interpose no obstacle, on condition, further than I desire that they may be delivered to him on the Muddy, ten miles in advance of this camp. President Young says Mr. Gerrish is, "supposed to be detained in Colonel Johnston's camp;" the supposition is erroneous; Mr. Gerrish started for the eastern States some weeks since. He has at all times been at liberty to go wherever he pleased, as is every other American citizen, without question from any one, except to Salt Lake City, or some position occupied by an armed body of Mormons opposed to the government; all intercourse with the enemy being prohibited by the 56th and 57th articles of war.

However unfortunate the position now occupied by that portion of the citizens of Utah belonging to the sect of Mormons, it is of their own seeking, and it is one from which they can be relieved by the mere act of obedience to the proclamation of Governor Cumming.[17] Having the question of peace or war under his own control, President Young would, should he choose the latter, be responsible for all the consequences.

I beg to ask of you the favor to communicate my reply to President Young.

With great respect, your obedient servant,

A. S. JOHNSTON
Colonel 2d Cavalry, Commanding

11. KANE ENTREATS JOHNSTON TO MODIFY HIS REPLY TO YOUNG [18]

ECKELSVILLE, March 16, 1858   8½ A.M.

SIR: At the request of his excellency Governor

---

[17] This Proclamation is printed below, in Part X.
[18] *Doc. 2,* pp. 90-91.

Cumming, I consent to bear the reply which you request me to communicate to President Brigham Young. I fear that it must greatly prejudice the public interest to refuse Mr. Young's proposal in such a manner at the present time. Permit me, therefore, to entreat you, most respectfully, to reconsider it; and, adverting to my offer made you orally on Sunday afternoon [March 14], ask permission to impart to you additional information with respect to the posture of affairs at Salt Lake City, if you can encourage me to believe that by so doing I may yet hope to modify your views.

I beg not to hasten your determination. My horse will not arrive from the range in time for me to proceed in search of the Mormons before tomorrow.

If I adopt the opinion that a more particular reply is called for from me to those portions of your letter which do not, in my opinion, necessarily connect themselves with the subject-matter of Mr. Young's letter, I shall feel at liberty to offer it at a future day.

I am, with great respect, your obedient servant,

THOMAS L. KANE

12. THOMAS L. KANE TO GOVERNOR CUMMING [19]

ECCLESVILLE Mar. 16, 1858 7 A.M.

MY DEAR SIR: In deference to your flattering view of the value of my personal efforts to the public service I submit to you reluctantly a reason which did not occur to me until after you left last night why I must limit the time to which I may consent to the postponement which you have so forcibly urged upon me.[20] It connects itself with the performance of one of the very

---

[19] Found in the Cumming papers, Duke University. This letter is not printed in *Doc. 2*.

[20] Cumming pays further tribute to Kane's patriotic effort in his letter of March 22nd, quoted below as no. 14.

duties which I have assumed, I mean that of proceeding in search of the Mormons in the field. The service I regard as one of the least noticeable peril, ever since the outrage upon Mr. Robinson; but, in case of accident – shd I not return I might rest under the stigma of having submitted to insult without having made an effort to exact redress.

I have this morning written a letter to Colonel Johnston entreating him to reconsider his reply to Brigham Young. Should I receive an answer from him declining peremptorily to do so, or shd I otherwise be satisfied that all hope is at an end of my being able to exert a personal influence upon his mind in favor of peace, I must consider it incumbent upon me to arrange my personal relations (past equivocation) as they shd. be without more delay.

Most respectfully and gratefully, Sir,   Your friend & servant   THOMAS L. KANE

13. GOVE REPORTS KANE'S MOVEMENTS AND THE ARMY HATRED OF KANE [21]

TUESDAY, 16th.   Cold, windy, and very disagreeable. I am officer of the day. Today a sergt. of a dragoon picket of some 20 men in the direction of Salt Lake came in and reported the loss of several mules by Mormons, men that evidently came out of Salt Lake City with Kane. The soldiers are very much incensed against this man Kane. It is thought that the Governor is completely fooled by him.

WEDNESDAY, 17th.   St. Patrick's Day, but little drunkenness as no whiskey.

MY DEAR MARIA,   two hours since I wrote the

---

[21] *Gove's Letters, op. cit.,* pp. 135-36.

sentence above, and what do you think I have stopped
so long for? You cannot divine. About 7 o'clock in the
evening I commenced, and it is now 9 o'clock and I
renew my letter. I have been in command of one of the
lunettes with my company and a detachment of artillery
with guns shotted for a fight. Several shots were fired
into camp, and then came my favorite alarm call and
the long roll on the drum of the 5th Inf. Co. In three
minutes we were in position and ready for a fight. The
Mr. Kane I have spoken of previously left this morning for Salt Lake City under a guard.[22] Tonight he
returned and says he got lost, that he fired these shots
to find his way into camp.[23] This we do not believe, as

---

[22] In the Cumming papers is found the following:

HEADQUARTERS DEPARTMENT OF UTAH
Camp Scott U. Ter.,   March 17, 1858

CAPTAIN THOS. H. MILL, 5th Infantry
Camp Scott, U.T.

SIR, The Colonel commanding directs me to inform you that he has
selected you to command an escort of 1 N.C. Officer and 9 Privates (mounted)
to Colonel Thomas L. Kane of Pennsylvania.

He wishes you to see Colonel Kane passed without interruption beyond our
lines to the Salt Lake Road and to accompany him thereon about 18 miles—
beyond which he will meet no one denying his right to go to Salt Lake City.

Colonel Kane was a bearer of communications from Brigham Young and
if perceived his presence will ensure you from molestation — You will however take every precaution to insure the safety of your party.

You will return to this Camp tonight.

I am Sir, very respectfully   Your Obedient Servant

F. J. PORTER,   Assist. Adjt. Gen.

[23] The *Newark Daily Advertiser* of May 24, as quoted in *Gove's Letters,*
p. 215, gives this information: "Col. Kane arrived at the camp from Salt
Lake City on March 12, and, after a conference with Gov. Cumming and
others went back for another interview with the Mormons, and after his
second return, he, with Gov. Cumming, on April 7 set out for Salt Lake City.
It is stated that when Col. Kane came into the camp the second time it was
night, and some pistol shots, which he fired by way of signal according to an
arrangement with the captain of his escort, being mistaken for a Mormon
attack, the whole army turned out. Col. Kane, being fired at by a sentinel at
two paces distance, had a narrow escape with his life."

his shots came directly over the camp. A patrol of the guard was sent out immediately, and one of my men shot at Mr. Kane and just missed him. My men have a reputation in that line, you may well believe. They brought him in and Mr. Kane was the most astonished man you ever heard of. He barely escaped and that was all, and a more frightened individual I never saw. He was sent with a guard to Camp Scott. My men were in the work and rifles loaded before you could turn round, anxious for a fight. I have no confidence in this man, and our men sleep on their arms tonight. His escort was seen by the Provost Sergt. (Preston), and if they molest us tonight they will be a sorry party. It was exciting in the extreme to see with what alacrity my men got in position. I would have given $500 to have had a fight. Tomorrow the whole army moves down to this post, and a nice little fight would have given us a brevet. We may have one yet. Tomorrow I will write you of this night. We shall sleep on our arms, and woe betide any of these scoundrels if they molest us. McCarty shot at him, and we all think he did it on purpose, as Mr. Kane thinks it hit his collar. The man says it was accidental. I heard the men talking about it and they say he shot at him. Had he killed him he should not have been hurt. Even if Mr. Kane's story is true he runs his own risks in coming into camp in that way. The military authorities think him a spy and there is no doubt about it, and the sooner he gets out of our reach the better.

THURSDAY, 18th.   Terrific snow storm. Camp Scott on the move. Headquarters came down in the morning. Snow storm from the N.E. commenced about 10 o'clock and has raged all day.   .   .

FRIDAY, 19th. Am officer of the day. Storm still raging. Old Bridger,[24] who is Col. Johnston's guide and who was driven out from his place by the Mormons, says that this is the equinoctial storm, and may last for some days, then comes the warm weather. Everyone in camp is miserable. The snow is so deep that the men cannot get much wood, and we are here about as destitute as the people in camp. . . 10 o'clock p.m. Storm raging still. . .

14. CUMMING ASKS KANE TO CONTINUE EFFORTS TOWARDS RECONCILIATION [25]

EXECUTIVE OFFICE, ECKELSVILLE,
G.R. COUNTY, UTAH TY. 22d March, 1858
COL. THOMAS L. KANE,

SIR: The storm so long impending, is now ready to burst upon the deluded inhabitants of this Territory. Whilst it is my duty to enforce unconditional submission to the authority of the United States, yet in the performance of that duty, I would gladly temper justice with mercy, and prevent the unnecessary effusion of blood. Especially I would shield women and children from the sufferings incident to civil war.

I am not unmindful of the great effort already made by you, in the spirit of exalted patriotism, nor of the perils and fatigue which you have so bravely encountered in the effort to induce the Mormons to realize their true position, and return to their allegiance. From the partial success which has attended your effort to procure that result, I think that it is desirable that you should continue to [rest of line blank] a rebellious population, that both duty and

---

[24] James Bridger, Mountain Man, and builder of Fort Bridger.
[25] Cumming Papers, Duke University.

policy indicate the necessity of immediate submission to the United States, and dictates an appeal to its clemency, for immunity for past offences.

I do therefore earnestly desire that you will persevere in your mission of mercy, and give up, for the present at least, your purpose of returning to Philadelphia.

Very respectfully &c, &c.   A. CUMMING

15. GOVE REPORTS KANE'S DEPARTURE FOR CONFERENCE WITH THE MORMONS [26]

FORT BRIDGER, U.T.   March 26, 1858

. . . Col. Kane went out yesterday morning to confer with the Mormon authorities. The nature of his business no one knows. I think all he gets out of Col. Johnston will not do him much good.

. . . Saturday, 27th. Col. Kane returned today. The result of his mission is not known.

16. COLONEL KANE'S DIARY [27]

MARCH 28, 1858. And now behold my first Sunday – the first time since I embraced this work, that I have heard the Order to Halt & Stand at Ease. I have returned from a trip on which I was *successful in* making arrangements for *introducing Governor C. into the Valley,* with the feeling that I have now done my last utmost, and may leave the future to a less finite Power. – It shall prove for me if there is any God – other than that which nailed Him to the Cross – whose groans are still heard.

This day I might indulge in journalizing for my darling, but I have not given me a holiday from *Duty,*

[26] *Gove's Letters,* pp. 141, 142.
[27] Winther, *op. cit.,* pp. 77-79.

and [one][28] commands me to rest my wearing being utterly. . .[29]

I put on my day clothes the one clean change – early, this morning: I anticipated enjoying it so much.– But this must be more wearing than that which I have been confronting.– Homesickness, Fears for them all – and, oh, my griefs, my griefs!

May I but return before this has changed me and I seem to the dear ones another than myself! – Elisha, my dear Elisha.[30]

I made one of the Qrmaster's men tie me in my tent from the outside – to keep me from intruders while I lay down – and my tears fell till sun down into the cups with which I held the cold water against my frost bitten cheeks. I then arose – prayed to the memory of my Prince, and, asking forgiveness for my regrets, promised my best to *keep strong* and not to think of returning home before I saw plainly it was my duty.

I ought to regret if my adventurous service is ending, for another reason. I am evidently the child of a more heathen day than my dear wife and the saintly to whom her life most naturally belongs. But, in my coarser way – while I am for Good's sake spending my time among rude risks – I think I lift my heart as high to heaven as theirs. This is the discipline adapted for my nature, and I should have more of it. I should live in the stone fortress on the Rocks of the moon till the "change of some kind comes over me."– Now, I am but on the *mournful journey,* through the wild tangled paths of the snow clad valleys.

---

[28] Editor Winther's insertion.

[29] The omission here and those later in this diary were made by Dr. Winther. We have quoted here the entire extract that he gives.

[30] Col. Kane's brother, the arctic explorer, whom he now appreciated more than ever.

– This passage of my darling's book came into my mind on Thursday, just after I had recovered the trail and saw the storm approaching – the *magical* storm I called it – which soon broke on me in such wicked blindness.– Until it compelled an active struggle with the danger it threatened it was a grand & solemn enactment productive of the highest poetical impression.

Doing nothing now which it will interest anyone to read the record of – it is time that I shd. like others make entries in my Diary. Well, Monday & Tuesday [March 29 and 30] have been devoted to tasks connected with striking the tents for a removal from Camp Scot to Camp Bridger – and running conversation with the Governor.– (protracted to 12 last night). He will go with me to the Salt Lake. Identified as Robt. Williams,[31] best preacher & Oath ready. In the evening a good dip. . .

WEDNESDAY Mar. 31. Called on Col. Johnston and endeavored to induce him to review his decision respecting the mails.[32] Gave him my mind also about the Indian matter.[33] When he told me what he had said to Little Soldier, congratulated him at not having given that Little Traitor any thing to misrepresent in a garbled form as he undoubtedly wd. otherwise to his friends the Mormons. At which understood thrust he winced. All civil however. . .

THURSDAY APRIL 1. *Draughted letter to President.* . . And with this entry I close this book – which if anyone as young as I was 10 years ago could read and

---

[31] Before he actually goes, he decides to proceed in his official capacity as Governor.

[32] The mail to Utah had been stopped.

[33] It was charged that the troops and Indian Agent Hurt had endeavored to turn the Indians against the Mormons.

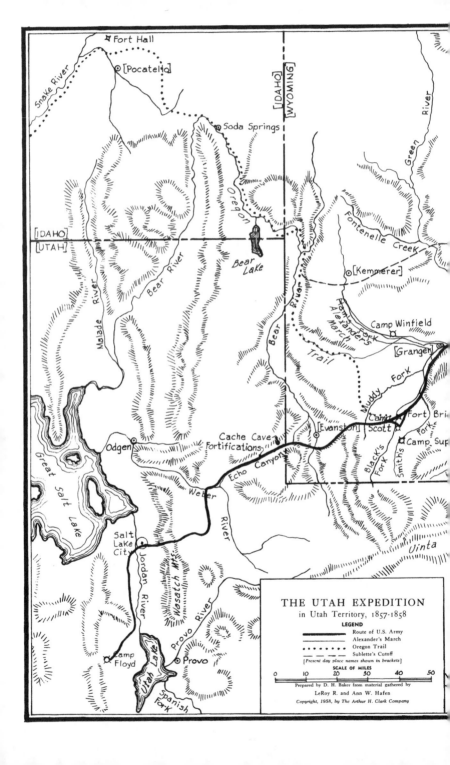

THE UTAH EXPEDITION
in Utah Territory, 1857-1858

LEGEND

⎯⎯⎯⎯⎯ Route of U.S. Army
⎯ ⎯ ⎯ Alexander's March
• • • • • Oregon Trail
⎯ · ⎯ · Sublette's Cutoff
[Present day place names shown in brackets]

SCALE OF MILES
0   10   20   30   40   50

Prepared by D. H. Baker from material gathered by

LeRoy R. and Ann W. Hafen

Copyright, 1958, by The Arthur H. Clark Company

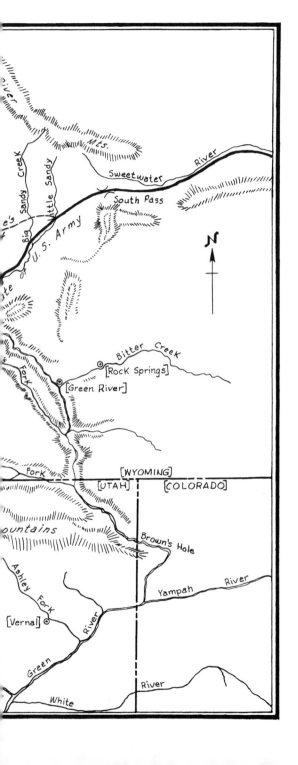

understand – understand what thoughts were in my mind when some remarks were made in it, what when the many more were omitted concerning things better meriting remembrance but which could not be trusted to it[34] – I think that too truthful picture of a passage of hours life – in one man's life and a great nation's history wd overpower him & surely he wd break his heart or he wd blaspheme.

17. REQUEST FOR EQUIPMENT AND SUPPLIES FOR THE TRIP TO SALT LAKE CITY[35]

EXECUTIVE OFFICE, NEAR CAMP SCOTT

COL. A. S. JOHNSTON   3 April, 1858

SIR: I respectfully request that you will order the proper officers to furnish me with the property and other articles contained in the above schedule and oblige,   Respectfully yrs. &c.   A CUMMING

P.S. In addition to the mules required by me, Col. Kane desires that Col. Johnston will give the necessary orders which will enable him to receive his own horse and mule now in the general herd. at the same time I am desirous of leaving Camp at nine o'clk on Monday morning [April 5th] next. Please advise me whether it will be necessary to send for the Commissary stores today, & also whether I am sufficiently explicit. I am &c &c.   A. CUMMING

List of Quarter Master's property required for contemplated expedition to G.S. Lake City, alluded to in preceding letter of Col. Johnston.

Eight Strong Mules.
Four setts Harness for light sp. wagon.

---

[34] The army distrust of Kane made it inexpedient for him to commit to paper much of his thoughts, feelings, and intentions.

[35] Cumming papers, Duke University.

One light spring wagon.
Two grease buckets with grease.
One watering bucket.
Ten Picket Ropes.
Ten iron Picket Pins.

Commissary Stores Required.

100 lbs white sugar
100 lbs Coffee
20 lbs Rice
25 lbs Beef
10 lbs Candles

A. CUMMING, GOVERNOR

18. GOVERNOR CUMMING REPORTS HIS RECEPTION [36]

EXECUTIVE OFFICE, G.S.L. CITY, U.T.
15th April 1858

COL. A. S. JOHNSTON,

SIR: I left camp on the 5th inst. en route to this city, in accordance with a determination communicated to you on the 3d inst., accompanied by Col. Kane, as my guide, and two servants. Arriving in the vicinity of the Spring, which is on this side of the "Quaking Asp" hill, after night, Indian camp fires were discovered on the rocks, overhanging the valley. We proceeded to the Spring, and after disposing of the animals, retired from the trail beyond the mountain. We had reason to congratulate ourselves upon having taken this precaution, as we subsequently ascertained that the country lying between your outposts and the Yellow is infested by hostile renegades and outlaws from various tribes. I was escorted from "Bear River Valley" to the western

[36] Cumming's Letter-press book (Duke University); and also printed in *Doc. 2*, pp. 72-73. The Governor's subsequent actions are traced in Part X, which follows.

end of "Echo Canon," the journey for the most part being performed after night. It was about eleven O'clk, p.m. when I arrived at "Weber Station." I have been every where recognized as the Governor of Utah, and so far from having encountered insults or indignities, I am gratified in being able to state to you that in passing through the settlements, I have been universally greeted with such respectful attentions as are due to the representative of the Executive authority of the U.S. in this Territory.

Near the "Warm Springs" at the line dividing Great Salt Lake and Davis Counties, I was honored with a formal and respectful reception by many gentlemen, including the Mayor and other municipal officers of the city, and by them escorted to lodgings previously provided. The mayor occupied a seat in my carriage.

Ex-Governor Brigham Young paid me a call of ceremony, as soon as I was sufficiently relieved from the fatigue of my mountain journey to receive company. In subsequent interviews with the Ex-Governor, he has evinced a willingness to afford me every facility which I may require for the efficient performance of my administrative duties. His course, in this respect, meets, I fancy, with the approval of a majority of this community. The Territorial seal with other public property has been tendered me by Wm Hooper, Esqr., late Acting Secretary pro. tem.

I have not yet examined the subject critically, but apprehend that the records of the U.S. Courts, territorial library, and other public property are unimpaired.

Having entered upon the performance of my official duties, in this city, it is probable that I will be detained for some days in this part of the Territory.

I respectfully call your attention to a matter which demands our serious consideration. Many acts of depredation have been recently committed by Indians upon the property of the inhabitants, one in the immediate vicinity of this city.

Believing that the Indians will endeavour to sell the stolen property at or near the camp, I herewith enclose the Brand Book (incomplete) and Memoranda (in part) of stock, lost by citizens of Utah, since Feby 25th 1858, and two letters addressed to me on the same subject by Wm H. Hooper, Esqr., late Acting Secretary pro. tem. which may enable you to secure the property and punish the thieves.

With feelings of profound regret I have learned that Agent Hurt is charged with having incited to acts of hostility the Indians in Uintah valley. I hope that Agent Hurt will be able to vindicate himself from the charges contained in the enclosed letter from Wm Hooper, late Sec. pro tem. yet they demand thorough investigation.

I shall probably be compelled to make a requisition upon you for a sufficient force to chastise the Indians alluded to. Since I desire to avoid being compelled to call out the militia for that purpose.

Very respectfully,   Yr obt servant

A CUMMING
Govr Utah Ty.

P.S. The gentlemen who are entrusted with this note, Mr. John B. Kimbal, & Mr. Fay Worthing, are engaged in mercantile pursuits here, and are represented to be gentlemen of the highest respectability. They have no connection with the church.

Should you deem it advisable or necessary, you will

please send any communication intended for me by them. I beg leave to commend them to your confidence and courtesy. They will probably return to the city in a few days. They are well known to Messrs Gilbert, Perry and Barry, with whom you will please communicate.

Very respectfully   A. CUMMING   Govr.

[Colonel Kane remained in Utah for more than a month. He witnessed the general exodus of the Mormons to the south, of which more will be said later. Kane accompanied Governor Cumming to Utah Valley, and upon their return journey they met 800 wagons and numerous herds of cattle and sheep between Springville and Salt Lake City.[37]

On May 13 Kane and Cumming left Salt Lake City on their return to Fort Bridger.[38] From this point Kane continued eastward, accompanied by a Mormon escort. His arrival at the Missouri River is reported in the following document.]

19. COLONEL KANE RETURNS TO THE STATES [39]

Today, (June 8) Col. Kane, the special agent of the President to the Mormons, with an escort of five men, viz: Maj. Howard Egan, and Messrs. Murdock, West, Knowlton, Van Ettan, and Worthing, arrived at Florence, N.T., only 23 days out, having started on the 13th ult. Col Kane is bearer of important dispatches from Brigham Young and Gov. Cumming, to the authorities at Washington, and starts in continuation

[37] Journal History, *op. cit.,* under date of May 6, 1858.

[38] *Ibid.,* May 13.

[39] The *Crescent City Oracle* (Council Bluffs, Iowa), June 11, and reprinted in the *Deseret News,* July 21, 1858.

The Journal History of May 31st records the arrival of W. S. Godbe and John Hunt at Provo, having brought a trunk and sack from San Bernardino for Col. Kane. They had made the round trip in 20 traveling days, the "quickest trip on record," but did not arrive until after Col. Kane had started on his trip eastward. The baggage items were later sent after the Colonel.

of his journey to-morrow. We visited Col. Kane today, and conversed freely with himself and his party and have learned full particulars in regard to the state of affairs in the West. From his long and arduous travels and exposure to some five months of the worst season of the year, the Col. is in delicate health, and somewhat worn and indisposed, yet seems cheerful and patient, and shows himself as, not only a humane man and a philanthropist, but an intelligent gentleman.

The Col. crossed over from California in the winter and after a short stay at Salt Lake City, and having a talk with Brigham, proceeded to Camp Scott where he staid for some time, returning with Gov. Cuming, who had received invitation to come into Salt Lake City and assume the responsibilities of his office. After proceeding a short distance they were stopped by a large armed force of Mormons, who, after being informed who they were, escorted them into the city, where they were received kindly by the people, who honored them with music, feasting, and every kind attention. Brigham gave over to Gov. Cuming the gubernatorial authority, books, papers, &c. The Gov. examined the court records, library, and other public property, papers and records, and to his astonishment every thing was found and in their place and perfect order, and not destroyed as had been reported and sworn to by the rascally officials who formerly returned and succeded in getting up this difficulty. A great number of families had gone and were still starting South, in anticipation of allowing the troops to come in, and thereby avoiding a collision with the Government.

The women and children had nearly all left the city and settlements north, but their destination southward

was a secret the party could not penetrate – some con-
jectured they would go to Mexico, Sonora, or the
valleys to the interior, to the south, they have recently
been exploring where sugar, cotton, rice and vines
grow profusely. The governor followed in the route of
the emigration, some 50 miles southward, overtook
large companies and desired them to return to their
houses, farms and homes, and although the Mormons
everywhere treated them respectfully and kindly, they
were firm, kept their own secrets, and moved on, the
watchword being "to the south." From all that could
be gathered, it seemed that the Mormons had determined to emigrate in mass from the valleys of Utah
rather than come in contact with the troops and authority of their own nation and country, and for their
loyalty to the American flag they would once again
leave their homes, firesides and possessions – as far as
his power extended the Governor offered overtures of
peace and desired that the emigration be arrested – and
Col. Kane, with an escort, was immediately despatched
to Washington with important business, touching the
settlement of difficulties. They all left Great Salt Lake
City on the 13th ult., arriving at Camp Scott on the
16th, where they found the army nearly destitute of the
means of subsistence, having but ten days short rations
in store, and soldiers very much dissatisfied, and many
deserting. General Johnston seemed in bad humor
towards the Governor and mankind generally, at the
peaceful indications being made. . . Tonight the
Col. gives the members of his party a supper, with kind
expressions of his gratitude for their attention and
watchfulness over him on so long and toilsome a
journey – dismissing all but Major Egan, who accom-

panies him to Washington. . . Col. Kane speaks highly of the manner in which he was received by Brigham and the Mormons, and the kindness and hospitality of the people there. Col. Kane is entitled to much credit for the daring perseverance and energy evinced in making this lengthened journey in mid winter; and we congratulate him and the country generally upon the successful result of his mission.– *Crescent City Oracle,* June 11.

20.   THOMAS L. KANE ARRIVES HOME [40]

Arrival of Col. Thomas L. Kane.– This gentleman – the self-appointed Peace Commissioner to the Mormons – arrived at his home in this ward, on the evening of June 18, in buoyant spirits and hearty good health, after one of the most romantic, dangerous and successful expeditions on record. He proceeded to Washington, on the 19th, with dispatches from Gov. Cumming for the Government.   *Germantown Telegraph,* Phila., June 23.

21.   BRIGHAM YOUNG'S LETTER OF APPRECIATION TO KANE [41]

G.S.L. CITY, U.T.   Jany. 14th 1859

COL. THOMAS L. KANE

MY DEAR FRIEND: Though having nothing direct from you, yet I feel to improve the opportunity of private conveyance.

We have thus far passed the ordeal without being forced into a collision, or even an outward quarrel with our enemies; although a few have spared no pains to involve us therein. But the Lord has frustrated and

---

[40] *Germantown Telegraph* (Penn.), June 23, 1858.

[41] Letter reproduced in Winther, *op. cit.,* pp. 59-62.

thwarted their purposes, and left them to sip of their own folly. . .

I am happy to learn, tho' through an indirect source, that you have recovered your health, and sincerely hope that you are quite yourself again. . .

You, Colonel, are daily and hourly remembered by us all in our supplications to the throne of power, and in the domestic circle. We shall ever appreciate the good, the generous, the energetic and talented little Col. . . Excuse me Col., and do not feel that I am intruding, knowing your views are so different from ours,[42] as I express not only my own, but the sentiments of all around me – those and many, very many more than you associated with while we were favored with your presence in this so far distant retreat. . .

May the God of Abraham bless you Col.; your dear wife and children; your Mother and all your reverend Father's family, with all that pertain to you and them; and may you rejoice continually in the prosperity and success which shall attend all your efforts, and the Holy One of Israel guard and protect you from every evil.

The health of my self, family and friends generally is good.

Sincerely and truly your friend,   BRIGHAM YOUNG

---

[42] This would seem to refute the frequently repeated statement that Kane was a Mormon.

X

Governor Cumming's Reports
and Correspondence

For chief executive of Utah Territory, President James Buchanan chose Alfred Cumming to replace Brigham Young. Mr. Cumming, a native of Georgia, had recently been Superintendent of Indian Affairs at St. Louis, with jurisdiction over the Upper Missouri and the Upper Platte and Arkansas Agencies.[1]

Governor Cumming proved to be a good choice for a difficult position. A man of character and resolution, he was to chart an independent course between the pressures exerted by the military on one hand, and the Mormons on the other.

The actions and opinions of Governor Cumming are well exhibited in his reports and letters. The fine collection of his papers, carefully preserved and arranged at Duke University, were graciously placed at the disposal of the editors by the University.

Governor Cumming set out from Fort Leavenworth on September 17th, with an escort headed by Captain

---

[1] Alfred Cumming was born in Augusta, Georgia, Sept. 4, 1802, of a socially and politically prominent family. He was mayor of Augusta in 1839. He was sutler with Scott's army in the War with Mexico. In the 1850s he was Indian Agent on the upper Missouri. After his governorship in Utah he returned to Georgia and remained in retirement. *Dictionary of American Biography* (N.Y., Charles Scribner's Sons, 1930), IV, pp. 592-93 and the sources there cited.

The extensive collection of Cumming papers at Duke University was made available by gracious Miss Mattie Russell, Curator of Manuscripts.

St. George Cooke.[2] He reached Fort Laramie October
23rd and arrived at Camp Scott, near Fort Bridger, on
November 19th, after enduring the severe storm that
nearly paralyzed the military expedition.

1. GOVERNOR CUMMING TO BRIGHAM YOUNG [3]

GREEN RIVER COUNTY, NEAR FT. BRIDGER
Utah Terr. 21st Nov. 1857

To BRIGHAM YOUNG Ex-Gov. of Utah Terr.

Sir: On the 11th July, 1857, I was appointed by
the President to be Governor of this Territory.[4]

Since my arrival within the limits of the Territory,
I regret to have found that many acts of violence have
been committed on the highways, in the destruction &
robbing of property belonging to the United States.
These acts which indicate that the Territory is in a
state of rebellion, are ascribed, how truly I do not
know, to yourself.

A proclamation, purporting to have issued from you,[5]
and papers signed by your authority found upon the

---

[2] Col. Johnston offered Cumming the choice of an escort under Cooke, or to
accompany the colonel commanding (Johnston). The Governor's decision to
go with Capt. Cooke and thus be a little more independent of the military
leadership may have offended Col. Johnston and may have contributed to the
later friction that developed between the two men.

[3] This is the first letter in the Letter-press Book kept by Cumming as
Governor. The Governor's letter-press books and other papers were ex-
amined by the present editors at Duke University in February, 1957. The
University then permitted these papers to be microfilmed for the Brigham
Young University Library.

[4] The original of the official appointment is in the Cumming papers at
Duke University. Also, the oath of office taken at St. Louis, July 27, 1857,
and renewed before Judge D. R. Eckels, Chief Justice of the U.S. Supreme
Court of Utah at Eckelsville, Green River County, Feb. 2, 1858.

A U.S. Treasury Department letter to Cumming of Sept. 10, 1857, says the
Governor's salary is $2500 per year, starting from the date of his commission,
but that none was to be paid until he entered upon his duties in the Territory. This condition may be one of the reasons for the early setting up of
the Territorial government at Camp Scott.

[5] Brigham Young's Proclamation of Sept. 15, printed above, in Part III.

person of Joseph Taylor,[6] have been submitted to my inspection. The matter contained in these papers authorizes and commands violent & treasonable acts; acts tending to the disruption of the peace of the Territory, and which subjects their actors to the penalties accorded to traitors.

If these papers referred to, be not authentic, I trust you will promptly disavow them.

I herewith enclose a copy of my Proclamation to the People of Utah Territory.

You will oblige me by acknowledging the receipt of this by the returning messenger.

I am, Sir, very respectfully,   Yrs. &c. &c. &c.

A. CUMMING

2. GOVERNOR CUMMING'S PROCLAMATION TO THE PEOPLE OF UTAH [7]

GREEN RIVER COUNTY, NEAR FORT BRIDGER,
Utah Territory, 21st November, 1857

On the 11th of July, 1857, the President appointed me to preside over the executive department of this Territory. I arrived at this point on the 19th of this month, and shall probably be detained some time, in consequence of the loss of animals during the recent snow storm. I will proceed at this point to make the preliminary arrangements for the temporary organization of the territorial government.

Many treasonable acts of violence having been committed by lawless individuals, supposed to have been countenanced by the late executive, such persons are in a state of rebellion. Proceedings will be instituted against them in a court organized by Chief Justice

---

[6] Major Joseph Taylor was captured and on him were found Gen. Wells' instructions relative to the destruction of U.S. army supplies, etc. This is reproduced in Part IV, document 19.

[7] Printed in *Doc. 71, op. cit.,* pp. 75-76.

Eckels, held in this county, which will supersede the necessity of appointing a military commission for the trial of such offenders. It is my duty to enforce unconditional obedience to the Constitution, to the organic laws of the Territory, and to all the other laws of Congress applicable to you. To enable me to effect this object, I will, in the event of resistance, rely, first upon a *posse comitatus* of the well disposed portion of the inhabitants of this Territory, and will only resort to a military *posse* in case of necessity. I trust that this necessity will not occur.

I come among you with no prejudices or enmities, and, by the exercise of a just and firm administration, I hope to command your confidence. Freedom of conscience, and the use of your own peculiar mode of serving God, are sacred rights guarantied by the Constitution, with which it is not the province of the government, or the disposition of its representatives in this Territory, to interfere.

In virtue of my authority as commander-in-chief of the militia of this Territory, I hereby command all armed bodies of individuals, by whomsoever organized, to disband and return to their respective homes. The penalty of disobedience to this command, will subject the offenders to the punishment due to traitors.

A. CUMMING,
Governor of Utah Territory

3. GOVERNOR CUMMING
TO SECRETARY OF STATE LEWIS CASS [8]

CAMP SCOTT, UTAH TERRITORY 28th Nov. 1857

SIR: Lieut. Col. Cooke, commanding the escort of the civil officers of Utah, formed a junction with the

---

[8] Cumming Letter-press Book.

army on the 19th instant at this point, which is little more than one hundred miles from Salt Lake City. On the 20th I had an interview with Colonel A. S. Johnston, Commanding, on the subject of future movements, who informed me that he could not for the present advance beyond this Camp (near Bridger) in consequence of the loss of animals during the snow storms encountered near Green River and its tributaries.

Under existing circumstances I will remain with the command, lest by advancing I might retard rather than promote the public interest.

New developments will shape my future action.

I am accompanied by Sec. Hartnell, Chief Justice Eckels, Dist Atty Hockaday, Marshal Dotson, Supt. Forney, Agent Hurt, & Postmaster Morell.[9]

It is much to be regretted that the associate Judges have not arrived.

A proclamation, purporting to have emanated from the late Governor, a commission to Joseph Taylor signed D. H. Wells, and various depositions taken by Judge Eckels, all exhibit a rebellious spirit on the part of the leaders of the people, and the audacious acts of violence committed on the highways, plainly indicate that no inconsiderable portion of the masses sympathize with the insane movements of their leaders.

I will use all honorable means in my power for the suppressing this effort of deluded fanatics to disturb the peace of our country.

I am satisfied in my judgment that the territory is now in a state of rebellion, and I would gladly receive from the President such orders and instructions as will distinctly define my military rights and duties. if it

---

[9] The other Judges, John Cradlebaugh and Charles E. Sinclair, were to come later.

prove necessary that the Governor, ex officio commander in chief of the militia of Utah Territory should be associated with a mixed (?) [10] command at war with rebels.

On the 21st inst I addressed a communication to the People of Utah, and a letter to Brigham Young, Esq., late Gover copies of which are herewith submitted to your inspection.

Chief Justice Eckels will organize a court in this country, for the trial of such cases as may properly come before it. If in consequence of our great remoteness we shall be delayed in subduing the rebellious spirit, it may be well to consider the propriety of modifying the powers of the Executive, and Judges, in relation to the establishing a seat of Government, places of holding courts, &c. &c.

Since my arrival here, I am, if possible, more satisfied that a secret service fund ought to be placed at the command of the Governor or somebody else. It also seems to me important that the arrangement for funds for the Marshal should be changed. Would it not be well to give him a liberal fixed salary, instead of fees, until quiet is restored. In this connection I will take the liberty of suggesting, that if the President is satisfied with the character of the parties appointed to office in this Territory, it may be well to consider the propriety of calling upon Congress to increase their compensation, as the present arrangement is rather too strong a draught upon their patriotism to be permanent.

I am, Sir, respectfully, Yr. obt. servant,

A. CUMMING Gov. Utah Ter.

---

[10] Not decipherable.

4. GOVERNOR CUMMING TO SECRETARY CASS [11]

CAMP SCOTT, UTAH TER.   13 Dec. 1857

SIR: The causes alluded to in my note of the 28th Nov. continue to paralyse the military movements of the army. Since my arrival I have endeavoured to re-establish the authority of law, by the organization in this (Green River) County of a court, and by other means which seem most conducive to that end.

We continue to be almost entirely isolated from the population of the Territory.

I herewith enclose a note received by the officer in command from the late Governor of the Territory. It abounds, as you will perceive, with evidences of the same tone of mind, which characterized former communications from him to Col Alexander, whilst that gentleman remained in Command. Copies of the papers above referred to, were transmitted by General Johnston to the Commander in Chief, Lt. Gen. Scott, without having been submitted to me. Should you deem it desirable to call upon Genl. Scott for those papers, they can be designated as follows:

Col. Alexander to Brigham Young Oct. 2d, 10th, 12th, 18th, 19th & Nov. 1st.[12]

Brigham Young to Col. Alexander Oct. 7th, 14th, 16th, 28th.[13]

D. H. Wells order to Joseph Taylor, Oct. 4th.[14]

Note to Col Alexander Oct. 8th.

John Taylor to Capt. Marcy, Oct. 21st.[15]

---

[11] Cumming Letter-press Book.

[12] The letters here listed are printed in *Doc. 71,* on the pages here enclosed in parentheses: Oct. 2 (p. 35), 12 (pp. 83-85), 18 (p. 85), 19 (p. 54), and Nov. 1 (p. 56).

[13] These letters are found in *Doc. 71* as follows: Oct. 7 (p. 47), 14 (pp. 48-50), 16 (pp. 50-54), and 28 (pp. 54-55).

[14] Found in *Doc. 71,* pp. 56-57.

[15] *Ibid.,* pp. 57-64.

The above enumerated letters were this morning exhibited to me for the first time. Considering them important as evidences of the character of public sentiment in the Territory, I regret that I have been deprived hitherto of an opportunity of furnishing the Department with copies. As soon as I received permission to peruse these papers in the Adj. General's Office,[16] I requested copies, which in due time will be forwarded by mail. I also requested the Adgt. Genl to retain the originals, subject to the order of the Court, in the event of their being required as evidence.

I am, Sir, &c. &c. &c.   A. CUMMING
                                          Govr. Utah Ty.

5. CUMMING REPORTS TO SECRETARY CASS [17]

CAMP SCOTT, GREEN RIVER CO.   UT. TERRY.
                                    5 Jany 1858

SIR: The present crippled condition of the military force in this valley, which arose from the great loss of animals, on their march through the mountains in November has compelled the officer in command to establish himself in winter quarters at this point.

Pending the present condition of affairs, I have deemed it inexpedient to advance toward Great Salt Lake City. The civil officers are therefore with *me* in this Territory.

As soon as I am in a condition to re-establish and maintain the authority of the U.S. there, I will proceed without delay to the city, and endeavour to restore order and obedience to the Law. I herewith enclose a communication purporting to be the Proclamation of

---

[16] This would be the office of F. J. Porter, Asst. Adjt. Gen. to Col. Johnston. Evidence of lack of cooperation between the civil and military authorities is here apparent.

[17] Cumming Letter-press Book.

Brigham Young, in which an attempt is made by assertions, and, the most puerile reasoning, to justify his own treasonable acts, and those of his associates in rebellion.[18]

William Stowell was arraigned yesterday, before the District Court for this County, under an indictment for treason. Stowell pleaded "not guilty," and on motion of his Counsel the case was postponed until next term, and he remanded.

The indictment under which he was arraigned, includes Brigham Young, Heber Kimball, D. W. Wells and others.[19]

Stowell will be made as comfortable as is compatible with imprisonment for an unbailable offence, and every legal facility be afforded him in securing counsel, witnesses, &c, &c.

The operations of the civil authorities here seem distasteful to the gentlemen constituting the Legislative Assembly. You will perceive by referring to their proceedings that they have endeavoured to disorganize this County by resolution.[20]

Respectfully, &c, &c.   A. CUMMING
                                Govr. Utah Terry.[21]

---

[18] Young's letter of Sept. 29, 1857, and his Proclamation of Sept. 15, which accompanied the letter. Printed in *Doc. 71*, pp. 33-35.

[19] For indictments of Young and others see documents 13 and 14, below.

[20] The legislature passed a resolution to disorganize Green River County, Utah.

[21] Some other letters of Cumming to Cass that follow in the Letter-press Book are not of sufficient importance to justify their reprinting here. However, we refer to the contents of some: In a letter of Jan. 24 Cumming says: I believe the opinion prevails among intelligent men, that Brigham Young & his associates will fight at as early a day as possible, with a view to anticipate the arrival of re-inforcements to this Command. Previous to their more open acts of hostility we shall doubtless be subjected to the annoyance of predatory parties." He also reports the departure of Hartnett, Sec. of Utah Terr., for St. Louis.

Cumming's letter to Cass of Feb. 6 reports that all the civil offices of the

6. CUMMING REPORTS PRESENCE
OF COLONEL KANE [22]

CAMP SCOTT, UTAH TY.　24 March, 1858

HON LEWIS CASS
Secretary of State,　Washington, D.C.

SIR: A highly respectable gentleman arrived in this Camp a few days since from G.S.L. City. Whilst there he had several conversations with Brigham Young, and other prominent persons. The gentleman referred to addressed a letter by this mail to another gentleman in Washington, which will be exhibited to you.

The weather is becoming very mild. The snow will soon cease to be an impediment to mountain travel.

It is my present intention in a short time to visit G.S.L. City, where I can have communication with the people before the army advances.[23] The other civil officers will await my return.

Very respectfully,　Yr. obt. servant

A. CUMMING,　Govr Utah Ty.

7. GOVERNOR CUMMING REPORTS
FROM SALT LAKE CITY [24]

EXECUTIVE OFFICE

G.S.L. City, Utah Ty.　May 2d 1858

HON. LEWIS CASS

SIR: You are aware that my contemplated journey was postponed in consequence of the snow on the moun-

---

Territory have been vacated by the incumbents. Another letter of Feb. 6 reports the Governor's appointment of David A. Barr as Justice of the Peace for Green River County.

Cumming's letter of March 22 to T. L. Kane is published above, as number 14 in Part IX.

[22] Cumming Letter-press Book.

[23] Here is indication that the Governor is planning to accompany Kane to Salt Lake City, although they do not leave until April 5th. Cumming's relations with Kane are presented above, in Part IX.

[24] Cumming Letter-press Book.

tains and in the canons, between Fort Bridger and this city. In accordance with the determination communicated in former notes, I left camp on the 5th April and arrived here on the 12th instant.

Some of the incidents of my journey are related in the annexed note addressed by me to Col. A. S. Johnston on the 15th April. . .[25]

This note omits to state that I met parties of armed men at Lost & Yellow Creeks, as well as at Echo Canon. At every point, however, I was recognized as the Governor of Utah, and received with a military salute. When it was arranged with the Mormon officer in command of my escort that I should pass through Echo Canon, at night, I inferred that it was with the object of concealing the barricades and other defences. I was therefore agreeably surprised by an illumination in honor to me. The bonfires kindled by the soldiers from the base to the summit of the walls of the Canon, completely illuminated the valley, and disclosed the snow-covered mountains which surrounded us. When I arrived at the next station I found the emigrant road of the "Big Mountain," still impassable. I was able to make my way, however, down "Echo Canon."[26]

Since my arrival I have been employed in examining the records of the Supreme and District Courts, which I am now prepared to report as being perfect and uninjured. This will doubtless be acceptable information to those who have entertained any impression to the contrary.[27]

I have also examined the legislative records, and other books belonging to the office of the Secy of Utah,

[25] This letter of April 15 is reproduced above, in Part IX.

[26] This should be the canyon of Weber River, leading to Ogden.

[27] That the court records had been destroyed was a report frequently repeated.

which are in perfect preservation. The property return, though not made up in proper form, exhibits the public property for which the estate of A. W. Babbitt[28] is liable, that individual having died, whilst in the office of Secy of State for Utah. I believe that the books and charts, stationary and other property appertaining to the Surveyor General's office, will, upon examination be found in the proper place, except some instruments, which are supposed to have been disposed of by a person, who was temporarily in charge of the Office. I examined the property, but cannot verify the matter, however, in consequence of not having at my command, a schedule or property return.

The condition of the large and valuable territorial library also commanded my attention, and I am pleased in being able to report that Mr. W. C. Staines, the Librarian, has kept the books of records in most excellent condition. I will at an early day, transmit a catalogue of this library, and schedules of the other public property, in the certified copies of the Records of the Supreme and District Courts, exhibiting the character and amount of the public business last transacted in them.

On the 21st inst. I left Great Salt Lake City and visited Tuilla and Rush vallies, in the latter of which lies the Military Reserve, selected by Col. Steptoe.[29] I endeavoured to trace the lines upon the ground from field notes, which are in the Surveyor General's Office.

An accurate plat of the Reserve, as it has been measured off, will be found accompanying a commu-

---

[28] Babbitt had been killed, presumably by Indians, on his journey back to the States.

[29] Col. E. J. Steptoe had been appointed Governor of Utah, but did not qualify and assume the office.

nication, which I shall address to the Secretary of War upon this subject.

On the morning of the 24th inst, information was communicated to me, that a number of persons who were desirous of leaving the Territory, were unable to do so, and considered themselves to be unlawfully restrained of their liberty.

However desirous of conciliating popular opinion, I felt it incumbent on me to adopt the most energetic measures to ascertain the truth or falsehood of the statements. Postponing therefore a journey of importance, which I had in contemplation, to one of the settlements of Utah County, I caused public notice to be given immediately of my readiness to assist all persons, who were, or deemed themselves to be aggrieved, and on the ensuing day, which was Sunday, I requested the following notice to be read in my presence, to the people at the Tabernacle.

NOTICE

It has been reported to me that there are persons residing in this, and in other parts of the territory, who are illegally restrained of their liberty. It is therefore proper that I should announce that I assume the protection of all such persons, if any there be, and request that they will communicate to me their names and places of residence, under seal, through Mr. Fay Worthing, or to me in person during my stay in the city.

A. CUMMING, Govr. Utah Ty.

I have since kept my office open, at all hours of the day and night, and have registered no less than 56 men, 33 women, and 71 children as desirous of my protection and assistance in proceeding to the States.[30] The large majority of these people are of English birth, and

---

[30] The names of all these persons are given in the Gov. Cumming papers at Duke University.

state that they leave the congregation from a desire to improve their circumstances, and realize elsewhere more money by their labor. Certain leading men among the Mormons, have promised to furnish the flour, and assist them in leaving the country.

My presence at the meeting in the Tabernacle, will be remembered by me as an occasion of intense interest. Between three and four thousand persons were assembled for the purpose of public worship. The hall was crowded to overflowing; but the most profound quiet was observed when I appeared. President Brigham Young introduced me by name as the Governor of Utah, and I addressed the audience from the stand. I informed them that I had come among them to vindicate the national sovereignty; that it was my duty to secure the supremacy of the Constitution and the laws, that I had taken my oath of office to exact an unconditional submission on their parts to the dictates of the law. I was not interupted in a discourse of about thirty-five minutes duration. I touched, as I thought best, upon all the leading questions between them and the general government. I remembered that I had to deal with men embittered by the remembrance and [word omitted] of many real and some imaginary wrongs, but did not think it wise to withhold from them the entire truth. They listened respectfully to all that I had to say, approvingly even, I fancied, when I explained to them what I intended to be the character of my administration. In fact, the whole manner of the people was calm, betokening no consciousness of having done wrong, but rather as it were, indicating a conviction, that they had done their duty to their religious and to their country. I have observed that the Mormons profess to view the

Constitution as the work of inspired men, and respond with readiness to appeals for its support.

Thus the meeting might have ended but, after closing my remarks, I rose and stated that I would be glad to hear from any, who might be inclined to address me upon topics of interest to the community. This invitation brought forth in succession several powerful speakers, who evidently exercised great influence on the masses of the people. They harangued on the subject of the assassination of Joseph Smith, Junior, and his friends; the services, rendered by a Mormon battalion to an ungrateful country – their sufferings on "the plains," during their dreary pilgrimage to their mountain home, etc. etc. etc.

The Congregation became greatly excited, and joined the speakers in their intemperate remarks, exhibiting more frenzy than I had expected to witness among a people, who habitually exercise great self control.

A speaker now represented the federal government as desirous of needlessly "introducing the national troops into the Territory," whether a necessity existed for their employment to support the authority of the civil officers or not. The wildest uproar ensued. I was fully confirmed in my opinion that this people with their extraordinary religion and customs, would gladly encounter certain death, than be subjected to the mockery of a trial by a jury, composed of the followers of a camp. In my first address I had informed them that they were entitled to a trial by their peers, that I had no intention of stationing the army in immediate contact with their settlements, and that the military posse would not be resorted to until other means of arrest had been tried and failed. I found the greatest difficulty in explaining these points, so great was the excitement. Eventually, however, the efforts of Brigham Young were successful in calming the tumult, and restoring order before the adjournment of the meeting. It is proper that I should add that more than one speaker has since expressed his regret at having been betrayed into intemperance of language in my presence.

The President and the American people will learn with gratification the auspicious issue of our difficulties here. I regret the necessity which compels me to mingle with my congratulations the announcement of a fact, which will occasion you concern.

The people, including the inhabitants of this city, are removing from every settlement in the northern part of the territory. The roads are every where filled with wagons loaded with provisions and household furniture. The women and children, often without shoes or hats, are driving their flocks, they know not where. They seemed, not only resigned, but cheerful. "It is the will of the Lord," and they rejoice to exchange the comforts of home for the trials of the wilderness.[31]

---

[31] A policy of retreat instead of one of resistance was adopted by the Mormon leaders in March, 1858. It had been hinted at previously, to Captain Van Vliet in September, 1857, and on occasion subsequently. But now, in a council of the leaders on March 18, and by a general conference of the people on the 21st, it became the grand strategy. In early April many families from the northern settlements, with their teams and livestock were moving through Salt Lake City on the way south.– Journal History, March 21, 1858.

Mary Ann Young, a wife of Brigham Young, said: "I am very comfortably situated, but I would be sorry to think that one good brother's life was lost in defending my home. I would rather leave peaceably. We shall be innocent and God will bless us with his holy spirit and we shall be happy on the desert."– Journal History, March 23, 1858.

John R. Young, who traveled from California to Utah in April, began to see the effects of the exodus as far south as Parowan. "Horses, oxen and cows," he noted, "were harnessed or yoked to wagons and carts and one family by the name of Syphus was pulling their effects on a handcart with a

Their ultimate destination is not, I apprehend, definitely fixed upon.[32] "Going South," seems sufficiently

pair of yearling steers. Mothers and children walked along as merrily as if going to a corn husking; each family moving its little bunch of cows and flock of sheep, and all starting on the journey (that was never completed) to Sonora, in Mexico. At times we were compelled to drive our wagon for miles outside the beaten road. . ."– copied in the Journal History under date of Feb. 25, 1858.

George A. Smith in a letter of April 5, wrote: "It is a general time of health and everybody appears in good spirits. The people are vacating Salt Lake City and flying to the mountains. About three hundred families left last week, as it is understood here that the Government has ordered large reinforcements to Utah, for the extermination of the faithful, who will be found, probably (if found at all) in rocks and deserts, or, like the ancient saints, hid deep in dens and caves of the earth. . .

"I had hoped my family might have enjoyed a little rest and eaten the fruit of my little orchard, containing one hundred and fifty assorted trees, many of which are budded for fruit.

"I have been driven from Missouri, where I left a good property and planted fruit trees for somebody else to eat. I passed through the same ordeal in Illinois. I preferred leaving my homes to renouncing my religion. The government expelled me from Nebraska, although they were well aware of my intention to leave in a few months, for the mountains; and I can go again and again, until death shall furnish me a quiet resting place, should our insane countrymen continue to trample the sacred rights of freemen, guaranteed by the institutions and blood of their fathers, under their feet with impunity."

[32] The Mormons looked about for a place to go. On April 7 President Young issued an order to W. H. Dame of Parowan to raise sixty or seventy men in his district, to fit them out with tools, seed, grain, and water barrels and to explore the desert to the west and north. The expedition failed to find a suitable place for settlement.– Journal History, April 7 and 25, 1858.

Proposals for migration of the Mormons to Central America were made by representatives who came from New York. John R. Young was guide for a Mr. Cooper and associates on their way from California to Utah. He reports: "At last we reached Provo, where the Church leaders had made their temporary headquarters. In the evening I visited Pres. Young and made known to him the object of Mr. Cooper's visit. Two days later he gave audience to Messrs. Cooper, Mathewson, and Hardin. They held a lengthy conversation in which Mr. Cooper, in glowing language, told the Mormon leader what a splendid opportunity it was for them to lead their people to Central America, where, he said, they could found an empire that would crown the stirring life of Brigham Young and his associates with endless glory.

"I can still hear the ringing words of Brigham Young's answer: 'Gentle-

definite for most of them, but many believe that *their ultimate destination is Sonora.**

men,' said he, 'God Almighty made these everlasting hills to be bulwarks of liberty for the oppressed and downtrodden of the earth. We shall never leave here and go to a country where we should have six hundred miles of sea coast to defend and where any nation at their pleasure could send war ships to bombard our cities. Furthermore, gentlemen, should the desire ever come we have hundreds of boys just as capable of going to Nicaragua and of taking possession and holding it too, as Gen. Walker of New York. Gentlemen, you have your answer.' "– Journal History, Feb. 25, 1858.

In the Journal History of May 24, 1858, is another account of the meeting at Provo of John B. Cooper and James M. Harbin with Young and other Mormon leaders to consider the proposition from Col. Kinney to sell to the Mormons the mosquito country in Central America. Cooper had power of attorney from Kinney to deal regarding the region. He brought a book describing the country. Young said the United States would be annexing the country and added: "If Kinney owned all Central America and would give it to me for nothing I would not go there. I am satisfied the climate is unhealthy." Young said, "the political pulse of the United States is to annex the whole world." He also said, "we will not move from this territory as we are just where we want to be, and where we intend to stay, and all hell cannot move us from here; but I can settle the Mosquito coast from other countries so fast that it would make them howl from north to south."

On the 25th Cooper and Harbin left an official document for President Young, containing a proposition to sell Col. Kinney's claim to 30,000,000 acres on the Mosquito Coast at ten cents per acre.– Journal History, May 25.

On May 30 Messrs. Clarkson and Booky of San Francisco called on President Young. "Clarkson said the proposition to sell the Mosquito Coast was known to President Buchanan, and all operations of the army were suspended until the results of Mr. Cooper's mission was ascertained, as it was expected that we would accede to the proposition, he believed that the government would give us from 12 to 13 million dollars and pay our transportation, as they had spent eight million dollars now, to no purpose in the war against us.

"Clarkson said it was the belief of the administration that if the authorities of the Church would leave this country that about one-third of the people would follow; the rest would settle down here and be good citizens. Mr. Clarkson was told that if we purchased the Mosquito Country we would send the poor there first. He said he thought we would send the rich first and then the poor could not get away."– Journal History, May 30, 1858.

* On the aftn of Sunday last, President Brigham Young is reported to have spoken in the Tabernacle as follows: "I have a good mind to tell a secret right here; I believe I will tell it anyhow. They say there is a fine country down there; *Sonora* is it, is that your name for it? Do not speak of this out of doors, if you please." [Cumming's note.]

Young, Kimball, and most of the influential men have left their commodious mansions, without apparent regret, to lengthen the long train of wanderers. The masses every where announce to me that the torch will be applied to every house indiscriminately, throughout the country, so soon as the troops attempt to cross the mountains.

I shall follow these people, and attempt to rally them. Numbers whom I have met appear to be in dread of the Indians, whom the distressed conditions of the whites has encouraged to commit extensive depredations. I may at least quiet the apprehensions of these persons, and induce some of them to return. A military force could overwhelm most of these poor people, involving men, women and children in a common fate. but there are among the Mormons many brave men, accustomed to arms and to horses, men who would fight desperately as guerrillas, and if these settlements are destroyed, will subject the country to an expensive and protracted war, without any compensatory results. They will, I am sure, submit to *trial* by their *peers,* but they will not "brook the idea of trials by juries composed of teamsters and followers of the Camp, nor of an army encamped in their cities, or dense settlements.

I have adopted means to recal the few remaining Mormons in arms, who have not yet, (it is said) complied with my request to withdraw from the Canons and the Eastern frontier. I have also taken measures to protect the buildings, which have been vacated in the northern settlements. I am sanguine that I will be able to save a great deal of the valuable improvements. I shall leave this city for the South tomorrow. After I have finished my business there, I shall return as soon as possible to the army, to complete the arrangements which will enable me before long, I trust, to announce that the road between California & Missouri may be travelled with perfect security by teams and emigrants of every description. I shall restrain all operations of the military for the present, which will enable me to receive from the President additional instructions, if he deems it necessary to give them. Very respy Yr obt servant, A. CUMMING Govr of Utah.

8. GOVERNOR CUMMING TO SECRETARY CASS [33]

EXECUTIVE OFFICE 12th May 1858
G.S.L. City Utah Terry.

HON LEWIS CASS

SIR: I have returned from the South after having seen and conversed with large numbers of the Mormons, who are journeying in that direction. I have reason to hope that my intercourse with these persons has contributed to allay fears on their part which are perhaps unreasonable. I regret to have been an eyewitness, however, to scenes of great trial and suffering.

I have the gratification of authorizing you to announce that the road is now open between Missouri and California, and that emigrants and others, adopting the usual precautions for their safety against Indians, may pass through Utah Territory, without hindrance or molestation. Parties will do well, however, to report themselves at Bridger, where any information which I may be possessed of, of importance for their guidance will be communicated to them.

I am, Sir, &c. &c. A. CUMMING, Governor

---

[33] Cumming Letter-press Book.

9. GOVERNOR CUMMING TO PRESIDENT YOUNG[34]

G.S.L. CITY,   May 12, 1858

MY DEAR SIR: I regret to be obliged to answer your letter of the 6th inst. in haste. I would thank you for the complimentary notice of myself, which it contains, but more for the tender you make of your continued exertions to advance the public good. I know the value of your services and exhort you patriotically to persevere.

I trust particularly that you will succeed in persuading those who respect your opinion, and who are moving south, that there is no ground for the apprehension, which they appear to entertain. You may assure them that no effort on my part will be spared to restrain the troops at Bridger from a further advance, until a reply is received by me to dispatches, which I have transmitted from this city to the secretary of State at Washington.

I am sir, Very respectfully, Your obedient servant,
ALFRED CUMMING

10. GOVERNOR CUMMING TO JOHNSTON[35]

EXECUTIVE OFFICE, CAMP SCOTT, U.T.

21 May, 1858

BREV. BRIG. GENL. A. S. JOHNSTON,

SIR: After careful investigation, I am gratified in being able to inform you, that I believe, there is at present no organized armed force of its inhabitants in any part of this territory, with the exception of a small party, subject to my orders, in or near Echo Canon.

I therefore respectfully request that no hindrance

---

[34] Journal History of May 12, 1858.
[35] Cumming Letter-press Book. Gov. Cumming has returned to army headquarters at Camp Scott.

may hereafter be presented to the commercial, postal or social intercourse throughout the territory.

I am, Sir, very respectfully,   A. CUMMING
                                        Govr. Utah Ty.

11. GENERAL JOHNSTON TO CUMMING [36]

HEADQUARTERS, DEPARTMENT OF UTAH
Camp Scott, Utah Territory,   May 21, 1858

SIR: I have the honor to acknowledge the receipt of your letter of this date, and have to say in reply, that, with the assurance your excellency gives me of your "belief, after a careful investigation, that there is at present no organized armed force of its inhabitants in any part of this Territory," with the exception mentioned, it gives me great satisfaction to reply that the troops under my command will oppose no further obstruction to the carrying of the mails, or to the commercial pursuits, or to a free intercourse of the inhabitants of that Territory.

With great respect, your obedient servant
           A. S. JOHNSTON,   Colonel 2d Cavalry
        and Brevet Brigadier General, U.S. Army
                                      commanding

12. GOVERNOR CUMMING TO MARSHAL DOTSON [37]

EXECUTIVE OFFICE,   CAMP SCOTT   25th May, 1858
MR. DOTSON,

SIR: I have your note of this date before me.

Please inform me when and where the District Court of the United States in the First Judicial District of Utah Terry. will hold its next term.

In your communication you assert that this territory

---

[36] *Doc. 2, op. cit.,* (Ser. 998), p. 102.
[37] Cumming Letter-press Book, p. 49.

is now in a state of rebellion. What evidence have you that the *Government* considers it in a state of rebellion? Does not that branch of the government which is authorized to declare Utah in a "state of rebellion" permit Bernheisel to retain his seat in the house of Representatives as delegate from Utah?

I wish to call your attention to the following extract from my "Proclamation to the people of Utah, dated 21 Nov. 1857, "I will, in the event of resistance, rely, first, upon a posse comitatus of the well-disposed portion of the inhabitants of this Territory, and will only resort to a military posse in case of necessity."

Have you met with the "resistance" referred to in the above extract, which would render it necessary for me to employ the posse spoken of above?

I have yet to learn that you have met with such resistance in arresting "Brigham Young and sixty six others."[38] If I am mistaken, please inform me.

Yrs. &c.   A. CUMMING, Govr.

13. GOVERNOR CUMMING TO JOHNSTON [39]

Ex. OFFICE, NEAR CAMP SCOTT   25th May, 1858
GENL JOHNSTON,

SIR: Marshal P. K. Dotson has this day requested me to place such a possee under his command as will enable him to serve writs upon Brigham Young and sixty-six others indicted for treason and other felonies by the Grand Jury in Green River Co. Utah T. Please inform me whether you can furnish the military posse, if specifically demanded by Marshal P. K. Dotson.

Very respy &c &c.   A. CUMMING, Govr.

---

[38] See the two following documents.
[39] Cumming Letter-press Book, p. 50.

14. JOHNSTON REPLIES REGARDING A POSSE [40]

HEADQUARTERS, DEPARTMENT OF UTAH,
Camp Scott, U.T. May 26, 1858

HIS EXCELLENCY A. CUMMING,
Governor of Utah Territory

SIR: I have just received your letter of yesterday's date, and I have to say in reply that, should a requisition be made upon me by the civil authority for troops to be employed as a posse to serve writs upon Brigham Young and others, indicted for treason and other offences, I will not at this time be able to comply with such requirement.

With great respect, your obedient servant,

A. S. JOHNSTON, Colonel 2d cavalry
and Brevet Brigadier General U.S. Army
commanding.

15. GOVERNOR CUMMING'S PROCLAMATION OF PARDON [41]

To the inhabitants of Utah and others whom it may concern:

WHEREAS James Buchanan, President of the United States, at the city of Washington, the sixth day of April, eighteen hundred and fifty-eight, did by his proclamation offer to the inhabitants of Utah who submit to the laws a free and full pardon for all treasons and seditions heretofore committed; [42] and

WHEREAS The proffered pardon was accepted, with the prescribed terms of the proclamation, by the citizens of Utah;

---

[40] *Doc. 2,* p. 104.

[41] *Doc. 2,* p. 113. The speed with which he issued this (on June 14) would indicate his eagerness to restore peace and normalcy – and to do so ahead of the Peace Commissioners.

[42] The President's action for reconciliation and his tentative pardon of April 6th will be discussed in Part XI.

NOW THEREFORE I, Alfred Cumming, governor of Utah Territory, in the name of James Buchanan, President of the United States, do proclaim that all persons who submit themselves to the laws and to the authority of the federal government are by him freely and fully pardoned for all treasons and seditions heretofore committed. All criminal offences associated with or growing out of the overt acts of sedition and treason are merged in them, and are embraced in the "free and full pardon" of the President. And I exhort all persons to persevere in a faithful submission to the laws and patriotic devotions to the Constitution and government of our common country.

Peace is restored to our Territory.

All civil officers, both federal and territorial, will resume the performance of the duties of their respective offices without delay, and be diligent and faithful in the execution of the laws. All citizens of the United States in this Territory will aid and assist the officers in the performance of their duties.

Fellow citizens, I offer to you my congratulations for the peaceful and honorable adjustment of recent difficulties.

Those citizens who have left their homes I invite to return as soon as they can do so with propriety and convenience.

To all I announce my determination to enforce obedience to the laws, both federal and territorial.

Trespasses upon property, whether real or personal, must be scrupulously avoided.

Gaming and other vices are punished by territorial statutes with peculiar severity, and I commend the perusal of these statutes to those persons who may not have had an opportunity of doing so previously.

In testimony whereof I have hereunto set my hand and caused the official seal of the Territory to be affixed, at Great Salt Lake City, in the Territory of Utah, this fourteenth day of June, one thousand eight hundred and fifty-eight, and of the independence of the United States the eighty-second.

A. CUMMING

JOHN HARTNETT [HARTNELL], Secretary

[SEAL, By the Governor.]

16. GOVERNOR CUMMING TO JOHNSTON [43]

EX. OFFICE, G.S.L. CITY, U.T. 15 June, 1858

GEN. A. S. JOHNSTON,

SIR: I left Camp Scott on the 3d of June, and arrived here on the 8th inst., having been detained on the road by accidents to my wagons. On the 11th & 12th of June, a conference was held between the President & leaders of the Church of Latter-day Saints and the Peace Commission. I was present at the conference by invitation, and heard a statement made by President Young to the effect that he had evidence of your intentions to advance the army on the 14th or 15th of this month without waiting for communications from the Commissioners or myself.

To this statement I gave a prompt and positive denial; alledging that General Johnston would not violate a pledge made by him to the Commissioners and to myself on the 30th of May at Camp Scott.[44] Secy Hartnell left Fort Bridger on Friday the 11th

---

[43] Cumming Letter-press Book, p. 52.

[44] See Johnston's answer in the next document. In the *Deseret News* (VIII, pp. 75 and 96) account of the council of June 11-12 it is reported that Young told the Peace Commissioners and Cumming that he had information that Johnston was going to move before he heard from the Commissioners. "Gov. Powell assured Gov. Young that it would cost Johnston his commission if he should move without authority from them."

(being the first day of the Conference at G.S.L. City,) arrived here on the 13th inst. and to my great surprise informed me that you had requested him to inform the Commissioners and myself of your intention to take up the line of march for this city on the 15th of June.

As the time when this communication was made to Secretary Hartnell, the conference had only commenced, you could not therefore have received any communication from the Commissioners or myself. We should necessarily wait to know the result of the conference before communicating with you.

I earnestly request that you will make such disclosures as may be made without detriment to the public service which may enable me to reconcile this apparent discrepancy between my Statement and that recently communicated through Mr. Hartnell.

I am aware that you will probably have received communications from the Commissioners announcing the termination of the conference, previous to the day appointed for your departure from Camp, but this does not affect the question.

I stated to President Young that you were pledged not to march until you had received communications from the Commissioners or from myself, that you had told me that you would issue a proclamation setting forth your intentions. Now it is obvious, that without some explanation on your part, I may be suspected of duplicity in regard to my statement to President Young, and be compelled to resort to some means of defence & explanation. I must therefore endeavour to impress upon you the necessity of furnishing me with the desired information to combat the distrust which may otherwise arise in the minds of the People.

Very respectfully, &c.

A. CUMMING,   Gov Utah Tr.

17. JOHNSTON'S REPLY TO GOVERNOR CUMMING [45]

HEADQUARTERS DEPARTMENT OF UTAH
Camp on Yellow creek, U.T.,   June 19, 1858

SIR: Your letter of the 15th instant was received today. At the conference with the commissioners at your tent – it being understood that I could not commence the march from Fort Bridger before the arrival of the supplies, and that the preparation for the march, depending upon their arrival, could not probably be made before the 15th or 20th instant, and understanding from them that they believed before that time they would be able to ascertain the result of their mission – *I did say,* as represented by you, that "I would delay the march of the troops until I heard from them;" but by no means did I intend to give to what I said the binding force of a pledge, should it be in confliction with a good military reason for pursuing a different course, nor did I suppose the commissioners and yourself so understood it. As I used the language asserted by you to President Young, the distrust, if any is incited, should rest upon me; and I now disclaim any intention of misleading any one.

The instructions of the President to the commissioners were positive that the army should occupy the Territory of Utah, and my orders do not allow the discretion of making delay, unless reasons should be offered for so doing which should appear to me sufficiently cogent.

It was not foreseen by me that the supplies would arrive as soon as they did, and that the grass in every direction within convenient reach would be so rapidly consumed. The last circumstance alone made it neces-

---
[45] *Doc. 2,* pp. 116-17.

sary to move; and had it been expedient to halt, marching as slowly as it is necessary to do on account of the very large train indispensable at this distance from the source of supply, it I thought could easily be made known to me. It was designed by me, and I so informed you, that I would give notice of my march from Fort Bridger. But as commissioners were appointed to confer directly with the people, I did not deem a formal notice necessary, and thought the message sent by Mr. Hartnett would subserve every purpose.

I have the honor also to acknowledge the receipt of your excellency's letter of the 17th instant.[46] I beg leave to say in reference to the subjects mentioned that, in the execution of my orders, I have only to select suitable military sites for posts; such as are healthy and have good water, plenty of wood and grass.

It is not essential to a good selection that it should be contingent to a city or near any settlement, nor would it be desirable to those in command. In marching through any part of the Territory the greatest care will be taken that no one is improperly treated or injury to their property sustained.

The commissioners I understand intend to meet the army at the camp we expect to make between the two mountains. I would be glad, if you can do so, if you will make the visit with them, and to receive the information you have of different parts of the valley, which I am sure will be valuable to me.

With great respect, your obedient servant,

A. S. JOHNSTON,   Colonel 2d Cavalry
and Brevet Brigadier General U.S. Army,
Commanding

---

[46] This letter follows as the next document.

18. CUMMING TO JOHNSTON [47]

EX. OFFICE, G.S.L. CITY, U.T.

GEN. A. S. JOHNSTON,   17 June, 1858

SIR: I have this moment received your note of the 16th, covering your address to the people of Utah, under date of the 14th of June.[48] I will cause your address to be as generally circulated as circumstances will admit. The present excited condition of the public mind demands the utmost caution on your part in approaching the valley. The houses in this city and the northern settlements are closed and abandoned. The population has "gone South" with the exception of a small body of civil police. The fields and gardens are very insufficiently protected by fences. The grazing grounds or commons are indispensable to the comfort of the population. The introduction of masses of hired followers of your Camp, would cause unnecessary excitement. In short, with a full knowledge of the condition of affairs in the Territory, whilst I desire that you should continue your march, as soon as you are in possession of such facts as will enable you to select and occupy suitable camps, yet it is my duty to protect against your occupancy of positions in the immediate vicinity of this city or any other dense settlement of the population.

Should you resolve to act in opposition to my solemn protest you may be assured that it will result in disastrous consequences, such as will not meet the approval of our Government.

Respectfully, &c &c.   A. CUMMING   Gov of Utah

---

[47] Cumming Letter-press Book, p. 55.
[48] This Address to the People of Utah is reprinted in Part XI.

19. GOVERNOR CUMMING TO SECRETARY CASS [49]

EXECUTIVE OFFICES   G.S.L. CITY   UTAH TR.

18 June 1858

HON. LEWIS CASS,

SIR: The military peace commission arrived in this city a few days since, and held a conference on the 11th and 12th inst. with Brigham Young and other leaders of the Church. I was present at the conference by invitation.

The aspect of affairs remains as favorable as before the arrival of the Commission.[50]

At a conference with the commissioners and the officer in command at Camp Scott on the 30th May, it was my impression that General Johnston pledged himself not to march before the 20th June, at any rate, until he had heard from the Commissioners. Under that impression I communicated with Brigham Young.

At the conference on the 11th Young stated with much apparent warmth, that he had in his possession the evidence that the army would march on the 14th or 15th June. This statement I promptly contradicted. On the 13th I was notified that Genl Johnston would take up the line of march on the 15th June. The Genl was on Bear River and issued an address to the people of Utah on the 14th.

I regret the apparent discrepancy between my statement and the General's action, for such occurrences tend to diminish public confidence. I have written a formal note to the Commissioners requesting them to

---

[49] Cumming Letter-press Book, pp. 58-60.

[50] An inference that the Peace Commission was unnecessary and might have upset the peace arrangements.

inform me substantially their remembrances of this pledge of the General. The gentlemen have deferred answering this note for several days. I have since written to Genl Johnston, requesting him to give me such information as will enable me to combat the distrust likely to arise from the matter if left unexplained.

By reference to the first "Instructions" to the commissioners, I perceive that the President says "Of course your instructions in no manner interfere with his (the Governor's) powers." The first instructions are withdrawn, and in the second, this quoted sentence is entirely omitted. But I shall continue to exercise the functions of my office, until I am otherwise specifically advised by the President.

Respectfully &c.   A. CUMMING,   Govr. of Utah

XI
The Peace Commission
and Settlement of Difficulties

INTRODUCTION

A Mormon complaint which Captain Van Vliet had carried back to Washington in October, 1857, was that the Government had despatched troops upon unfounded rumor, without first making an investigation. In response to Mormon objections, Van Vliet had said in early September that the Government might "yet send an investigating committee to Utah."[1] John M. Bernhisel, Utah Delegate to Congress, who accompanied Van Vliet from Utah to the East, pressed the same point before members of the Administration and of Congress.

When the army was finally stalled in the Green River Valley, and was forced to spend the winter in the Fort Bridger area, there was ample time for the government in Washington to appraise its actions and give re-consideration to its policies. Congress and the press became critical of Buchanan's administration for getting itself into such a position. (See Part VIII above, for Congressional reactions.)

The President had welcomed Colonel Kane's effort to attempt reconciliation, but the Colonel's mission was an unofficial undertaking. On January 27, 1858, a Joint

---

[1] See above, Part II.

Resolution was introduced in the Senate. It proposed the appointment of commissioners to examine into the difficulties in Utah with a view to their peaceful solution.[2] The same day the House passed a resolution calling upon the President "to communicate to the House of Representatives the information which gave rise to the military expeditions ordered to Utah Territory, the instructions to the army officers in connexion with the same, and all correspondence which has taken place with said army officers, with Brigham Young and his followers, or with others, throwing light upon the question as to how far said Brigham Young and his followers are in a state of rebellion or resistance to the government of the United States."[3]

In early February the New York Herald reported that Dr. Bernhisel, Utah's Delegate, had had several long interviews with the President in which he proposed that the "troops be withdrawn and that a commission be dispatched to the territory to arrange for the settlement of the difficulties."[4]

Finally, Buchanan decided to send official representatives as a Peace Commission. The men chosen were Lazarus W. Powell, Ex-Governor and Senator-elect from Kentucky; and Major Ben McCulloch of Texas. These were men of recognized stature and ability. The President entrusted them with a signed proclamation of pardon, which was to be issued if conditions warranted it. The work of the Commissioners is detailed in the documents that follow.

---

[2] Senate Resolution no. 14, in *Cong. Globe,* Jan. 27, 1858, p. 428.

[3] The response to this resolution was the extensive *Doc. 71,* of 215 pages, heretofore referred to.

[4] *New York Herald,* Feb. 5, 1858.

1. LEWIS CASS REPORTS DECISION
TO SEND PEACE COMMISSIONERS [5]

DEPARTMENT OF STATE
WASHINGTON   April 7th 1858

To HIS EXCELLENCY, ALFRED CUMMING
Governor of the Territory of Utah

SIR: The President has determined to send two persons as Commissioners to Utah to explain to the inhabitants, the views and purposes of the Government, and to endeavour to recall them to a sense of their duty and to submission to the laws. Mr. Powell of Kentucky and Mr. McCullough of Texas have been selected for that purpose, and they will proceed upon their mission without delay. I enclose you a copy of the proclamation, issued by the President upon this subject,[6] and of the instructions under which these gentlemen will act. As you will perceive, they have been directed to communicate freely with you and the President desires I should state to you, that you enjoy his entire confidence, and that he is sure you will heartily co-operate in carrying these measures into effect, and will afford the commissioners all the aid and information in your power.

I am, Sir   Your Obt. Sevt.   LEWIS CASS

2. SECRETARY FLOYD'S INSTRUCTIONS
TO MESSRS. POWELL AND McCULLOCH [7]

WAR DEPARTMENT, WASHINGTON,   April 12, 1858
GENTLEMEN: You will proceed with all practicable

---

[5] Alfred Cumming Papers, Duke University. This letter by Secretary of State Cass precedes by some days the actual appointment.

[6] The Proclamation is reproduced below, as *Doc. 3* in this Part.

[7] Printed in *House Ex. Doc. 2,* 35 Cong., 2 Sess., pp. 160-62 (Hereafter referred to as *Doc. 2*).

despatch to the Territory of Utah, and it is hoped you will reach the forces commanded by General Johnston, before hostilities shall have been actually renewed. You will carry with you the President's proclamation to the people of Utah, dated on the 6th instant, and give such extensive circulation to it as you may be able to effect amongst them. This will clearly point out to them the unfortunate relations in which their present attitude places them towards the government and people of the United States.

The duties committed to you by the President are of great importance, though you are not authorized to enter into any treaty or engagement with the Mormons. It is the great object of the President to bring these misguided people to their senses, to convert them into good citizens and to spare the effusion of human blood. He relies much upon your high character, patriotism, and prudence to accomplish these results, by convincing them, should the opportunity offer, how desperate is their effort to resist the authority of the government, and how much in accordance it will be with their own true interests to return to their allegiance, and submit promptly and peaceably to the Constitution and laws of the United States upon the assurances contained in the President's proclamation.

To restore peace in this manner is the single purpose of your mission. To this end, you may place yourselves in communication with their recognized leaders, should this be deemed expedient under their circumstances, on your arrival in Utah.

Much must necessarily be left to your discretion and wisdom in any communication you may have with the Mormon people. You can repeat the assurances heretofore given by the President, that the movement of the army to Utah has no reference whatever to their religious tenets or faith. Whilst they obey the laws and perform their duty as citizens, no power in this country has either the right or the disposition to interfere with their religion. In the language of the proclamation addressed to the Mormons, "If you obey the laws, keep the peace, and respect the just rights of others, you will be perfectly secure, and may live on in your present faith, or change it for another at your pleasure. Every intelligent man among you knows very well that this government has never, directly or indirectly, sought to molest you in your worship, to control you in your ecclesiastical affairs, or even to influence you in your religious opinions."

It is the duty and determination of the federal government to see that the officials appointed and sent out by the President shall be received and installed, and due obedience be yielded to the laws and to their official acts. When this shall have been fully accomplished, a necessity will no longer exist to retain any portion of the army in the Territory, except what may be required to keep the Indians in check and to secure the passage of emigrants to California.

You will communicate freely with General Johnston and Governor Cumming, and act in concert with them. At this distance it is impossible to anticipate what may be the condition of affairs on your arrival in Utah, but the President was determined to leave no effort unessayed to bring these rebellious people to a sense of their duty before it be too late.

In the month of December last Colonel Thomas L. Kane, of the city of Philadelphia, impelled thereto by ancient kind feelings for the Mormons, deemed it to be his duty to repair to Utah for the purpose of influencing that people to do their duty to the government of the United States, and, if possible to spare the effusion of blood. He acted under a deep conviction of duty, against the advice of his excellent father, Judge Kane, since deceased, and other members of his family. Having determined upon this course, the President, whilst he recognized him in no manner as a government agent, addressed him two letters under date of 31st December last, copies of which are now communicated to you.[8] Colonel Kane is probably at this time in Utah, and if you should find him there he may render you essential service in accomplishing the object of your mission.

All orders for facilitating your journey shall be given to the officers in command of the troops and stations along the line.

I am, gentlemen, very respectfully, your obedient servant,

JOHN B. FLOYD,   Secretary of War

3.   A PROCLAMATION [9]
By James Buchanan
President of the United States of America

WHEREAS the Territory of Utah was settled by certain emigrants from the States and from foreign countries, who have for several years past, manifested a spirit of insubordination to the Constitution and laws of the United States. The great mass of those settlers, acting under the influence of leaders to whom they seem to have surrendered their judgment, refuse to be

---

8 These letters are reproduced above, in Part IX.

9 *House Exec. Doc. 2,* 35 Cong., 2 sess., vol. I (Ser. 997), pp. 69-72.

controlled by any other authority. They have been often advised to obedience, and these friendly counsels have been answered with defiance. Officers of the federal government have been driven from the Territory for no offence but an effort to do their sworn duty. Others have been prevented from going there by threats of assassination. Judges have been violently interrupted in the performance of their functions, and the records of the courts have been seized and either destroyed or concealed. Many other acts of unlawful violence have been perpetrated, and the right to repeat them has been openly claimed by the leading inhabitants, with at least the silent acquiescence of nearly all the others. Their hostility to the lawful government of the country has at length become so violent that no officer bearing a commission from the Chief Magistrate of the Union can enter the Territory or remain there with safety; and all the officers recently appointed have been unable to go to Salt Lake or any where else in Utah beyond the immediate power of the army. Indeed, such is believed to be the condition to which a strange system of terrorism has brought the inhabitants of that region, that no one among them could express an opinion favorable to this government, or even propose to obey its laws, without exposing his life and property to peril.[10]

After carefully considering this state of affairs, and maturely weighing the obligation I was under to see the laws faithfully executed, it seemed to me right and proper that I should make such use of the military force at my disposal as might be necessary to protect the federal officers in going into the Territory of Utah,

---

[10] These are serious charges to have made with little or no dependable evidence.

and in performing their duties after arriving there. I accordingly ordered a detachment of the army to march for the City of Salt Lake, or within reach of that place, and to act, in case of need, as a posse for the enforcement of the laws. But, in the meantime, the hatred of that misguided people for the just and legal authority of the government had become so intense that they resolved to measure their military strength with that of the Union. They have organized an armed force far from contemptible in point of numbers, and trained it, if not with skill, at least with great assiduity and perseverance. While the troops of the United States were on their march, a train of baggage wagons, which happened to be unprotected, was attacked and destroyed by a portion of the Mormon forces, and the provisions and stores with which the train was laden were wantonly burnt. In short, their present attitude is one of decided and unreserved enmity to the United States and to all their loyal citizens. Their determination to oppose the authority of the government by military force has not only been expressed in words, but manifested in overt acts of the most unequivocal character.

Fellow-citizens of Utah, this is rebellion against the government to which you owe allegiance. It is levying war against the United States, and involves you in the guilt of treason. Persistence in it will bring you to condign punishment, to ruin, and to shame; for it is mere madness to suppose that, with your limited resources, you can successfully resist the force of this great and powerful nation.

If you have calculated upon the forbearance of the United States – if you have permitted yourselves to suppose that this government will fail to put forth its strength and bring you to submission – you have fallen into a grave mistake. You have settled upon territory which lies geographically in the heart of the Union. The land you live upon was purchased by the United States and paid for out of their treasury. The proprietary right and title to it is in them, and not in you. Utah is bounded on every side by States and Territories whose people are true to the Union. It is absurd to believe that they will or can permit you to erect in their very midst a government of your own, not only independent of the authority which they all acknowledge, but hostile to them and their interests.

Do not deceive yourselves nor try to mislead others by propagating the idea that this is a crusade against your religion. The Constitution and laws of this country can take no notice of your creed, whether it be true or false. That is a question between your God and yourselves, in which I disclaim all right to interfere. If you obey the laws, keep the peace, and respect the just rights of others, you will be perfectly secure, and may live on in your present faith, or change it for another, at your pleasure. Every intelligent man among you knows very well that this government has never directly or indirectly sought to molest you in your worship, to control you in your ecclesiastical affairs, or even to influence you in your religious opinions.

This rebellion is not merely a violation of your legal duty; it is without just cause, without reason, without excuse. You never made a complaint that was not listened to with patience. You never exhibited a real grievance that was not redressed as promptly as it could be. The laws and regulations enacted for your government by Congress have been equal and just, and their enforcement was manifestly necessary for your own welfare and happiness. You have never asked their repeal. They are similar in every material respect to the laws which have been passed for the other Territories of the Union, and which everywhere else (with one partial exception) have been cheerfully obeyed. No people ever lived who were freer from unnecessary legal restraints than you. Human wisdom never devised a political system which bestowed more blessings or imposed lighter burdens than the government of the United States in its operation upon the Territories.

But being anxious to save the effusion of blood, and to avoid the indiscriminate punishment of a whole people, for crimes of which it is not probable that all are equally guilty, I offer now a free and full pardon to all who will submit themselves to the authority of the federal government. If you refuse to accept it, let the consequences fall upon your own heads. But I conjure you to pause deliberately, and reflect well, before you reject this tender of peace and good will.

Now, therefore, I, JAMES BUCHANAN, *President of the United States,* have thought proper to issue this, my PROCLAMATION, enjoining upon all public officers in the Territory of Utah, to be diligent and faithful, to the full extent of their power, in the execution of the laws; commanding all citizens of the United States in said Territory to aid and assist the officers in the performance of their duties; offering to the inhabitants of Utah, who shall submit to the laws, a free pardon for the seditions and treasons heretofore by them committed; warning those who shall persist, after notice of this proclamation, in the present rebellion against the United States, that they must expect no further lenity, but look to be rigorously dealt with according to their deserts; and declaring that the military forces now in Utah, and hereafter to be sent there, will not be withdrawn until the inhabitants of that Territory shall manifest a proper sense of the duty which they owe to this government.

In testimony whereof, I have hereunto set my hand, and caused the seal of the United States to be affixed to these presents.

Done at the city of Washington, the sixth day of April, one thousand eight hundred and fifty-eight, and of the independence of the United States the eighty-second.

[L.S.]   JAMES BUCHANAN

By the President: LEWIS CASS, Secretary of State

4. POWELL AND McCULLOCH REPORT FROM FORT LEAVENWORTH [11]

FORT LEAVENWORTH,   April 25, 1858

HON. J. B. FLOYD

Secretary of War, Washington, D.C.

DEAR SIR: We reached this place without accident or delay. At St. Louis we selected five ambulances and harness which were promptly purchased by Colonel Crossman, quartermaster at that place, and shipped the next day for this place. We have completed our arrangements and will start on the plains to-day. Our party consists of a sergeant and five dragoons, a wagon master, five teamsters and a guide. Our teamsters are armed; each ambulance is drawn by four mules, we take three saddle horses. Colonel Munroe, the commander at this place, Colonel Tompkins the quarter-

---

[11] *Doc. 2,* pp. 163-64. The Report is sent to Sec. Floyd.

master, and the commissary, promptly furnished us with everything we desired. The officers in every department of the service with whom we had business did everything in their power to facilitate our departure. We were most kindly received and hospitably entertained by Colonel Munroe, during our sojourn here.

We take very little baggage. The ambulances are so comfortable that we find it unnecessary to take a tent. We have been fortunate in procuring excellent teams. We can carry in the ambulances sufficient forage for our animals. We expect to make thirty-five miles a day. We will reach General Johnston's camp at the earliest possible moment.

We have the honor to be, very respectfully, your obedient servants,

L. W. POWELL,   BEN MCCULLOCH

Commissioners to Utah

N.B.   We will avail ourselves of every opportunity to advise you of our progress.   Respectfully,

L. W. POWELL   BEN MCCULLOCH

5.   REPORT TO SECRETARY FLOYD FROM FORT KEARNY [12]

FORT KEARNEY,   May 3, 1858

DEAR SIR: We reached this place yesterday evening at six o'clock. We left Fort Leavenworth at half past three on the evening of the 25th last month. We were seven days two and a half hours out from Leavenworth. . .

We will leave here in the morning, and expect to reach Fort Laramie in eight days. . .

We met two days since a party consisting of a

---

[12] *Ibid.*, pp. 164-65.

merchant and others from Camp Scott, they informed us that they left General Johnston's command the 21st of March. They report General Johnston's army in good condition; they met Colonel Hoffman's command thirty-five miles this side of Fort Laramie. From information received from these gentlemen, we expect to reach Camp Scott by the time Colonel Hoffman does.

We were informed by these gentlemen that General Johnston would not advance until he was reinforced by Colonel Hoffman and Captain Marcy.

We have the honor to be, very respectfully, your obedient servants,

L. W. POWELL, BEN McCULLOCH,
Commissioners to Utah

6. REPORT TO FLOYD FROM CAMP SCOTT [13]

CAMP SCOTT, U.T., June 1, 1858

DEAR SIR: We have the honor to report that we reached this camp on the 29th of last month. We found General Johnston's command in good health and spirits.

The advance of Colonel Hoffman's command has arrived. Colonel Hoffman with the remainder of his command will reach this place in seven or eight days. General Johnston is of the opinion that the command of Captain Marcy will arrive in fifteen or twenty days; we have had full and free conference with General Johnston and Governor Cumming touching the object of our mission. Governor Cumming has recently returned from Salt Lake City; the governor is of the opinion that the military organization in Utah has been disbanded, with the exception of a few men that are under his control. Ex-Governor Brigham Young

---

[13] *Ibid.*, pp. 165-67.

has so informed the governor. From information received from Mormons and others recently from the City of Salt Lake, we fear that the leaders of the Mormon people have not given the governor correct information as to the condition of affairs in the valley; Governor Cumming having communicated the result of his visit to the Great Salt Lake City to the government we deem it unnecessary to state anything concerning it.[14]

We will set out for Great Salt Lake City at ten o'clock tomorrow morning, accompanied by Governor Cumming. We expect to reach the city in three or four days, and place ourselves in communication with the recognized leaders of the Mormon people; we have strong hopes that the Mormons may be induced to submit quietly to the authority of the government. . . They have abandoned their more northern settlements, and are moving their women and children and their supplies of provisions to the southern part of the Territory; this indicates in our judgment an intention on the part of the Mormons to leave the Territory, or to place themselves in an attitude to fight the army when it shall enter the valley. It may be their object to prevent their families from coming in contact with the army and the civil authorities that may be established in the Territory. . .[15]

---

[14] Cumming's letter of May 2, printed above, in Part X.

[15] The decision to abandon their homes and move south had been made at a conference of Mormon leaders on March 21. See the Journal History of March 21 for an account. "The meeting resolved itself into a special conference to take into consideration the policy of abandoning this city and moving the inhabitants thereof to the south instead of fighting the United States army that is now on our borders. Pres. Young said: 'I would rather see this city in ashes than have one good Elder killed.'" The remarks of Wilford Woodruff are given in the *Deseret News*, VIII, p. 26.

General Johnston is of the opinion that the command of Colonel Hoffman and Captain Marcy will arrive in fifteen or twenty days, and that at the end of twenty days he will be ready to march to Salt Lake City; the general is confident that when the officers and reinforcements arrive he will have sufficient force to march to Salt Lake City should he be resisted by the best army the Mormons can bring into the field. We will use every effort to see and confer with the Mormon people, and to make known their intentions to General Johnston by the time he is ready to march.

It affords us pleasure to state that General Johnston most heartily and cordially co-operates with us, and has done everything in his power to facilitate the object of our mission. We find the best order and most cheerful feeling prevail in the command, and that the command have borne the severe trials and difficulties by which they have been surrounded in a manner becoming American soldiers.

From information received from Mormons and others recently from Salt Lake City, we are induced to believe that great disaffection exists among the Mormons, and that large numbers of them would leave Utah were they not deterred by fear of injury from the Danite band;[16] hence the necessity that such as wish to leave should have the protection of the flag.

We have the honor to be, respectfully, your obedient servants,

L. W. POWELL   BEN McCULLOCH
Commissioners to Utah

---

[16] A supposed band of "Destroying Angels."

7. COMMISSIONERS REPORT
FROM SALT LAKE CITY [17]

GREAT SALT LAKE CITY, U.T.,   June 12, 1858
HON. JOHN B. FLOYD

DEAR SIR: We have the honor to report that we reached this city on the 7th instant. We lost no time in placing ourselves in communication with the chief men of the Mormon people. After the fullest and freest conference with them we are pleased to state that we have settled the unfortunate difficulties existing between the government of the United States and the people of Utah. We are informed by the people and chief men of the Territory that they will cheerfully yield obedience to the Constitution and laws of the United States. They consent that the civil officers of the Territory shall enter upon the discharge of their respective duties.[18] They will make no resistance to the army of the United States in its march to the valley of Salt Lake or elsewhere. We have their assurance that no resistance will be made to the officers, civil or military, of the United States in the exercise of their various functions in the Territory of Utah.

The people have abandoned all the settlements north of this, and all the families have left this city, only about fifteen hundred persons remaining here to take charge of the property and to burn it if the difficulties had not been settled. The people from this city and north of it have gone south to Provo, fifty miles south of this and to points beyond.

We will visit Provo and the settlements south in a day or two, and see and confer with the people and

17 *Doc. 2,* pp. 167-68.
18 The Governor had already entered upon his duties.

inform them that the difficulties have been settled, and thus induce them to return to their homes. We have written to General Johnston by the messenger who will bear this, informing him of what has been done, and that he could march his army to the valley whenever he desired to do so. We intend to remain and visit the people and converse with them until General Johnston's army arrives. We think it important that we remain until the army is located in the valley. We have but a moment to write as the express will start in a few moments. We will in a few days forward a detailed report.

We have the honor to be, very respectfully, your obedient servants,

L. W. POWELL,   BEN McCULLOCH
Commissioners to Utah

8. PEACE COMMISSIONERS TO GENERAL JOHNSTON [19]

GREAT SALT LAKE CITY, U.T.,   June 12, 1858

DEAR SIR: We have the pleasure of informing you that after a full and free conference with the chief men of the Territory we are informed by them that they will yield obedience to the Constitution and laws of the United States; that they will not resist the execution of the laws in the Territory of Utah; that they cheerfully consent that the civil officers of the Territory shall enter upon the discharge of their respective duties; and that they will make no resistance to the army of the United States in its march to the valley of Salt Lake or else-where. We have their assurance that no resistance will be made to the officers, civil or military, of the United

---

[19] *Doc. 2,* pp. 119-20.

States, in the exercise of their various functions, in the Territory of Utah.

The houses, fields, and gardens of the people of this Territory, particularly in and about Salt Lake City, are very insecure. The animals of your army would cause great destruction of property if the greatest care should not be observed in the march and in the selecting of camps. The people of the Territory are somewhat uneasy for fear the army, when it shall reach the valley, would not properly respect their persons and property. We have assured them that neither their persons nor property would be injured or molested by the army under your command. We would respectfully suggest, in consequence of this feeling of uneasiness, that you issue a proclamation to the people of Utah, stating that the army under your command would not trespass upon the rights or property of peaceable citizens during the sojourn in, or the march of your army through, the Territory. Such a proclamation would greatly allay the existing anxiety and fear of the people, and cause those who have abandoned their homes to return to their houses and farms.

We have made enquiry about grass, wood, &c., necessary for the subsistence and convenience of your army. We have conversed with Mr. Ficklin fully on this subject, and given him all the information we have, which he will impart to you. We respectfully suggest that you march to the valley as soon as it is convenient for you to do so.

We have the honor to be, very respectfully, your obedient servants,

L. W. POWELL   BEN MCCULLOCH
Commissioners to Utah

9. GENERAL JOHNSTON
TO PEACE COMMISSIONERS [20]

HEADQUARTERS DEPARTMENT OF UTAH
Camp on Bear river, June 14, 1858

GENTLEMEN: Your communication from Salt Lake City was received today. The accomplishment of the object of your mission entirely in accordance with the instructions of the President, the wisdom and forbearance of which you have so ably displayed to the people of the Territory, will, I hope, lead to a more just appreciation of their relations to the general government and the establishment of the supremacy of the laws.

I learn with surprise that uneasiness is felt by the people as to the treatment they may receive from the army. Acting under the twofold obligations of citizens and soldiers, we may be supposed to comprehend the rights of the people, and to be sufficiently mindful of the obligations of our oaths not to disregard the laws which govern us as a military body. A reference to them will show with what jealous care the general government has guarded the rights of citizens against any encroachment.

The army has duties to perform here in execution of the orders of the Department of War, which, from the nature of them, cannot lead to interference with the people in their various pursuits, and if no obstruction is presented to the discharge of those duties there need not be the slightest apprehension that any person whatever will have cause of complaint against it. The army will continue its march from this position on Thursday, 17th instant, and reach the valley in five days. I desire

[20] *Ibid.,* pp. 120-21.

to encamp beyond the Jordan on the day of arrival in the valley.

With great respect, your obedient servant,

A. S. JOHNSTON,   Colonel 2d Cavalry
and Brevet Brigadier General, U.S. Army,
commanding

10.   TO THE PEOPLE OF UTAH [21]

The commissioners of the United States, deputed by the President to urge upon the people of this Territory the necessity of obedience to the Constitution and laws as enjoined by his proclamation, have this day informed me that there will be no obstruction to the administration and execution of the laws of the federal government, nor any opposition on the part of the people of this Territory to the military force of the government in the execution of their orders. I therefore feel it incumbent on me, and have great satisfaction in doing so, to assure those citizens of the Territory who, I learn, apprehend from the army ill treatment, that no person whatever will be in anywise interfered with or molested in his person or rights, or in the peaceful pursuit of his avocations; and, should protection be needed, that they will find the army (always faithful to the obligations of duty) as ready now to assist and protect them as it was to oppose them while it was believed they were resisting the laws of their government.

A. S. JOHNSTON,   Colonel 2d Cavalry
and Brevet Brigadier General, commanding
HEADQUARTERS DEPARTMENT OF UTAH
Camp on Bear River, June 14, 1858

[21] *Ibid.,* p. 121.

11. COMMISSIONERS REPORT FROM UTAH [22]

GREAT SALT LAKE CITY, U.T.,   June 26, 1858

DEAR SIR: In our hurried note of the 12th instant we had the honor to report that we reached this city on the 7th of this month, and at once put ourselves in communication with the recognized leaders and chief men of the Mormon people.

When we arrived ex-Governor Young and other chief men of the Mormon church were at Provo, a city fifty miles south of this, to which place and to points beyond, the inhabitants of the settlements north of this and the larger portion of the people of this city had gone with their families and personal property.

On our arrival we made known to the people here the object of our mission.

On the evening of the 8th we were waited on by a committee of three gentlemen who informed us that it was the desire of the people of the Territory that we confer with ex-Governor Brigham Young concerning the difficulties between the United States government and the people of Utah, we informed the committee that we would with pleasure confer with ex-Governor Young and such others as the people of Utah should indicate as their representatives, at such time and place as was convenient to them.

On the evening of the 9th we were informed by the committee that they had made known to ex-Governor Young and others that we were ready to confer with them, and that ex-Governor Young and other chief men of the Mormon church would be in this city on the

---

[22] *Ibid.,* pp. 168-72. To Secretary Floyd.

evening of the 10th, and that they would be ready for conference on the morning of the 11th, at 9 o'clock.

On the evening of the 10th ex-Governor Brigham Young, Heber C. Kimball, Lieutenant-Governor [Lieutenant General] Wells, who constitute the first presidency of the church of Latter Day Saints, and several of the twelve [apostles] and other chief men of the Mormon church, reached this city.

When advised of their arrival we addressed a note to ex-Governor Young informing him that we were ready to confer with him and such others as the people had indicated at such time and place as he might name, to which note we received a reply fixing the 11th at 9 o'clock p.m., and the large room in the council-house in this city as the place for conference. On the evening of the 10th we had an interview with ex-Governor Brigham Young, Heber C. Kimball, and Lieutenant-Governor Wells, and explained to them the object of our visit. We met the three gentlemen last named and many other leading men of the Mormon people at the time and place named in ex-Governor Young's note.[23]

We stated the object of our mission, and distinctly made known to them the views and intentions of the President concerning the people of Utah. We stated that we had no power to make any treaty or compact with them, the object of our mission was to make known to them the policy the President intended to pursue towards the people of Utah, and to induce them to submit quietly and peaceably to the authority of the United States.

---

[23] An account of this council is given in the Journal History of June 10, 1858; and in the *Deseret News,* VIII, p. 75; and VIII, p. 96.

A fuller account of the meeting on June 11 is given in the Journal History of that date, with a summary of the remarks of each speaker. The same is true of the speeches on the 12th.

We informed them that it was the determination of the President to see that the authority of the United States be maintained in Utah, and that the Constitution and laws of the nation should be enforced and executed in this Territory.

That the President would send the army of the United States to the valley of Great Salt Lake in such numbers, at such times, and to such places in the valley or other parts of the Territory as he might think the public interests demanded, and retain it there as long as he should think the interest of the United States required him to do so; that such military posts would be established in the Territory of Utah and in the valley of Great Salt Lake as the Secretary of War should think necessary to protect the emigration to and from the Pacific, prevent Indian depredations, and to act as a *posse comitatus* to enforce the execution of civil process should it be necessary.

We stated that the object of the President in sending a portion of the army to Utah was to enforce the execution of the laws and protect the civil officers of the government in the exercise of the duties of their respective offices; that, in the event the inhabitants of the Territory quietly and peaceably submitted to the execution of the laws of the United States, and would peaceably receive the officers of the government appointed for Utah, and permit them, without resistance, to exercise the various functions pertaining to their respective offices, there would be no necessity for the army to be used to enforce obedience to the civil authority. If they should refuse to receive in a peaceable manner the officers of the government, or should in any way resist the execution of the laws of the United

States within the Territory, the President would employ, if necessary, the entire military power of the nation to enforce unconditional submission and obedience to the Constitution and laws of the United States; if the civil officers of the Territory were peaceably received, and no resistance made to them in the discharge of their official duties, the army then in the Territory, or such portion of it as might hereafter be sent there, would only be used to protect emigrants and inhabitants from Indian depredations.

We informed them it was not the intention of the President in sending a portion of the army to the Territory to deprive the people of Utah of any of their rights, but to see that the authority of the United States was respected and the civil officers protected, and obedience yielded to the Constitution and laws, as enjoined by the President in his proclamation; should they quietly and peaceably submit to the authority and laws of their country, the army will be used as promptly to protect them in all their constitutional rights as it would be to compel obedience to the authority of the United States.

We called their attention to the Proclamation of the President which had been distributed among them. We stated that the President, in order to avoid the effusion of blood and to cause them to return to their allegiance to our common country, had deputed us to make known to them the designs and intentions of the government and the policy that would be pursued towards the people of Utah, which we had now done. We stated that the President asked nothing of them but what it was their duty as good citizens to perform, and that we trusted our mission would result in the restoration of peace, quiet, and order in the Territory.

We stated that we wished a free conference with them and were ready to hear what they had to say. Ex-Governor Brigham Young, Lieutenant-Governor Wells, Mr. Erastus Snow, Mr. Clements, and Major Hunt spoke. They expressed their gratification that the President had sent commissioners to Utah; they stated that they were attached to the Constitution and government of the United States; they spoke harshly of many of the officials who had held office in the Territory; they spoke of the wrongs and injuries heretofore done them; they said they desired to live in peace under the Constitution of the United States. They denied that they had ever driven any official from Utah, or prevented any civil officers entering the Territory; they admitted that they burnt the army trains and drove off the cattle from the army last fall, and for that act they accepted the President's pardon. All the charges that had been made against them, except the one last named, they denied.

After a session of several hours the conference adjourned until nine o'clock the next day; on the evening of the 11th, we had a lengthy conversation with ex-Governor Young, Heber C. Kimball and Lieutenant-Governor Wells, on matters touching our visit.

On the morning of the 12th, at 9 o'clock, we again met at the council house, a large number of citizens were present; Elder John Taylor, Colonel George A. Smith, General Furgison, and ex-Governor Young made speeches; they expressed attachment to the Constitution and government of the United States, said they desired to live in peace under the Constitution of the United States, spoke harshly of certain officials who had been in the Territory, denied all the charges that had been made against them, except burning the army

trains, which they admitted. The general tone and
sentiments expressed, were averse to the army coming
to the valley of Salt Lake. We are pleased to state that
the conference resulted in their agreeing to receive
quietly and peaceably all the civil officers of the government, and not to resist them in the execution of the
duties of their offices, to yield obedience to the authority
and laws of the United States. That they would offer no
resistance to the army; that the officers of the army
would not be resisted or molested in the execution of
their orders within the Territory; in short, they agreed
that the officers civil and military of the United States,
should enter the Territory without resistance, and
exercise peaceably and unmolested all the functions of
their various offices. At the close of the conference, we
made a short address to a large audience, expressing
our gratification that the people had agreed to submit
peaceably and amicably to the authority of the United
States, and we assured them that whilst they acknowledged the authority of the United States, and were
obedient to the Constitution and laws of the country,
they would be protected by the government in all their
constitutional rights. That the army which would in a
few days be in the valley of Great Salt Lake, would not
molest or injure any peaceable citizens, in person or
property. We announced to the people that they could
return to their homes without danger of interruption
from the army. All present appeared gratified at the
result of the conference. On the evening of the 12th
instant, we despatched a messenger to Brevet Brigadier
General Johnston, advising him that the people of this
Territory had agreed to submit peaceably to the authority of the government, and suggesting that he issue a

proclamation to the people of Utah, and march to the valley at his earliest convenience. General Johnston replied to our note on the 14th inst, and enclosed us his proclamation to the people of Utah. We send enclosed with this a copy of our note to General Johnston, and copies of his reply and proclamation. It was the intention of the people, if a peaceable adjustment had not been made, to have burned their houses, destroyed the growing crops, and retreated to the mountains on the approach of the army. With this view they had removed their women and children, and their household and personal property from this city and the settlements north of it, to the southern part of the territory, and had stored large quantities of grain and provision in the mountains.

On the evening of the 16th instant we addressed a large crowd of the people at Provo, and on the evening of the 17th we addressed the people at Lehi.[24] They seemed pleased that peace had been restored in the Territory.

It is to be hoped that peace, order and quiet may hereafter prevail in this Territory, and that the people of Utah may ever be loyal, true and faithful to the Constitution and flag of the Union.

His excellency Governor Cumming was present at most of our conferences and heartily co-operated with us in carrying out the object of our mission.

Brevet Brigadier General Johnston, commanding the army at Utah, cordially co-operated with us in our efforts to carry out the wishes of the President.

The governor, secretary of state, chief justice,

---

[24] Powell's address at Provo is printed in the *Deseret News,* VIII, p. 87; and his talk at Lehi in VIII, p. 120.

marshal, superintendent of Indian affairs and post-master are in the Territory, and have entered upon the duties of their respective offices. The special justices have not yet reached the Territory. Brevet Brigadier General Johnston with the army under his command reached the valley of Great Salt Lake this morning, and will to-day, march through this city and encamp just beyond its limits. The general will in a few days select the locations for his permanent posts; peace and quiet prevail in the Territory. We will set out for Washington in a few days.

We have the honor to be very respectfully, your obedient servants,

GEORGE [LAZARUS] W. POWELL, BEN MCCULLOCH
Commissioners to Utah

12. COMMISSIONERS REPORT TO SECRETARY FLOYD [25]

GREAT SALT LAKE CITY, U.T., July 3, 1858

DEAR SIR: On the 26th of last month General Johnston marched the army under his command through this city, and encamped on the banks of the River Jordan, just without the limits of the city.[26]

---

[25] Doc. 2, pp. 172-74.

[26] The Journal History of June 26 reports that the army passed through the city in the strictest order, and that not a lady was seen. It says that Capt. St. George Cooke rode with his head uncovered in respect for the Mormon Battalion which he had led in the march to California during the Mexican War.

Col. R. T. Burton, who had led the advance Mormon troops to scout the army's approach in Sept., 1857, was in charge of guards stationed in Salt Lake City when the army marched through. His journal records: "Six a.m. roll call. Men ordered to remain in quarters. At 10 a.m. troops commenced passing through until 12:30, when those in the rear halted. At 2 p.m. again commenced to pass through until 5:30 p.m. There are reported to be 600 wagons, 6,000 head of animals, and 3000 men. They camped over Jordan, west of the city."– Journal History.

On the 27th Powell and others visited Gen. Johnston in his tent. The

The army remained encamped on the Jordan for two days. Wood and grass being scarce, the general moved twelve or fifteen miles west, near the foot of the mountains,[27] where wood and grass were more abundant; at which place the troops will probably remain until the general selects the place for a permanent post. . .

L. W. POWELL,   BEN MCCULLOCH
Commissioners to Utah

13. MINUTES OF THE CONFERENCE, JUNE 11 AND 12 [28]

WASHINGTON, D.C.   August 24, 1858
HON. JOHN B. FLOYD, Secretary of War
DEAR SIR: We have enclosed herewith a copy of a paper containing a concise statement of what was said in the conference held in Great Salt Lake City on the 11th and 12th of June last, which is certified by ex-Governor Brigham Young, as correct.

We have the honor to be, very respectfully, your obedient servants

L. W. POWELL,   BEN MCCULLOCH
Commissioners to Utah

In the conference held in Great Salt Lake City, on the 11th and 12th of June, 1858, L. W. Powell and Ben

---

Journal History account says that Lt. Col. Smith spoke illy of the Mormons. Someone said he might be heard by some Mormons. He replied that he "did not care a damn who heard him; he would like to see every damned Mormon hung by the neck."

[27] To Bingham's Fort.— Journal History of June 29.

[28] *Doc. 2,* pp. 175-77. An account is also found in the *Deseret News,* VIII, pp. 75 and 96. The report in the Journal History of June 11 summarizes the remarks of each speaker. The Journal History of July 1 and 2 reports that there was some controversy as to the correctness of the minutes kept by the Mormon clerks of the council between the Commissioners and the Mormon leaders. The minutes were finally submitted to both sides and approved by both. The wording of most of the statement indicates that it was written by the Peace Commissioners.

McCulloch, commissioners to Utah, and ex-Governor Brigham Young and others, touching difficulties between the United States government and the people of the Territory of Utah, Governor Powell in behalf of the commissioners, said in substance, as follows:

He stated the object of the mission, and distinctly made known the views and intentions of the President concerning the people of Utah. He stated that the commissioners had no power to make any treaty or compact with them. The object of the mission was to make known to the people of Utah the policy the President intended to pursue towards them, and to induce them to submit quietly and peaceably to the authority of the United States.

He stated that it was the determination of the President to see that the authority of the United States be maintained in Utah, and that the Constitution and laws of the nation should be enforced and executed in this Territory; that the President would send the army of the United States to the valley of Great Salt Lake, in such numbers, at such times, and to such places in the valley or other parts of the Territory, as he might think the public interest demanded, and retain it there as long as he should think the interest of the United States required him to do so.

That such military posts would be established in the Territory of Utah, and in the valley of Great Salt Lake as the Secretary of War should think necessary to protect the emigration to and from the Pacific, prevent Indian depredations and to act as a *posse comitatus* to enforce the execution of civil process should it be necessary. He said that the object of the President in sending a portion of the army to Utah, was to enforce the execution of the laws, and protect the civil officers of the government in the exercise of the duties of their offices, that in the event the inhabitants of the Territory quietly and peaceably submitted to the execution of the laws of the United States, and would peaceably receive the officers of the government appointed for Utah, and permit them without resistance to exercise the various functions pertaining to respective offices, there would be no necessity for the army to be used to enforce obedience to the civil authority. If they should refuse to receive in a peaceable manner the officers of the government, or should in any way resist the execution of the laws of the United States within the Territory, the President would employ if necessary the entire military power of the nation to enforce unconditional submission and obedience to the Constitution and laws of the United States.

If the civil officers of the Territory were peaceably received and no resistance made to them in the discharge of their official duties, the army then in the Territory, or such portion of it as might hereafter be sent there, would only be used to protect emigrants and inhabitants from Indian depredations.

We stated that it was not the intention of the President, in sending a portion of the army to the Territory to deprive the people of Utah of any of their constitutional rights, but to see that the authority of the United States was respected, the civil officers protected and obedience yielded to the Constitution and laws, as enjoined by the President in his proclamation; should they quietly and peaceably submit to the authority and laws of this country, the army would be used as promptly to protect them in all their constitutional rights as it would be to compel obedience to the authority of the United States.

We called their attention to the proclamation of the President which had been distributed among them.

We stated that the President, in order to avoid the effusion of blood, and to cause them to return to their allegiance to our common country, had deputed the commissioners to make known to them the designs and intentions of the government, and the policy that would be pursued towards the people of Utah, which we had now done. We stated that the President asked nothing of them but what it was their duty as good citizens to perform, and that we trusted our mission would result in the restoration of peace, quiet, and order in the Territory.

We further stated that the commissioners had no power to give an order to the army, but that we had conferred with General Johnston, and that his army would not march to the valley of Great Salt Lake until he received information from us; that we did not know where General Johnston would make his permanent posts when he arrived in the valley of Salt Lake. General Johnston, however, told us that it was not his intention to station his army in or very near one of their large cities; that such a location would be calculated to demoralize the army; that he wished to make his permanent posts where wood, water, and grass were abundant. Governor Young expressed a desire that the commissioners would investigate certain charges that had been made against the people of Utah, to wit: as to whether the Mormons had killed Lieutenant Gunnison's party and Colonel Babbit, and burned the records and library of the federal court, and the truth of the charges made by Judge Drummond and others. The commissioners declined to go into the investigation desired for the reason that such an investigation was not within their instructions, and that it was impossible for them to do so if they desired it, for want of evidence and time.

Ex-Governor Young and others state that they were, and had ever been attached to the Constitution and government of the United States, and desired to live in peace and quiet under the government; they denied all the charges that had been made against them, except the burning of the army trains and driving off the cattle from the army last fall; that they admitted, and for that they accepted the President's pardon; they claimed that they were more ardently attached to the Constitution of the United States than others who made charges against them. Upon the President's views and intentions being made known, as set forth herein, it was agreed that the officers, civil and military, of the United States should peaceably and without resistance enter the Territory of Utah, and discharge, unmolested, *all their official duties.*

GREAT SALT LAKE CITY,   July 3, 1858

I have examined the foregoing statement of the substance of what was said in the conference held at Great Salt Lake City, Utah Territory, on the 11th and 12th of June, 1858, by Governor Powell and Ben McCulloch, commissioners to Utah, and ex-Governor Young and others, touching the difficulties that existed between the United States government and the people of Utah; the statement in writing examined by me is contained in six pages, hereto attached, and is, in substance a correct synoptical statement of what was said in said conference; the above is correct as far as I can recollect at present.   BRIGHAM YOUNG

Appendix

A. MR. MAGRAW'S LETTER TO THE PRESIDENT [1]

INDEPENDENCE, MISSOURI, October 3, 1856.

MR. PRESIDENT: I feel it incumbent upon me as a personal and political friend, to lay before you some information relative to the present political and social condition of the Territory of Utah, which may be of importance.

There is no disguising the fact, that there is left no vestige of law and order, no protection for life or property; the civil laws of the Territory are overshadowed and neutralized by a so-styled ecclesiastical organization, as despotic, dangerous and damnable, as has ever been known to exist in any country, and which is ruining not only those who do not subscribe to their religious code, but is driving the moderate and more orderly of the Mormon community to desperation. Formerly, violence committed upon the rights of persons and property were attempted to be justified by some pretext manufactured for the occasion, under color of law as it exists in that country. The victims were usually of that class whose obscurity and want of information necessary to insure proper investigation and redress of their wrongs were sufficient to guarantee to the perpetrators freedom from punishment. Emboldened by the success which attended their first attempts at lawlessness, no pretext or apology seems *now* to be deemed requisite, nor is any class exempt from outrage; all alike are set upon by the self-constituted theocracy, whose laws, or rather whose conspiracies, are framed in dark corners, promulgated from the stand of tabernacle or church, and executed at midnight, or upon the highways, by an organized band of bravos and assassins, whose masters compel an outraged community to tolerate in their midst. The result is that a considerable and highly respectable portion of the community, known from the Atlantic to the Pacific, whose enterprise is stimulated by a laudable desire to improve their fortunes by honorable exertions, are left helpless victims to outrage and oppression, liable at any

[1] *Doc. 71, op. cit.,* pp. 2-3.

moment to be stripped of their property or deprived of life, without the ability to put themselves under the protection of law, since all the courts that exist there at present are converted into engines and instruments of injustice.

For want of time I am compelled thus to generalize, but particular cases, with all the attendant circumstances, names of parties and localities are not wanting to swell the calendar of crime and outrage to limits that will, when published, startle the conservative people of the States, and create a clamor which will not be readily quelled; and I have no doubt that the time is near at hand, and the elements rapidly combining to bring about a state of affairs which will result in indiscriminate bloodshed, robbery and rapine, and which in a brief space of time will reduce that country to the condition of a howling wilderness.

There are hundreds of good men in the country, who have for years endured every privations from the comforts and enjoyments of civilized life, to confront every description of danger for the purpose of improving their fortunes. These men have suffered repeated wrong and injustice, which they have endeavored to repair by renewed exertions, patiently awaiting the correction of outrage by that government which it is their pride to claim citizenship under, and whose protection they have a right to expect; but they now see themselves liable, at any moment, to be stripped of their hard earned means, the lives of themselves and their colleagues threatened and taken; ignominy and abuse, heaped upon them day after day, if resented, is followed by murder.

Many of the inhabitants of the Territory possess passions and elements of character calculated to drive them to extremes, and have the ability to conceive and the courage to carry out the boldest measures for redress, and I know that they will be at no loss for a leader. When such as these are driven by their wrongs to vindicate, not only their rights as citizens, but their pride of manhood, the question of disparity in numerical force is not considered among their difficulties, and I am satisfied that a recital of their grievances would form an apology, if not a sufficient justification, for the violation on their part of the usages of civilized communities.

In addressing you, I have endeavored to discard all feelings arising from my personal annoyances in the Mormon country, but have desired to lay before you the actual condition of affairs, and to prevent, if possible, scenes of lawlessness which, I fear, will be inevitable unless speedy and powerful preventives are applied. I have felt free to thus address you, from the fact that some slight requests made of me when I last left Washington, on the subject of the affairs of Kansas, justified me in believing that you had confidence in my integrity, and that what influence I could exert would not be wanting to terminate the unfortunate difficulties in that Territory; I have the pleasure of assuring you that my efforts were not spared.

With regard to the affairs and proceedings of the probate court, the only existing tribunal in the Territory of Utah, there being but one of the three federal judges now in the Territory, I will refer you to its records, and to the evidence of gentlemen whose assertions cannot be questioned; as to the treatment of myself, I will leave that to the representation of others; at all events, the object I have in view, the end I wish to accomplish for the general good, will preclude my wearying you with a recital of them at present.

I have the honor to be very truly yours, &c.

W. M. F. MAGRAW

B. JUDGE DRUMMOND'S LETTER OF RESIGNATION [2]

March 30, 1857

MY DEAR SIR: As I have concluded to resign the office of justice of the supreme court of the Territory of Utah, which position I accepted in A.D., 1854, under the administration of President Pierce, I deem it due to the public to give some of the reasons why I do so. In the first place, Brigham Young, the governor of Utah Territory, is the acknowledged head of the "Church of Jesus Christ of Latter Day Saints," commonly called "Mormons;" and, as such head, the Mormons look to him, and to *him alone,* for the *law* by which they are to be governed: therefore no law of Congress is by them considered binding in any manner.

SECONDLY. I know that there is a secret oath-bound organization among all the male members of the church to resist the laws of the country, and to acknowledge no law save the law of the "Holy Priesthood," which comes to the people through Brigham Young direct from God; he, Young, being the vicegerent of God and Prophet, viz: successor of Joseph Smith, who was the founder of this blind and treasonable organization.

---

[2] *Ibid.*, pp. 212-214.

THIRDLY. I am fully aware that there is a set of men, set apart by special order of the Church, to take both the lives and property of persons who may question the authority of the Church; the names of whom I will promptly make known at a future time.

FOURTHLY. That the records, papers, &c., of the Supreme Court have been destroyed by order of the Church, with the direct knowledge and approbation of Governor B. Young, and the federal officers grossly insulted for presuming to raise a single question about the treasonable act.

FIFTHLY. That the federal officers of the Territory are constantly insulted, harrassed, and annoyed by the Mormons, and for these insults there is no redress.

SIXTHLY. That the federal officers are daily compelled to hear the form of the American government traduced, the chief executives of the nation, both living and dead, slandered and abused from the masses, as well as from all the leading members of the Church, in the most vulgar, loathsome, and wicked manner that the evil passions of men can possibly conceive.

AGAIN. That after Moroni Green had been convicted in the district court before my colleage, Judge Kinney, of an assault with intent to commit murder, and afterwards, on appeal to the Supreme Court, the judgment being affirmed and the said Green being sentenced to the penitentiary, Brigham Young gave a full pardon to the said Green before he reached the penitentiary; also, that the said Governor Young pardoned a man by the name of Baker, who had been tried and sentenced to ten years' imprisonment in the penitentiary, for the murder of a dumb boy by the name of White House, the proof showing one of the most aggravated cases of murder that I ever knew being tried; and to insult the court and government officers, this man Young took this pardoned criminal with him, in proper person, to church on the next Sabbath after his conviction; Baker, in the meantime, having received a full pardon from Governor Brigham Young. These two men were Mormons. On the other hand, I charge the Mormons, and Governor Young in particular, with imprisoning five or six young men from Missouri and Iowa, who are now in the penitentiary of Utah, without those men having violated *any criminal law in America*. But they were anti-Mormons – poor, uneducated young men *en route* for California; but because they emigrated from

Illinois, Iowa, or Missouri, and passed by Great Salt Lake City, they were indicted by a probate court, and most brutally and inhumanly dealt with, in addition to being summarily incarcerated in the saintly prison of the Territory of Utah. I also charge Governor Young with constantly interfering with the federal courts, directing the grand jury whom to indict and whom not; and after the judges charge the grand juries as to their duties, that this man Young invariably has some member of the grand jury advised in advance as to his will in relation to their labors, and that *his charge thus given is the only charge known, obeyed, or received by all the grand juries of the federal courts of Utah Territory.*

Again, sir, after a careful and mature investigation, I have been compelled to come to the conclusion, heart-rending and sickening as it may be, that Captain John W. Gunnison, and his party of eight others, were murdered by the Indians in 1853, under the orders, advice, and direction of the Mormons; that my illustrious and distinguished predecessor, Hon. Leonidas Shaw, came to his death by drinking poisoned liquors, given to him under the order of the leading men of the Mormon Church in Great Salt Lake City; that the late secretary of the Territory, A. W. Babbitt, was murdered on the plains by a band of Mormon marauders, under the particular and special order of Brigham Young, Heber C. Kimball, and J. M. Grant, and not by the Indians, as reported by the Mormons themselves, and that they were sent from Salt Lake City for that purpose, and *that only;* and as members of the Danite Band they were bound to do the will of Brigham Young as the head of the church, or forfeit their own lives. These reasons, with many others that I might give, which would be too heart-rending to insert in this communication, have induced me to resign the office of justice of the Territory of Utah, and again return to my adopted State of Illinois.

My reason, sir, for making this communication thus public is, that the Democratic party, with which I have always strictly acted, is the party now in power, and, therefore, is the party that *should now* be held responsible for the treasonable and disgraceful state of affairs that now exists in Utah Territory. I could, sir, if necessary, refer to a cloud of witnesses to attest the reasons I have given, and the charges, bold as they are, against those despots, who rule with an iron hand their hundred thousand souls in Utah, and their two hundred thousand souls out of that notable Territory; but I shall not do so, for the reason that the lives of such gentlemen as I should designate in Utah and in California, would not be safe for a single day.

In conclusion, sir, I have to say that, in my career as justice of the Supreme Court of Utah Territory, I have the consolation of knowing that I did my duty, that neither threats nor intimidations drove me from that path. Upon the other hand, I am pained to say that I accomplished little good while there, and that the judiciary is only treated as a farce. The only rule of law by which the infatuated followers of this curious people will be governed, is the law of the church, and that emanates from Governor Brigham Young, and him alone.

I do believe that, if there was a man put in office as governor of that Territory, who is not a member of the church, (Mormon,) and he supported with a *sufficient* military aid, much good would result from such a course; but as the Territory is now governed, and as it has been since the administration of Mr. Fillmore, at which time Young received his appointment as governor, it is noonday madness and folly to attempt to administer the law in that Territory. The officers are insulted, harassed, and murdered for doing their duty, and not recognizing Brigham Young as the only law-giver and law-maker on earth. Of this every man can bear incontestible evidence who has been willing to accept an appointment in Utah; and I assure you, sir, that no man would be willing to risk his life and property in that Territory after once trying the sad experiment.

With an earnest desire that the present administration will give due and timely aid to the officers that may be so unfortunate as to accept situations in that Territory, and that the withering curse which now rests upon this nation by virtue of the *peculiar* and heart-rending institutions of the Territory of Utah, may be speedily removed, to the honor and credit of our happy country, I now remain your obedient servant,

W. W. DRUMMOND,
Justice Utah Territory

HON. JEREMIAH S. BLACK,
Attorney General of the United States, Washington City, D.C.

Index

Index

This brief index is for use until the comprehensive analytical index of the Series (volume XV) is available.

Other titles by LeRoy R. Hafen and Ann W. Hafen
available in Bison Books editions

Handcarts to Zion
The Story of a Unique Western Migration, 1856–1860

Journals of Forty-Niners
Salt Lake to Los Angeles

Old Spanish Trail